TAXI
FROM
HELL

TAXI FROM HELL

Confessions of a
Russian Hack

Vladimir Lobas

Translated from the Russian by
Tamara Glenny

First published serially in Russian in 1990 by the New
York Russian daily, *Novoe Russkoe Slovo*, under the author's pen name, Vladimir Lobas. Subsequently published the following year in Moscow, in three
installments, by *Novy Mir* and by *Ogonek*, and in book
form by Novy Mir Press.

Library of Congress Cataloging-in-Publication Data

Lobas, Vladimir, 1937–
    Taxi from hell: confessions of a Russian
hack / Vladimir Lobas; translated from the Russian
by Tamara Glenny.
    p. cm.
    ISBN 0-939149-58-3: $20.95
    1. Lobas, Vladimir, 1937–   . 2. Russian
Americans—New   York   (N.Y.)—Biography.
3. Jews, Russian—New York (N.Y.)—Biography.
4. Taxicab drivers—New York (N.Y.)—Biography.
5. Refugees, Political—New   York   (N.Y.)—
Biography. 6. New York (N.Y.)—Biography. I.
Title.
F128.9.R9L63   1991
974.7′1004924047—dc20   91-5680
                                CIP

Published by
Soho Press Inc.
853 Broadway
New York, NY 10003

Book design and composition by The Sarabande Press

To my comrades: white and black;
Americans and immigrants, from Russia
and Israel, Greece and Korea; to Arabs,
Chinese, Poles, and all the rest of the cab
drivers of New York City—as a mark of
deep respect for their inhuman labor this
bitter book is dedicated.

Had I not been fated to become a taxi driver I would never have learned much of what I know, half of which should be enough to poison several human lives.

From *Night Road* by Gaito Gazdanov, a White Guard officer and writer who became a taxi driver in Paris during the Russian emigration in the 1920s.

I wish to thank the editors of the Moscow
literary monthly *Novy Mir* for the three
million blue-covered copies of their
magazine that have brought my *Taxi From
Hell* to Russian-language readers.

CONTENTS

INTRODUCTION

M r. A. flew into New York and checked into one of the hotels overlooking Central Park. The next morning, as the visitor walked out of the hotel, he took a deep breath of the park's keen air and glanced at his watch. It was time to begin a bustling New York day, and he made for the taxicab at the head of the line drawn up at the entrance.

It seemed rather strange to Mr. A. that the drivers of the first two taxis in the line were not behind the wheel, as he thought they were supposed to be, but rather propping up the wall of the hotel and chatting. They ignored the customer peeping inside their cabs; indeed, it seemed they had no intention of going anywhere. After waiting for a minute and realizing that the conversation could go on indefinitely, Mr. A. finally decided to interrupt their cozy tête-à-tête and asked, "Excuse me, guys, are you working?"

"My cab's taken," one of the men replied, wincing slightly.

"Can't you see we're talking?" said the second, with a grating accent, and he shook his head, apparently lamenting the general prevalence of bad manners.

To avoid an argument, the gentleman headed for the third taxi in line, but as he reached for the door handle the driver of this cab, who *was* sitting where he was supposed to be, snapped the automatic lock. Mr. A.

had no idea what was behind this absurd boycott, which made it all the more offensive. He hailed a passing taxi and tried to forget what had happened as quickly as possible.

Some hours later, however, toward evening, when the visitor came out of the hotel once more, his clothes changed and his sweetly scented wife on his arm, this unpleasant episode was repeated. The rush hour had already begun, and in the stream of traffic pouring past there was not an empty taxi to be had; at the entrance was one lone yellow cab. A slovenly character with dull eyes—was it beer or just idleness?—sat on the hood, his legs dangling.

"Please, take us to Maxwell's Plum," the couple pleaded. "It's only a few blocks, and we would be *so* grateful . . . "

But the obtuse cabbie did not take the hint. He suppressed a yawn with an effort, and, when he had stopped blinking, said, "I'm not going anywhere. I'm on my break."

The doorman turned away, probably ashamed to witness this humiliation of the prestigious hotel's guests. Mr. A. had to raise his voice to summon him, and, admittedly, order was restored right away: the slovenly character got behind the wheel in a moment. But it is certainly no fun being driven by some foul-tempered cabbie who keeps muttering under his breath, "Who needs it? Who needs it?" while scowling and braking sharply at intersections just to spite you.

The couple on the backseat fell silent and stared at the back of his balding head above the grubby collar and at the flabby, unshaven cheeks visible in the rearview mirror. Fortunately, the ride lasted only a few minutes; when the cab stopped the meter showed $1.80. The incident was over. The driver was handed two singles and told to keep the change.

"Why did you do that?" Mr. A.'s wife said, in a fit of pique, as the lout remained glumly silent.

"You're right," agreed Mr. A. "Couldn't you say something, driver, when I'm giving you a ten percent tip after all this—"

"What do you mean, 'ten percent'?" the cabbie snarled. "It's less than a quarter. Take your money back!"

His English was excruciating. One could barely refrain from slamming the car door.

But the next day, when the A.'s were leaving New York, a miracle occurred at the hotel entrance. They had hardly started down the steps when one of the taxi drivers, dozing in the line, sighted them and honked his horn. Another, who resembled the obnoxious oaf of the day before, rushed up and literally grabbed the suitcases out of their hands, while a third, quick on his feet, forestalled the doorman and obligingly flung open the door of the cab: "Have a good trip!"

Mr. A. exchanged glances with his wife; she could barely keep from bursting out laughing. But this was nothing to the travelers' amazement when with their own eyes they saw the driver (definitely the same one as yesterday!) slam the trunk shut, run up to the doorman, and shove a bill into his hand. Yes, the cabbie was doing the tipping instead of the guests.

"Kennedy airport!" Mr. A. snapped, none too politely, not forgetting their recent encounter.

"Yes, sir!" the oaf responded cheerfully, and the taxi roared off toward a changing traffic light.

And now, in case you wonder how I found out—and in such detail—what went on between some couple visiting New York and the taxi drivers in front of the hotel, and what happened in the cab, and even about that ridiculous altercation over a twenty-cent tip, I will reveal all: the balding oaf with the unshaven cheeks and the dull eyes was none other than me.

———

You know, I have an uncomfortable feeling that you have hardly opened my book and you are already annoyed. Look, you're probably saying, this "author," this cabbie, won't tell you anything straight: why are these lazy drivers suddenly falling over themselves to put people in a cab? And then paying the doorman to boot! Most likely it's nonsense. Whoever heard of taxi drivers tipping anyone?

But I swear, there is not a word of lies in my artless book. It is just that you have never happened to hear about the money we pay doormen on the sly: one dollar for a trip to the nearer airport, LaGuardia; two to Kennedy, which is further away; and, at the time I began hacking, we occasionally forked over five bucks for Newark.

Not every doorman takes bribes from taxi drivers, of course, and I certainly have no intention of slandering all of them, especially since many are friends of mine; and I can tell you, for example, about a remarkable black giant named Angel, who stands at the entrance of the Essex Lane Hotel to this day, and who is famous among us New York cabbies for his irreproachable honesty.

At the time I got to know Angel, he had been at his post for about twenty years. He already owned a couple of houses in the Bronx, a couple in Brownsville, a laundromat, and a nice piece of land in Florida. It is nothing to marvel at: anyone of these stalwart fellows in top hats, so majestic and so nimble, who take your tips with a bow, is, as a rule, far better off than—well, let's just say than most of those doing the tipping.

Naturally, nobody gets these enviable sums for nothing. The doormen are numbed by cold and wind and soaked by rain; they often have to tote hefty suitcases; and, like many heavily built people, Angel was constantly hungry.

As if to spite him, opposite the hotel, by the fence outside Central Park, an old Arab woman would light a fire on her food stand every morning. The pink juices of the meat dripped onto the coals, and the breeze would send the tantalizing aroma of roasting shishkebab wafting toward us. Angel tried his hardest not to look in her direction, but he could never stand it for more than an hour and would send over one of the taxi drivers currently enjoying his favor to get him a portion. But what is one helping of shishkebab to such a big fellow, even if it comes with hot pita bread and lettuce? He turns away for an instant—and it's gone. Then he would try again not to look over toward the park. Meanwhile the greedy Arab woman kept raising the price of her tasty wares: she started at a dollar fifty, but somehow it very quickly went up to $2.75, while the portions got smaller and smaller. Angel complained to us that even the pieces of pita bread were getting minuscule, and we were openly indignant at her brazenness.

Angel stood at his post, tortured by a perplexing thought. Of course, he was thinking, I'm certainly not poor, but all things considered, am I really so rich that I can afford to pay $2.75 for a shishkebab with one hand and with the other dish out innumerable Essex Lane airport trips to these cab drivers for nothing—for a song?

We understood his torment better than anybody, and kept offering him an honest trade — LaGuardia for a dollar, Kennedy for two — but he was firm as a rock. "No, no, a thousand times no!" the incorruptible Angel would reply. Even if the Arab woman lost all shame, he was not about to dirty his hands and take a *risk* as well.

The fact is that "selling airports" to cab drivers is a grave sin not merely in the eyes of God. A doorman can lose his position because of his dealings with these wretched cabbies. Don't forget that although a taxi driver *voluntarily* slips his two dollars in the doorman's pocket, should the passenger he has paid for suddenly change his mind and tell the man to take him to the airport bus stop instead of JFK, the cabbie is liable to throw both the passenger and his luggage unceremoniously out of the car in the middle of the road, go back to the hotel, and make a big fuss about it with the doorman. You took my money, he says, and stuck me with what? A shorty!

He's ready to go for the doorman's throat over his miserable buck. How can you have dealings with people like that?

Of course, it is easy to stand by and pass judgment. Well, you say, then don't have any dealings with taxi drivers if the management doesn't allow it and if their money is dirty. But who's arguing? Sure the taxi drivers' dollars are dirty! But there are *lots* of them. Just work it out: for every two or three hundred guests leaving the hotel daily, a minimum of sixty hire a cab to LaGuardia and thirty to Kennedy; and a few fly out of Newark. Do you understand what that means? It's over a hundred bucks a day! And a month? A year? Now tell me what you would do if you found yourself in Angel's place. I am sure you would be no better at coming up with a workable solution than any doorman before Angel ever was. You would just stuff the forbidden cash into your pockets until you got fired, like Bob at the Sheraton or Joe at the Holiday Inn, and then kick yourself for blowing it.

I will never forget the day when the rumor began to spread among taxi drivers that Angel had started giving out airports. Someone had gotten a Kennedy and someone else a Newark, they said. All excited, I hurried over to the hotel, and what did I see? For guests without suitcases, Angel stopped cabs driving past, but when the bellboy rolled out a cart piled with luggage, the doorman called over the first taxi in the yellow line!

There was no doubt about it, Angel was definitely giving out airports. But, as it transpired, he was still not taking *money*.

Instead, this bright doorman had imposed a fee in kind on the cab drivers who hung around his hotel. He would take a duck leg from one, half a banana, an apple, or a hard-boiled egg from another. Angel gulped down these victuals indiscriminately and in any order. This native of British Guiana quite quickly grew accustomed to our Russian pirogi with cabbage and powerful, garlicky Ukrainian sausage, and stopped wasting his money on shishkebabs, for which the ferocious huckster hated him and started calling him names.

"Monkey!" she would yell across the street. But Angel was deaf to her stupid gibes. In his resplendent uniform, with gold aiguillettes and white gloves, he looked so unlike a monkey that neither the passersby nor the hotel guests could imagine why the Arab woman was yelling and whom her sarcasm was aimed at. On top of that, a policeman, who rented an apartment in one of the doorman's houses, found out that the Arab woman had some kind of problem with her papers, and she hastily had to sell her lucrative spot next to Central Park to a Greek—for only seventeen thousand, it was said.

But our good Angel, patron saint of taxi drivers, is still with us today. Ducking into a nook in the wall, he swallows a slice of rich Odessa strudel, snacks on a pickled herring tail, and loads me up with a Kennedy.

This doorman can look the manager of his hotel in the eye with a clear conscience. He may not be giving out airport trips for free, exactly, but not even the strictest boss would dare call a piece of chicken a bribe. And what cabbie could summon up the nerve to yell out in front of the whole street, Your customer changed his mind, give me back my gefilte fish? Impossible. Nobody would ever do that.

But why am I going on about Angel this and Angel that? As long as my story has somehow gotten around to doormen, let me introduce you to the doormen at the best hotels in New York; and believe me, even if you are rich and influential, these connections will come in handy. For example, you can leave your Mercedes for an hour or so in the heart of the city with any of my friends, with no risk of having it towed away. You want to snort or shoot up? Bet on a ballgame or put a little tenderness in your life? They will always make sure you get exactly what you are in the mood for, right now. And along with the doormen, you will meet a movie-star dog and a poor Albanian cabbie who got rich in the space of a few days; I will show you New York—a different New York—as cab drivers see it; and if you are curious, I can teach you how to steal a suitcase, too.

If you are honest and hard-up, I will gladly explain how you can make an extra fifty bucks in an evening without a yellow cab, in your own beat-up car. We will plunge into the disturbing twilight of the West Side, drive past the cordons of prostitutes around the ruins of an abandoned highway, leave behind the old pier where crowds of homosexuals promenade, and stop off at one of the undistinguished bars in the Wall Street area, deserted in the evenings—Harry's American, Harry's Hanover—or at a secret brothel on Greenwich Street. We will wait under the stars for a quarter of an hour or so, until the usual bunch of operators stumbles out from their spree, celebrating a big killing on the stock exchange that day. We will shout to them, "Discount limo! Double the receipt!" and you'll see: two of them, who think they're the soberest, will detach themselves from the uproarious gang. They want to *negotiate*, and the money's as good as in your pocket; all you have to do is stuff as many of those drunks into the car as possible. It doesn't matter if one of them shouts that he's going to Fort Lee and another wants Brooklyn Heights; try to cram every last one of them into the car, and just warn them that everybody pays separately.

But if you, reader, are a person with "standards," and have no desire to drive drunken sharpers around at night; if what you need is not fifty bucks but many thousands and the freedom they bring—I can teach you, too, how to attain that freedom, without changing your present life in any way; not by crippling yourself with drudgery or years of penny-pinching, but by irreproachably legal means which will work even if you have no savings. And if that is *all* you are interested in, you don't have to read my book, or even skim through it looking for the requisite advice: just turn to Chapter 19 and in twenty minutes you will know everything you need to know. You will only be mildly surprised at how simple it all is; and maybe, in some corner of your mind, the thought will occur to you that many of your acquaintances—for whom you have great respect—must have done something very similar.

But maybe you will find the adventures of a New York cabbie entertaining and funny: how a gypsy told his fortune (and whether it came true); how he learned to drive his Checker in *reverse*; how he once found in his cab the cobblestone his customers meant to bash him over the head with; how he solved Frank the doorman's riddle about the beggar and the doctor; how he made friends with a police commissioner; how he bought his own taxicab, and what came of it all. As you turn the pages, you may well get to the end without even noticing it, and discover, to your amazement, that for some reason you have no desire whatever to make use of your new knowledge of this simple and quite legal method — not even to free yourself and your wife from your dreary labors.

My taxi's free — hop in, reader! An extraordinary trip lies ahead. You won't tell me where to go, and I won't turn on the meter; and we will speed along the bumpy streets of New York, over the route I happen to have driven for three hundred thousand miles.

Vladimir Lobas
New York

Part One

THREE HUNDRED THOUSAND MILES AGO

Chapter One

- - - - - - - -

A PERFECTLY DECENT
MAN ONLY YESTERDAY

Each morning, when I wake up in my apartment on the nineteenth floor of a building that rises across the street from the ocean in Brooklyn, the first thing I do is look out the window to check whether my cab is where I left it the night before. The car is leased and I answer for it with my life; it has never been pinched, thank God, but cars are stolen so often in New York that I have developed the reflex anyway.

Convinced that my Checker is still there, topped by the forage cap of its advertisement, I quietly close the door to the bedroom where my wife is sleeping, and the other door to my son's room, and head for the bathroom, past my disused study. Last night I came back from work late and exhausted, and the result is that my left hand still trembles even now, after I have slept; and I have to contrive somehow to cup my hands to bring the water to my face. I have adapted to this, however; and as I wash I remember that yesterday, when I was parking in front of the building, I saw only two yellow cabs on our block, while just now, when I looked out the window, I noticed at least five. These cars belong to my neighbors, émigrés from Russia like me; they must have had to work well into the night and had come home even later than I.

In our building—or, rather, in the huge city housing project made up of six blocks that stand on the edge of a black neighborhood—many of the tenants, in fact nearly half, are "Russians."

Back in Russia we were not considered Russians. Under the heading NATIONALITY in our passports was written the word JEW, and we were allowed to leave only because we were Jews. But we had hardly crossed the Soviet border when everyone began calling us "Russians" since we talked in Russian, and we have become so used to this that now we even speak of ourselves as "Russians."

We were attracted to Brooklyn both by the proximity to the ocean and to the colony of our fellow countrymen in Brighton Beach—and, of course, by the conditions of the lease: for excellent, well-appointed apartments we pay half as much as the tenants of the privately owned buildings around us. We live in a poor man's paradise.

Needless to say, not everybody who wants to can enter paradise. Only families with an income inside a certain range—not higher and not lower than the set limits—have the right to live in our development. If a tenant's income rises, so does his rent, which is why every year we are obliged to give the authorities a special notarized declaration of our financial position.

Arriving in an alien country, before we had learned to say two words in its alien language, we "Russians" immediately grasped the very essence of the American way. We understood that the benefits to be had here are *real*, while the restrictions are *conventional*. The income scale, for instance, is a mere convention. When you put your name down on the waiting list for an apartment, the proper thing to do is not to declare your real income, but instead whatever figure the scale permits; and everything will be just fine. Nobody checks the figure. What is more, nobody checks the annual declaration either. And even the principle of the two- or three-year waiting list is nothing but a kind of allegory, a delicate allusion. To intelligent people who know what's what, the officials will grant a dwelling without bothering about the waiting list. For us, Soviet émigrés, this was entirely simple and natural; what Jew in the Soviet Union ever moves into an apartment without paying a bribe? Indeed, some of my bolder, more sharp-witted compatriots arrived at the realization that once you received an apartment from the city, you did not have to move into it. You could go on living right where you were—buy a house in Long Island if you could afford it—and, after jacking up the rent, sublet the cheap apartment to an émigré less savvy than yourself. Now, that's business! And Russians poured into our buildings, arousing the enmity of the old tenants.

Our émigrés' children, I noticed with surprise, were embarrassed by the language of their parents. A six-year-old friend of mine would tug at his mother's skirt when she chatted to me in the elevator: "Mommy, stop it! You ought to be ashamed of yourself." Scampering out to the playground, he sat down on a bench, looking askance at the noisy swarm of young ladies, and said with a sigh, "I like girls."

"Then why don't you play with them?"

"They say, 'You're Russian, you're bad.'"

"What manners! Want an ice cream?"

"Is it kosher?"

"What does that mean?"

"'Kosher' means really yummy."

At the ice-cream stand he saw a raddled old woman and sidled up to her with an obsequious smile.

"Do you like that lady?"

"She's rich."

"Why do you like rich ladies?"

"'Rich' means really smart."

This boy never asked any questions. He knew all of the answers to all of the questions. He was the son of the only one of my acquaintances who before long became a millionaire.

In this Brooklyn paradise I lived a strange, ghostly kind of life for over three years. Every day I bought a Russian-language newspaper. The books I read, though published in the West, were written in Russian. We shopped in Russian delicatessens for bread baked to a Russian recipe, for Russian dried mushrooms, Russian ham, and Russian mineral water.

Once a week I got on the subway and traveled clear across New York from the little pocket, where I lived out my Russian life in America, to another little pocket in a few rooms in a skyscraper on East Forty-second Street, occupied by an organization whose employees also spoke to each other in Russian and pecked away on Russian typewriters, and where stacks of *Soviet* newspapers (some subscribed to especially for me) teetered on library tables; and there I received my weekly check for one hundred and ninety dollars.

Every Friday at ten a.m. sharp I entered a special room, draped floor to ceiling with folds of material to absorb sound reverberations; closed the heavy soundproof door behind me, sat down facing the soundproof glass wall, and waited for the red signal to flash over my head. When it was lighted the microphone was on.

At the same moment the tall gray-haired man behind the glass wall nodded. I nodded back, and he pressed the button that switched on the prerecorded introduction:

"This is Radio Liberty. We now present the weekly program by our commentator Vladimir Lobas . . ."

Vladimir Lobas is my pen-name.

In order to prevent people from listening to us in Russia, Soviet cities were surrounded by networks of super-powerful radio stations, which never broadcast the news, or weather reports, or soccer games. Instead they transmitted around the clock the uninterrupted howl of high-frequency generators—"KGB jazz." It was war: for minds, for men's souls; and over the airwaves it turned to war between the Western transmitters and the Soviet jammers.

Only three and a half years before, if anyone had asked me, a self-confident thirty-five-year-old filmmaker whose name occasionally appeared in the press, what exactly made me give up a successful career and along with it some perhaps not very meaningful but all the same very pleasant trappings—the privilege of seeing Western movies unavailable to ordinary mortals, travel abroad forbidden to others, a comfortable apartment in a writers' cooperative bought on preferential terms for eight hundred rubles (a thousand dollars!); and what made me leave behind the graves of my mother and the nanny who brought me up, and part with my father and my friends—I would have replied: *that red light, that radio station*, which, I knew, existed somewhere out there, in far-off America.

Nothing about this impulse—which may seem strange to a Westerner—was personal, peculiar only to me. Millions of others, intelligent and stupid, winners and losers, swarming alongside me in that other

Soviet life, yearned, and still yearn, to break out of there by any means, at any price—on a tourist trip, a sports competition, a performing tour, an Israeli visa—or else at night, under gunfire, under barbed wire, in a rubber dinghy, with an aqualung, heedless of what lay ahead. For years, therefore, the thought burned in me that one day I would find myself in front of this microphone and be granted the opportunity of telling the truth to people who had had malignant lies drummed into their heads for generations. And that was why I did not worry too much about the money I would earn; or whether I would gain or lose by "cheating destiny."

As it happened, the money I earned at the radio station was quite sufficient for our needs. My wife and I made no sacrifices. Our son went to an excellent private school for which we paid not a penny; later he entered college, and, though I had no connections, he not only attended free of charge but also received some money for textbooks and other expenses.

I wrote in detail about our life in America to my father, who, albeit with some difficulty, nevertheless managed somehow to translate my letters into the Soviet way of thinking. He was not surprised, for example, that a student was paid a stipend. However, when I wrote him that my wife's mother, who had emigrated with us, was receiving a pension and renting a separate apartment, Papa got furious and yelled at me from beyond the ocean: lie if you want, just don't lie through your teeth! How could your mother-in-law get a pension in America when she's never worked a day there in her life?

In fact I had the same thought myself sometimes: really, how can this be?

But one day a quite different America came knocking at our door. I got a toothache.

Once again I traveled clear across New York, by subway and then by bus, to yet another little pocket, where, among glaring floodlights and cupboards full of instruments, there ruled a dentist who somehow— though with an accent, with effort—spoke Russian. Hearing my irreproachably pure speech, he asked me to pay for the examination and

X rays in advance, and then pronounced sentence: extraction of eight teeth and implantation of *two bridges*.

"But if only one tooth is aching," I exclaimed, "why do you want to extract eight?"

"Because they're dead," the dentist said mournfully.

"But I've never had a toothache."

"It's a problem for most émigrés. The change in lifestyle, food, and water creates stress."

The scientific discussion was over.

"And how much is this going to cost me?"

The bright light shining in my face went out with the flick of a switch.

"Four thousand eight hundred and fifty dollars," the dentist rapped out, and everything went dark before my eyes. I was not accustomed to dealing in thousands, you know. I had not made a thousand dollars in any one month since I had emigrated.

"Doctor, would you mind if, say, I gave you five hundred dollars now, and then paid you the rest in installments of three hundred or so every month?"

The dentist was offended. "Am I asking you for the whole lot at once? Of course I can wait a month or two. But I can't wait a year!"

On my way home, at the corner of Coney Island and Brighton Beach Avenues, I saw a future millionaire. He was standing under a garish umbrella hoisted over a brand-new cart, selling hot dogs.

"So, how's it going?" I asked.

"Good," Misha said, and added, "Volodya, I lost my shame the day after I landed in America!" (Back in Russia he had been an engineer — on paper.)

Misha held out a free hot dog, opened a can of Coca-Cola for me, and suddenly said, "Want to go into business with me?"

"Depends what," I replied weightily.

Misha looked me straight in the eye, and I knew he was going to say something awful. But he just breathed heavily and was silent. He stuck his hand deep in a pocket of his baggy Soviet-made pants, fumbled around in there a long time (he was obviously hesitating over whether to reveal whatever it was) and, finally making up his mind, plunked down on the counter of the cart a yellow metal disk about the size of a dollar. On the obverse I saw, stamped in relief, the head of the Statue of Liberty.

"Volodya, we're going to *coin* this broad!" He turned pale. "This is pure gold!"

"Look, Misha," I said with exasperation. "What do you need me for? I know nothing about gold, and I don't have any money."

"I know, I know," Misha whispered. "But you've got the language, Volodya!"

"What language? I speak English a hundred times worse than you do Yiddish."

"Who cares if you're worse and I'm better?" He was getting angry. "You haven't even heard me out!"

Misha turned over the disk, whose reverse side was smooth, and explained that I was holding a "memorial medal," which we would sell to the fortunate parents of newborn Americans. Once it was engraved on the smooth side with the infant's name and date of birth, what father or mother could resist the temptation of having a "memorial" for the rest of their lives? And so many children were being born in New York! And New York was only the beginning . . . In short, he, Misha, would go after the rabbis and the Jewish maternity hospitals, while I would take on the English-language territory, recruiting the Catholic, Protestant, and other goyishe clergy, who, taking advantage of their authority, would actively promote the sales of our medal.

"Why would they help us?" I said, puzzled, and then I saw the pain my vulgar naïveté was capable of inflicting.

"*Vo-lo-dya*—they'll get a piece of the action, of course!"

It happened somehow that just around this time, when I was trying to open my disfigured mouth as little as possible—when, after prolonged negotiations, the dentist had finally extracted my teeth, promising to cement *temporary* bridges, at no charge, as soon as my gums had healed—the first breath of doubt about the integrity of the free press in America began to stir in me. This occurred in that pleasant hour after dinner when a cool breeze was wafting in from the ocean, and I was sprawled in an armchair, deep in the *New York Post*. I found it hard to read the newspapers, but this time I bravely struggled through an article

9

on unemployment. There were not too many words in the article I did not know, since everyone around me—my neighbors in the building, television announcers, senators, the president himself—was constantly gabbling about the subject.

Hunger sated, I was nodding off, and in order to prolong the daily reading lesson, I began scanning the easiest section, the classified ads. Somewhere, someone was looking for:

FINANCIAL CONSULTANTS, PROGRAMMERS, MANAGERS, PRIVATE INVESTIGATORS, BODYGUARDS . . .

So why on earth were hundreds of people standing in line at the offices where they hand out unemployment compensation? HELP WANTED, shouted the ads, calling for COOKS, WAITERS, MESSENGERS, JEWELERS, HAIRDRESSERS, POSITIVE PEOPLE, ENERGETIC PERSONS . . .

Someone had paid for every one of these ads. Why were businessmen throwing their dollars away instead of phoning the unemployment office—which must have a card index—and asking them to send over an unemployed hairdresser or an "energetic person"? Evidently something important was going on here that I did not understand, so I told myself to stop bothering my head over government affairs and to think about more mundane matters, such as how to earn five thousand dollars on the side and exchange my temporary teeth for "real" ones. But no such luck: when I started going through the ads in earnest, it became apparent that finding a way of earning the most modest extra income for myself was a great deal harder than solving the problem of unemployment on a national scale.

I did not know anything about accounting or programming. I was not cut out to be a private investigator. I could not be a manager, if only because I had never supervised anyone and was incapable of doing such a thing.

Descending ever lower down the ladder of professional prestige, I came across the section DRIVERS WANTED, too long to fit into three columns. Drivers were wanted for trucks, limousines, minibuses, delivering bread, soda, gasoline . . .

I had never driven a truck, or a limousine, but for some reason this prospect pleased me. Merely dreaming about the dashing freedom of a driver's life was delightful!

TAXI DRIVER, BE YOUR OWN BOSS!

This ad I liked even more:

BRAND-NEW CABS. GET BEHIND THE WHEEL RIGHT AWAY!

My sense of responsibility protested, and prudence suggested that I ought not to get behind the wheel of any car, brand-new or decrepit. Still, I was busy at the radio station only on Fridays, and completely free the rest of the week . . . and anyway, why not at least give it a try?

> If you don't have a hack license we help you get it in three days.
> Don't pass up the chance to earn $600 per week!

Well, how could I pass up a chance like that?

My wife glanced over my shoulder at the newspaper. She had lost her position as a Russian typist in a translation bureau six months before, and since she was not yet really comfortable with the English language, she still had not been able to find a new job. Now, looking at the ad page, my wife was really frightened that somebody at a garage might take me on, and she tried to dampen my ardor: "Just stay where you are. 'Driver'! Who needs you?"

I called the number in the ad, quite certain nothing would come of it, but it was as if a treadmill had been set in motion. The flash of a camera, the fingerprints, the medical exam, and suddenly there I was, standing in some grungy shack in front of the examiners of the Taxi and Limousine Commission.

Even now I did not take the impending test very seriously, but before they gave out the question papers, when we were settling at our desks, I took note, just in case, of one Puerto Rican with a lively, intelligent face, and tried to get a seat next to him.

The first question on my sheet asked for the whereabouts of Rockefeller Center. I knew that one, of course. The answer to the second question, "Where is the Metropolitan Museum?" also posed no problems. So far things were not going too badly. But the third question—on the location of Penn Station—seemed more complicated. I had never been to that stupid station!

I could easily find my way around the New York subway, and casually explained to those new to it how to transfer from the D train onto the E or the RR; but when it came to the city aboveground my impressions were inexcusably foggy even for a novice cab driver. I glanced furtively around to make sure the examiner was not checking up on me, and squinted sideways at my neighbor's sheet. My spirits lifted immediately: our question papers were identical. And I had not been mistaken in my neighbor, he knew everything under the sun: the Waldorf-Astoria Hotel, Mount Sinai Hospital, the Chrysler Building . . .

We did not exchange a word, but, barely catching my eye, this Puerto Rican positioned his paper so it would be easier for me to copy his answers. Not for nothing do they say in Russia, "Jews can be good people too!"

The lisping examiner, who could also have done with a visit to the dentist, called me up to his desk. "You thpeak Englith?"

I replied that at the moment we were indeed speaking English.

He held out to me an open booklet and pointed to Paragraph 42. "Read that aloud!"

I read, "*A driver shall not refuse, by words, gestures, or any other means, to take a passenger. The penalty for violation of this rule is $100, for a second offense . . .*"

This dull American official clearly had no intention of having a heart-to-heart chat with me, as any Soviet personnel officer would have done in his place. The latter would undoubtedly have wanted to know why I had decided to drive a taxi; he would have said that honesty was the most important thing in my new profession, and might even have uttered some bromide out of the *Moscow Evening News:* did I understand the *responsibility* I bore, considering that a taxi driver was the "face of the city," the first person to meet new arrivals? I would have nodded and listened, and probably would have said a few words too—something about the very first taxi, for instance, which existed in ancient Rome and, though it consisted only of horses harnessed to a carriage, was nonetheless equipped with a real meter, constructed out of two concentric circular rims and mounted on the wheel hub. Every five thousand paces two of the openings drilled in the rims would coincide, and a pebble would fall through them into the special "cashbox."

Unfortunately the engineer and architect Vitruvius, who left us a detailed description of the first meters, tells us nothing about whether the cashboxes were sealed or not. After all, if they were not sealed, the rogues among the ancient Roman taxi drivers could quite easily have dropped in extra pebbles when they were driving drunken patricians, or, say, tourists from Carthage.

I did not know whether modern New York cabbies pulled such tricks now, since I had never been in a taxi here, but the scoundrels in the Eternal City itself had taught me a cruel lesson. When, during the recent period of émigré wanderings, our family got off the plane at Leonardo da Vinci airport and we, not knowing a word of Italian, held out a piece of paper with an address on it to the taxi driver, he fleeced us for a hundred dollars for the trip to the center of town and demanded more money—for the luggage!—and yelled at us, and would not give us back our suitcases, and all we had in the world was three hundred dollars, and we were faced with an indefinite wait in Rome for our American visas . . .

But the Taxi and Limousine Commission inspector was not about to start any kind of conversation with me, and as soon as I finished reading Paragraph 42 he declared the examination over. What my wife had feared and what I myself, deep in my heart, also feared, had come to pass. I had become a taxi driver, not knowing how to drive a car.

Chapter Two

THE ABC OF A NEW
PROFESSION

In the last year of my life in Russia, waiting for an exit visa, I decided that I must get a driver's license. Of course, a license could be bought, and it cost no more than a pair of shoes, but I really did want to learn to drive an automobile. Whether my fate abroad turned out well or ill, I thought, I would undoubtedly have to drive a car. And this time even my conservative father, who usually disapproved of all my schemes, and who, like me, had never owned a car, agreed with me: "Everybody drives over there. There it's essential."

Having struggled through the mandatory six hours' study with an instructor, I received a Soviet "driver's permit." In New York my exotic certificate was exchanged for a standard license, but I had no practical experience of driving at all, since I had never once gotten behind the wheel without an instructor.

It was a little late to back out now, and, promising my wife I would take the utmost care, I showed up for work at the same Brooklyn garage that had arranged my taxi driver's papers in such a short time.

As I had been told to do, I arrived at five in the morning. In the dispatcher's office I saw "Larry"—disgustingly bloated with fat—who was assuring somebody over the phone, "Yeah, it's me, Larry!" and who waved at me to wait. It seemed to be an important conversation: the dispatcher diligently wrote down on narrow red and green forms everything that was said; evidently he was taking early orders for cabs.

From corner to corner, limping like a warped pendulum, walked a frowning alcoholic with a porous nose that resembled a piece of cinderblock. A woman of about thirty sat hunched on a backless bench. She had probably been sitting that way for a long time; one could only imagine that her browless face might be pleasant at another time, in other circumstances.

I realized it would be better not to ask these two about anything, and I sensed, with a dim foreboding, that I was entering a strange, unknown world, inhabited by some very alien people.

"D? Like in Donna?" the dispatcher asked again. "Ten also?"

The door through which I had entered a quarter of an hour before opened slightly, and a disheveled head, level with the handle, poked through the crack into the office and bellowed: "Larry, is this lady going to get a cab?"

Larry's right hand went on writing, but his left slid into the desk drawer and tossed some car keys across the Plexiglas-covered desktop. The woman took them and went out. The lame man continued to pace back and forth, and the dispatcher went on writing. "F like in Frank? Ten?"

"Larry, is this gentleman going to get a cab today?"

Larry looked imploringly at the angry dwarf. "Donna—Linda?" His hand darted into the drawer. "Double?" The keys jingled. "Four?" The lame man went out.

Going up to the desk to remind Larry of my presence, I glanced at the ruled forms and saw that the dispatcher was taking down his notes on columns with headings such as AMOUNT AND TYPE OF BET, TRACK NAME, and RACE NUMBER. For the first time—a phrase I will have to use frequently from now on—I was looking at a real live bookmaker. Some kind of blue card with a photograph slid toward me across the Plexiglas. I picked it up. The photograph was mine. My name was printed next to it. And above the name glowered six bold figures, my hack number to this day.

"Don't forget the keys!" the dispatcher barked. "They'll come in handy!"

15

In the depths of the junk-cluttered yard stood two yellow Fords. One was brand new—forget that!—and I looked at it cautiously. The other was beat up and rusted through, and for that very reason suited me fine. No matter how I might maim this cripple, afterward I could say it had always been that way. Without further ado I made for the old car, and I was not mistaken: the key turned easily in the lock. The mangy cab was intended for me.

The engine roared. Now I had to accomplish a major acrobatic feat and turn the car toward the gates. I touched the steering wheel but it did not budge. I tried harder; no effect. The wheel would not turn to the right or the left; sweat broke out on my forehead.

"Yo, Larry!" The dwarf's head appeared alongside my car, and Larry came hurrying across the yard, wobbling and puffing.

"The wheel won't turn," I complained.

"Hey, buddy," Larry yelled, "all the cars here are like that! What's the matter, you don't get it? If the wheel jams, step on the gas. Then it'll turn."

"No, I don't get it," I said firmly. "When I have to turn the wheel, I step on the brakes, not the gas."

"But I don't have another car right now."

"Larry," the dwarf said reproachfully.

"Fine, just fine!" the dispatcher yelped. "I'm going to give him a cab with five thousand miles on the clock! But I want him to say it in front of you, Rabbit. Can I trust you with this baby?"

My mysterious defender, who for some reason was protecting my interests while appearing not to notice me, looked in my direction. I had to say something. I blushed and shook my head.

"No."

———

Professor Stanley Hoffman, a specialist in modern Russian history, who had been dismissed from his university post at the time of the Vietnam war and had ended up working in a hardware store, offered to give me some driving lessons free of charge.

I was a trying pupil. Stanley's long-suffering car, his only property, refused to obey me. I was afraid of my own uncertain movements, afraid of the cars that passed us, and I kept hugging the curb. However, over a weekend, the patient Stanley taught me to drive a car more or less straight, to make a turn, and even to turn around.

I felt my qualifications were increasing literally by the hour, but I still could not bring myself to reappear in front of either fat Larry or, worse, my strange friend, who—as I later learned from a talkative cab driver in a McDonald's—represented the local union at the Brooklyn garage where my debut had failed to take place. But there was no need to encounter the witnesses to my disgrace again; I was already the possessor of a blue card, a "certified" taxi driver, and taxi drivers were wanted everywhere. And so one morning, at the Freenat garage in the borough of Queens, a jumpy dispatcher named Louie shoved the keys to cab 866 at me through the window—and I ran off to look for my car!

It was getting light. Both sides of the lonely alley, which abutted the flank of the Queensboro Bridge, were lined with numbered Checkers. I went all the way around the block, which would have looked rather gloomy even in sunshine; my number was nowhere to be found. It remained to search under the bridge, where about fifty more cabs were parked, but I did not want to—it was dark out there . . .

Metal plates clanked underfoot. Beneath the low-slung girders of the bridge every sound echoed loudly. Hearing footsteps behind me, I looked around, stepped on a bottle, and nearly tripped. Two black men were following me along the wide alleyway! Their hair was held back by headbands, and a cigar box stuck out under each one's arm. Muggers carried revolvers in boxes like that, I had seen it in the movies.

The sinister pair was getting nearer, but I had already managed to spot cab number 866 and scuttled toward it a great deal quicker than dignity allowed.

The footsteps died away.

I squeezed into the driver's seat with difficulty; my Checker was parked between two others, both right up close. The starter squealed fearfully, I backed up, to get out from under the bridge as quickly as possible, and—got hooked on the bumper of the next car! I tried to rectify the error and hit the other cab.

A hand was thumping on the car roof above my head.

"Get out!"

17

I abandoned my refuge without the feeblest attempt at resistance. But the robbers did not lay a hand on me. Evidently it was the cab they wanted. The one who had knocked on the roof got into the driver's seat and in two maneuvers separated the coupled cars and stopped the Checker in the middle of the alleyway.

"Get in!"

Without looking up, I got a dollar out of my pocket.

"Put it away!"

The rear fender of my cab was pretty dented.

"Will they make me pay for this?"

"You talk too much! Get to work!"

And thus in the quiet hour before dawn on Sunday I found myself in a moving car, alone. It was July 3, my birthday, and my happiest as far back as I could remember.

How many times is a man granted the experience of happiness? How many times had *I* experienced that feeling? Well, the day I risked my life to swim across a tiny village pond, perhaps. But then that was not me. That was a consumptive boy from a deprived postwar Russia.

And I was happy again when I was teaching the haughty copper-haired receptionist from the beauty parlor on the next street to fly. I whispered to her, "Don't be afraid! Do as I do!" Copying my movements, she gracefully flapped her arms, and we soared into the air! But those were only dreams . . . And later, many years afterward, the first time I was allowed to use the editing table, I spliced together two sequences that happened to be at hand: one, in black and white, of a plane burning in the night sky and falling to earth, and another from a different film in color, a slow panorama of a field covered with scarlet poppies. I ran the roll through the moviola and felt a sudden shiver down my spine: the two sequences joined together had produced something unexpected that neither had possessed by itself, as if a spark had flared up in the cut! What was it?

And so it was now. I drove along, not knowing where, and was happy.

In the whole of this huge city I was probably the only taxi driver who was glad there were no passengers on the streets. I wanted to be by myself for a while, to get used to it all. I was even more glad when I saw that mine was the only car on the Queensboro Bridge.

Could I ever have dreamed that one day some madman would fill up

18

his car and give it to me for an entire day so I could go tooling around? Even the good Stanley would not do that.

And now this battleship, this Checker, is mine!

I am as free as a bird. I am going where I want. Not only that: for learning to drive a car, for getting to know a thrilling and still unfamiliar city, for my own pleasure, I—I! am going to be paid *money!* Do such things really happen? Can it be true?

I turned the wheel to the right, and the Checker veered toward the curb. I turned it to the left, and it straightened up again. I touched the brake, and it slowed down.

I realized that my car was sensitive and obedient. I drove more and more boldly; the speed took my breath away, the arrow on the speedometer was approaching 20. Now the main thing, I thought, was not to mix up the pedals—gas and brake!

———

Not a single taxi driver among the many I asked later on could recall his first passenger: who he was, where and whence he was going. I did not remember my first passenger either. But I did, of course, remember the first taxi driver who got talking with me.

Having crossed the bridge, I found myself in a still sleeping Manhattan, and, catching sight of an empty taxi outside Grand Central Station, I drew up behind it. I was longing to hobnob with my colleague, but he was sitting buried in his newspaper and, not venturing to disturb him, I began to look my Checker over.

It was roomy inside, in spite of the clear (bulletproof?) partition separating the driver from the passenger, the upper part of which slid aside. Sitting at the wheel, I could open and shut it and even flip the lock.

With the partition closed, passenger and driver could settle up using the change cup set into the Plexiglas, with a steeply sloping bottom that money could pass through, but not the barrel of a gun.

A meter with a flag was fixed to the dashboard. When a passenger got into the cab, I was supposed to push down the flag and the meter would show the initial sixty-five cents, the "drop." To the right of the meter, inserted in a special frame, my blue card shone in all its glory.

I got out of the car, admired the Checker's hypertrophied bumpers, which gave it reliable protection both front and rear, and glanced at the

19

passenger section. I wondered if a customer sitting in the backseat could read my name and number on the card in case he wanted to complain about me. I flopped down onto the black cushion and immediately jumped as though I had been stung: the meter had clicked—sixty-five cents!

"Hot seat," said a mocking voice. The middle-aged cabman was standing next to me holding his newspaper. "Didn't they tell you?"

Sure they had, but you can't remember everything. Now, before I had earned a penny, my first sale of the day had put me in the red. Sixty-five cents to pay.

"Who the hell thought up this contraption?" I growled. "I'm not going to forget to put the meter on when a customer gets in."

"You might put it on, but someone else might not."

"And why not?"

"He'd take the money and pocket it. Cabbies are that sort of people. You've got to watch them all the time."

It was not a pleasant remark, but it had no ill effect on me, since I did not consider myself a cabbie.

"Is it true that taxi drivers make six hundred dollars a week?" I asked.

"Depends."

"Well, how much do you make, on average, for instance?"

My new acquaintance looked at me in amazement. "You think I'm a taxi driver?"

I realized I had made some kind of blunder.

"If you're going to drive a cab, you'd better learn to tell people apart!"

What did he mean?

"Don't you see the way I'm dressed?"

A grubby necktie; a crumpled black suit jacket, despite the heat. His colorless face was lined, he looked drawn.

"The owner of this cab is a friend of mine. I don't work for a garage like you. If I have any spare time, I occasionally go out for a few hours."

Our conversation was taking place at six o'clock on a Sunday morning.

"So why do you need to drive around as if you were a cabbie?"

"Good question. I meet new people, make connections, acquire information. I'm a businessman."

No matter how engrossed I was in thoughts about myself, no matter how proud of my new persona, I could still see that he was ashamed of his lot, of his yellow cab. And I felt the more sorry for him because my own position was so different. After all, I knew for certain that I was not and never would be a taxi driver; quite the contrary, I would have been flattered if someone had mistaken me for a real cabbie. But my thoughts became confused when I asked myself whether I, who had always believed wholeheartedly that no *work* of any kind could be shameful, would want just then to run into somebody from the radio station or a neighbor from my building. The gaunt artist from the sixteenth floor? His ugly wife? The future millionaire? Oh, no, certainly not.

We stayed outside Grand Central for a long time. Nobody came up to us; the conversation petered out. Pondering how to accommodate my beliefs to my present situation, I concluded that driving a cab was no worse than any other kind of job, but if it was still demeaning, wasn't it because a taxi driver is offered and accepts tips—a lackey's wages? And with this thought I drove away.

———

I still see no passersby on the streets, and the cars around me are only yellow, only taxis. All of them empty, without passengers. And all of them hurrying somewhere—where?

How stupid, I think. As far as I can tell, a taxi driver should go fast when he's carrying a customer; but if he doesn't have one he should go slowly, so as not to let a chance slip by. In fact, wouldn't the most sensible thing be to stop and wait? Whoever needs a taxi will see my Checker himself.

I stopped on a corner and began to wait. Five minutes. Ten. The cabs rushed by, on and on. And not alongside the sidewalk, but right down the middle of the avenue.

Suddenly I noticed a strange figure: a girl in an evening gown. It was an absurd sight—the city flooded with sunlight, and she in a long dress drooping from its slender straps, tangled hair and bleary eyes.

The girl could barely walk; she was swaying. But she was headed toward me. For some reason, however, when she neared the curb, only a few steps from my Checker, she raised her arm. And instantly a cab, speeding down the middle of the road, shuddered like a wounded bird stumbling in flight and veered sharply in our direction. Indignant that

21

some smart guy was taking "my" fare away from me, I honked the horn, but the yellow predator's door slammed smugly, and in the place where the party girl had been teetering a second before, a bluish-gray cloud was already evaporating. . . . I decided that in her hungover state the customer had simply not noticed my cab was empty.

I had thought it all through: the money I would take from customers, the money I would not. Only one detail was missing—where was I going to get those customers?

How long had it been since I rejoiced that the streets were empty? A dead Sunday in July.

Don't worry, I kept telling myself encouragingly, my fares will find me. But it seemed my fares had not woken up yet. Maybe they had left New York altogether? What would they be doing on a weekend in the stuffy city? The Checker had already gotten hot in the sun; the air inside was thick and sticky.

Everything conspired against me that first day. The next customer, who appeared on the corner where I lay in wait for my quarry, deceived me just as the tipsy maiden had. He did not wobble; he was not drunk. He could see me perfectly well, but for some reason he stopped a *moving* cab. I realized—instinctively rather than intellectually—that in order to get a fare, I had to *keep moving*.

At the end of the block that my Checker was meandering along, a passerby raised his hand. He was on my side, my "territory," but a cab racing down the center lane darted swiftly toward him—and he was gone.

A little way down the street a couple stopped at the curb. Instantly, two cabs headed toward them and nearly collided. But the couple waved the importunate ones away with all four hands, as if to say, We don't need a taxi! And both cabs departed empty.

Quite close by, fifty yards from me, a youth ran out from a doorway yelling "Taxi! Taxi!" But I did not get him either. Another cab hurtled across my path from the other side of the street; I barely managed to brake in time.

Now it became clear to me where the empty taxis were hurrying; they were trying to overtake each other. It was a real race. The cabbie who won the race got the prize—the fare. But I could not take part in this contest. I stood no chance of winning. I tried to wait it out, to let the contestants pass, but to no avail—the yellow cars streamed past in an uninterrupted flow.

I decided to look for another thoroughfare with fewer cabs, and found one right away. It was Fifth Avenue, all shining with shop windows. But the stores were still closed, and I drove from Central Park to Forty-second Street without seeing a single pedestrian. Only some homeless people were sleeping here and there on the sidewalks, and one morose policeman strolled up and down, guarding the Aeroflot office from Jewish activists. However, the time was not exactly wasted: I was learning to drive a car. After all, had my father not said, "Everyone drives over there"? And here I was at last, like everyone else, driving too.

———

A few hours later, when the city had at last awoken and gradually begun to fill up with crowds, and I had already taken somebody somewhere, and my meter had already clicked on a good six or seven bucks, it became apparent—even in such a well-regulated area as Manhattan, where the streets are numbered, and their numbers determine the direction of the traffic, east- or west-bound—that innumerable surprises lie in wait for the new driver, and none of them pleasant. All of a sudden my way would be blocked, now by the Pan Am Building, now by the main post office. The treachery of the roads through Central Park knew no bounds. One of them, to famous Tavern-on-the-Green, suddenly threw my cab out of the park somewhere near Columbus Circle. Another, along which I set off across the park toward the Metropolitan Museum—checking with the map this time—bore me off to the wastelands of Harlem. And the numbers that jerk Broadway pulled! Without any warning it would turn into Amsterdam Avenue one minute, Seventh the next. And even Park Avenue, seemingly such a reliable thoroughfare, you would think a beginner taxi driver could at least depend on that one, yet it played a dirty trick on me, too. I drove down Park Avenue for exactly a mile without making a single turn, and found myself on Broadway again! But if only that were all.

Hardly had my first passengers gotten into the cab—and I had to talk to them willy-nilly: "Where are you going? How do I get there? Why didn't you tell me where to turn sooner?" — than all the drivers around me started to do the most terrible things.

A respectable limousine hurtled around a corner and came tearing toward me down a one-way street. And he even had the gall to honk! As it turned out, neither of us was to blame; it was blasted Sixty-sixth Street, which, muddling the general odd-even rule for Manhattan, led westward. I was heading east. Of course I lost my nerve as a result of this muddle and had to stop to catch my breath. Scarcely had I recovered and pushed off from the curb again when a lady, driving past in an open-top car, nearly bashed in the side of my Checker. Where was she looking? I rebuked the lady sternly, but what could I do about the rest of these crazy New Yorkers? The streets and avenues teemed with irresponsible motorists who had no interest whatever that my cab was moving off, or that my passenger had asked me to make a left turn from the right-hand lane. I moved along the streets in a constant screech of brakes, while a torrent of curses and abuse rained down on me.

I realize that when you learned to drive a car, you too experienced the feeling of "flying into space," perhaps got annoyed, broke a headlight, or bent a fender. But not like this—under a flood of invective.

You learned on quiet streets. Behind *me* sat a customer who made me go wherever he fancied, and along a route that suited *him*.

The passengers were constantly in a hurry and even more nerve-racking than the loony drivers. Admittedly, my customers did not lose their tempers when it became obvious that the cabbie had no idea how to get from the Port Authority to SoHo (it is my belief they even enjoyed giving orders— "Make a right! Make a left!"), but as soon as the question of the tip came up, nearly all of them became agitated:

"What's this? Why didn't you leave yourself thirty cents? I told you to, didn't I?"

"He probably wants more."

"Who cares what he *wants!*"

"Okay, give him another quarter. Here you are. Have fun!"

"You new to this? Worked in the movies? Eisenstein!"

I bit my tongue and never breathed another word about the movies.

But what have we here? Into the dusty interior of my fleet cab, whose glass has never seen a wipe in its life, a radiant marvel comes flitting.

Never had I seen such a beautiful woman before. Twice she had to tell me how to get to Beekman Place and twice remind me she had to buy a newspaper on the way. But then, stopping at a newsstand, without giving the lady time to collect herself, I leaped swiftly out of the car and presented her with the seven pounds of Sunday *Times* as if it were a basket of flowers.

On the cobbled driveway in front of the building a sullen cabbie and the doorman were loading luggage into another taxi. Helping my passenger out of the car, I relieved her of the awkward, messy paper, and when the lady paid me she rewarded my gallantry with a dollar fifty! However, I would not dream of taking even a lavish tip from the dazzling beauty.

"Permit me to refuse this," I babbled.

The eyebrows flew up in amazement. "You are incredible."

I was flattered.

"I haven't been driving a taxi long, you see. I'm a teacher by profession."

"For heaven's sake, lady, don't feel sorry for him!" The other cabbie suddenly poked his nose in. "Just thank God this idiot doesn't teach children anymore. 'Teacher,' my ass!"

The taxi driver, whom I had never seen before, was ready to punch me out.

Why did he hate me so?

———

Our life is made up of compromises. I had resolved not to take tips, and what had become of my resolution? Another soap bubble burst; and all that remained in my soul was another dirty puddle.

Sticking to my policy of avoiding the perilous and unprofitable race, I turned off the broad avenue onto a narrow street. There were not many people about, but I went on for a few blocks and was stopped by some children.

A boy and a girl. Seven or eight years old. Spotting my cab from a distance, they waved their skinny arms. I drove up to them unhurriedly—there were no yellow predators on this street, ready to snatch my modest booty away.

A dark-haired woman popped up in a plateglass window adorned with

intertwined lighted neon tubing depicting something incomprehensible. She waved to show she would be out in a minute, and the kids, who
were also dark-haired and dark-eyed, scrambled into the Checker. They
banged around inside, crashing the jumpseats and crawling about, and I
began to count the day's takings. I already had two five-dollar bills, seven
singles, and a whole handful of change. The meter clicked; sixty-five
cents became seventy-five, and at that moment a little arm flashed past
my face. Snap!

"What did you switch off the meter for?" I asked the boy, who was
hanging up to his waist through the open partition.

"I didn't switch it off."

"So what did you do?"

"I stopped the *timer*." He meant the device that computed the fare by
the minute when a cab was not in motion.

The kid was smiling slyly; it was impossible to be cross with him.

"Mister, give me a quarter," he requested.

I gave him one.

"What about me-ee?" The little girl poked her head through the
window. I had to give her one too.

"Please!" the boy whispered urgently. "Give me another one."

I did not care for this at all, but he reproached me. "Look how many
you have!"

At long last the father and mother appeared, bringing with them more
children. Again the cab was filled with laughter, fidgeting, excited
childish whispers, and again the begging hands were stretched out.
"Give us some too!"

I turned around and looked at the parents; they maintained a smiling
neutrality. What sort of people could they be?

The father told me the way and at the same time engaged in an odd
interrogation.

"Tell me: who are taxi drivers?"

I did not understand exactly what he wanted to know.

"Blacks?"

"Of course."

"Japanese?"

"Some."

"How about Gypsies? Have you ever seen a Gypsy drive a cab?"

26

I shrugged my shoulders as if to say, I've no idea.

"You've never seen one and you never will!" the man pronounced.

"Why ever not?"

"Because a cab driver works hard," the mother explained, "and we don't like to work!"

Only then did I guess what the intertwined neon tubes in the window signified, beside which I had waited for these customers. It was the upturned palm by which a fortune teller predicts the future. The same palm, only in blue neon rather than red, flickered in the window of the house where we stopped. The meter showed $1.90, and I was given two dollars. However, the husband and wife evidently felt slightly awkward, and the gypsy woman decided to pay the cab driver something extra in her own way.

"Want me to tell your fortune?

I was silent.

"For free!" She held out her hand, and I gave her mine.

"Oh!" Barely glancing at my palm, she exclaimed in rapture and clicked her tongue. "Oh, what do I see! You're going to get rich soon! That's right. Someone will leave a bag of money in your cab."

I smiled sourly, but the seeress said, "You don't believe me? You'll see."

It was three o'clock in the afternoon. At around four I had to get back to Queens, to the garage; the night-shift driver would be waiting for the cab. "Let's call it a day," I decided. I was hungry, and went into a pizzeria.

According to my calculations, my entire take, including the small change, should come to twenty-six dollars, and for a day shift a driver was supposed to make sixty-five. However, there was no point in getting upset about not filling the "quota"; it was early days yet. I took a gulp of my Coke, bit off the end of a fiery piece of pizza—and let out a groan. Heavens, I didn't have all of those twenty-six dollars! As ill luck would have it, when I left the house I had on me just enough to pay for two subway tokens and a pack of cigarettes. Meanwhile, I owed the garage sixty-five cents for my adventure with the "hot seat"; the gypsy kids had cadged a dollar from me, the pizza cost a dollar, and I had refused all tips.

My peculations were not large, but how was I going to explain them? Big or little, a taxi driver's take has to be turned over to the last penny. What would I say? How was I going to shout through the dispatcher's window that you couldn't turn down kids who asked you for a piece of change while the hacks coming off the shift would be standing by, listening?

As if sneering at my misfortunes, Columbus Avenue saw me off to the garage amid cries of "Taxi! Taxi!" Now that I had finished work, an upraised hand loomed at every corner. Coming up to my Checker, I noticed a young couple loaded with shopping bags.

"Where are you going?" I asked, shoving the key in the lock and committing my first taxi-driver's crime: *A driver shall not ask a passenger for a destination until the passenger is seated. The penalty for violation of this rule is $100.*

"I'm going back to Queens, to the garage," I told the customers, who were looking at me pleadingly, and suddenly I remembered that I had committed a second crime: *A driver shall not indicate by word, motion, or gesture that he is restricting his direction of travel or destination. The penalty for violation of this rule is $100.* What was the total of the punishment I had earned by now?

"Queens happens to be exactly where we're going," the young man said brightly.

What a piece of luck! I opened the trunk and we loaded up the packages. The girl, who was about fifteen, winked at me conspiratorially.

"You don't waste any time!"

"What do you mean?"

"You know what I mean!"

She was so happy, so proud; no one would have dared contradict her over anything just then. I was not about to try to read her mind.

The boy, who must have been all of twenty, had returned from a long voyage the night before. A sailor. Hadn't been home for five months. Yesterday the girl had met him when the ship docked. Now she was clinging to him; the trunk was stuffed with presents.

"Let's take the tunnel."

"If you tell me the way."

He showed no surprise at my ignorance and did not fall into the schoolmasterish tone. He was telling a cab driver how to find the tunnel linking Manhattan and Queens, and on his lips it sounded as natural as his stories about the sea voyage.

Canada, Norway, Portugal, Egypt, China . . . He didn't like Reds; some riffraff in Greenwich Village, he said indignantly, had organized a socialist party recently.

"Recently? I thought it happened eighty years ago."

He laughed. "You got it wrong somewhere. Our guys said last year for sure."

And the girl nodded, she remembered it well: last year for certain.

The conversation was interrupted when we entered the tunnel. For me this was a test of survival.

The squalid little house where our trip ended leaned up against an abandoned factory. Six dollars and five cents.

"What do we owe you?" the girl asked, for some reason, and she watched me—slyly, as if testing me.

I pointed silently at the meter.

"Hey, and you call yourself a cabbie? You forgot about the tunnel? You forgot about the trunk? And I thought—"

For the trip through the tunnel I had indeed paid seventy-five cents, but charging passengers for using the trunk was forbidden; I had had strict instructions about that at the garage.

"Don't argue. I know better!" the girl said aggressively. "My dad's a cab driver."

The boy cut our pointless argument short by holding out to me my biggest bill of the day—ten bucks, keep it!

I tried to refuse; they were a lucky fare for me anyway, without them I would have had to go to Queens empty. I thrust the change back with the feeling that my gesture was thoroughly insincere. After all, I needed the money so badly.

"Don't worry about us," the sailor said persuasively. "I brought home six grand."

"Yes, he did!" the girl confirmed.

We spent a long time saying goodbye, shaking each other by the hand. There were many more times to come when I would experience that special joy that comes from a sudden welling up of affection toward strangers.

"Don't forget to charge fifty cents for the trunk!" were the girl's parting words. "It helps. And take care of yourself. Don't even think of picking up blacks!"

———

The next morning I tried again to win the race for the early customer. I gathered speed, overtook one cab, then another, a fifth, and now, as far as the eye could see, there were no yellow sharks in front.

I was a shark myself! My Checker raced down the middle of the roadway, the arrow on the speedometer was approaching 50—I held dominion over Lexington Avenue!

The winner of the race is he who is the fastest. The first passenger I see will be mine. Well, where is he, then? Where?

At the end of the next block a pedestrian stopped at the curb and waved. I stepped on the gas and bang! The wheel hit me in the chest; I was tripped by a red light. But the passenger was mine anyway. He was not going to disappear. The other cabs were left behind. I fixed my eyes on the traffic light: so hurry up then, hurry!

But it was not to be. A Ford that I had overtaken a while back, bowling smoothly along behind me, was not tripped by the red light. I started up with a jerk! Floored the gas pedal! But a Checker's engine has only six cylinders; it is not a Jaguar or a Porsche. I had lost the race again. A race where you do not know the distance or the number of participants and where the fastest, it had turned out, was not necessarily the winner. But if it was not the fastest, then who?

I turned off the racetrack and, after ten minutes or so circling around quiet cross streets, calmly picked up a customer. Dropped him off. Prowled around for a quarter of an hour and found another. Thus I developed my own, original style of working. Let the fools run their wild race without judges or rules. I was getting my passengers with no strain on the nerves whatever. True, there were not many of them; but, on the other hand, the treacherous post office blocked my way less and less often; the drivers around me grew quite tame; I heard the curses and screech of brakes less and less often. There was only one big drawback: I brought back half as much money to the garage as the other cabbies. At the end of the week Mr. Forman, the manager, called me in.

"Do you know how much you'll get for your first week?"

I could guess that the paycheck would be modest at best.

"You receive 43 percent of your bookings. On Sunday you earned twelve dollars, Monday fourteen, Tuesday eleven. Do you understand why it's so little?"

Naturally, I understood that I still did not have the knack, that I had not managed to get the hang of it yet.

"Those are all roundabout explanations which don't teach you anything," the manager interrupted. "Do you want to learn how to make money?"

You bet! A science like that I was ready to soak up the way a sponge soaks up moisture.

"You waste a lot of time *waiting* for a customer to approach your cab. You're from Russia, over there people are used to getting cabs at taxi stands. Here in New York we do things differently. A New York taxi driver is always in motion!"

I listened, open-mouthed.

"Your second and biggest mistake. When it's slow, you scour the cross streets, while the customers are hailing cabs on the *avenues*."

Sitting in his windowless kennel in the garage, how on earth did the manager know where I was "scouring the streets"? He had read about taxis in Russia somewhere. But what about my "original style" that I was so proud of? How could he have found out about that?

I could endure it no longer. "How did you find out where I look for passengers?"

"I took a look at your trip sheets. You wrote right here that at 5:50 a.m. you picked up a customer at 260 East Sixty-seventh Street, and another fare half an hour later outside 88 West Eighty. Twenty minutes after that you got a fare at 65 East Sixty-fifth. Those aren't corner buildings, and that means you're cruising the *cross streets*. But when a New Yorker wants to pick up a taxi, he doesn't wait for a chance cab in front of his house; he goes out onto the *avenue*. That's what he's used to."

Harry Forman is not a made-up name but a real one, and I give it here because the manager of the Freenat garage was the *only* one of all the taxi drivers' bosses (whom I later had occasion to come across) who sent for me not to bawl me out, fine me, or take away my papers, but to help me. He could have had no other reason, for he already knew his garage was not going to make any profit out of me, simply because I lived in Brooklyn while the garage was in Queens, and so as soon as I had learned the business the least bit better, I would leave.

————

I lost the race many times after this conversation. Fainthearted, I would give up the struggle and retire to the quiet backwaters of the cross streets to trawl for a chance minnow. But one day, guessing the rhythm of the changing traffic lights correctly, catching the crest of the "green wave," I allowed two or three overeager taxi drivers to pass me, and, when they were tripped by a red light, went smoothly around them—and picked up a passenger!

The customer I had won, my living Grand Prix, was in no hurry to get into the cab, however. First he wanted to make an oral agreement with the taxi driver about the conditions of the forthcoming trip.

"You will take me to the corner of Third Avenue and Thirty-second Street," he said with a semi-interrogatory intonation, "write me a receipt, and indicate on it thirty-five cents more than the amount on the meter?"

"The conditions you propose are not bad, sir," I replied, trying to answer in kind. "Sit up in front, you'll be more comfortable."

The freckled face broke into a smile. However, he was beaming not because he was stupid, but because he was seventeen years old and carrying a small case that jingled with the tools of his trade.

"You must be quite an expert if the company pays for your taxi rides."

Yes, he's a pretty good electrician. This is his fourth month on the job. The pay's still modest, but he's already been promised a raise. And that's all the more important because the increase will allow him to settle down with his family and run his own life.

"Have you known your fiancée long?"

Oddly enough, this simple question elicited some contradictory explanations. There was no fiancée yet. There wasn't even a steady girlfriend, actually. And anyway it wouldn't be easy for him to find someone who would share his interests.

I was intrigued. "I don't think you'll have much trouble finding your helpmate, sir. [This was perfectly sincere; he was a good-looking boy.] It's probably your interests that are complicating things."

He was silent.

"You're a secretive sort of person," I said reproachfully, but of course that did not help. Once again I had to start up my shameless drill of flattery, which the fragile armor that protected the young man's ego could not withstand. He was going to get married as soon as he could because of a conflict with his father.

Well, everyone knows the sort of filial interests fathers are opposed to. *In time,* I said preachily, he would understand his father's point of view, but it might come too late, when what now seemed an innocent bottle of beer or "joint" would already have done its destructive work.

But I had fallen wide of the mark. For my information, there were many more exciting things in the world than marijuana and all that . . . For instance? Well, if it came to that, how about game machines?

"Hey, such foolishness!" I got angry. "How can you feed your first working wages to machines?"

But I had guessed wrong again. For the second time in the last two minutes it became obvious that banality and wisdom are not bedfellows. My passenger could not care less about gambling. With his earnings he *bought* machines, and not those you play for money but those you play for pleasure: pinball machines.

"And how many of these machines do you have?"

"Six."

"But they're expensive."

That was the point, they were not at all expensive. He looked for old, broken ones, and repaired and restored them. He loved them. He had built a totally new machine himself that didn't exist anywhere else, Cosmic Rain. He had an idea for another one, Submarine War. He had a lot of ideas!

"So why is your father against it?"

"We have a small apartment. There's no more space in my room, and Mom won't let me put them in the kitchen."

We had already arrived, but the boy still had not left, although he had paid and I had given him the receipt. He seemed to be trying to say

33

something else. At last he got it out: "I wish I could learn to drive like you one day!"

———

I was riding the subway, roaring with laughter. People looked warily in my direction and sidled away, but I could not calm down. In the thunderous underground hell, where, as always in the hot weather, the air conditioners were switched off, I counted up my victories, and they were numerous. To begin with, I really had learned to drive a car. I had had to.

In the last two weeks I had traveled one *thousand* miles! And not in the blissful quiet of the suburbs, but along seething avenues, tunnels, and bridges; and I had not hit a pedestrian or maimed myself, my Checker, or anyone else's car.

After more than three years in America I had spent my first days among real live Americans, and I could not help observing that the behavior of these "foreigners"—always hurrying somewhere, alien to me in their language and in their way of thinking—was unquestionably regulated by a desire not to degrade, by word, gesture, or any other means, the human dignity of a duffer cab driver. Over two hundred people had already used my cab, but not one of my customers had expressed the suspicion that I was driving him around and around Central Park or the Pan Am Building on purpose, unable to find the Commodore or the Biltmore Hotel. (Do you remember those names?) Not one had demanded that I pay for my mistakes out of my own pocket, either. One secretary actually found herself in my cab *twice* in those two weeks. What trials fate sometimes sends people. Both times she had to "run over" for an interview during her lunch hour: she was working out her last week at her old job. Because of me she was late getting to the interview the first time; three days later, when this unlucky girl, having barely opened the door of the yellow cab, instantly recognized the valiant cabbie, she gasped. She did not tell me to go to hell, she made herself get into my Checker—though I candidly advised her not to. And, of course, we were late again.

How could it happen that two weeks in a row my cab had been taken exclusively by patient, benevolent, and unassuming people? Why, later on, were they transformed into boors, misers, and troublemakers? Nor were all my miscues as innocent as my constant failure to make a turn in time. Now and then I actually forgot to check whether the second passenger had gotten into the cab, and I took off while one of the customer's feet was still on the sidewalk. How many times, as I pulled away, did I hear a bloodcurdling shriek? But neither the old man who dropped his glasses because of my actions, nor the portly nurse, nor the teenage saxophonist, whom I nearly crippled, cursed me out or harassed me with lectures. And who cared if after one hundred and fifty working hours I had broken out in a cold sweat one hundred and fifty times, and earned barely a dollar an hour—all the same, I had won!

And though tomorrow, before crack of dawn, I would have to get up again and drag myself across the city on the subway, at least it would not be to the artificial Russian microcosm in the middle of New York which only yesterday had been all America to me. Two weeks before I had felt that I was slowly dying. Now, collapsing from exhaustion, I felt alive!

Chapter Three

KALEIDOSCOPE

Thus began my "double life." I was up at four, at half-past got on the subway, and by a quarter to six I would leave the garage to join the morning race.

My shift ended at four in the afternoon. I arrived home at five, had something to eat, lay down on the couch, and glanced through the Soviet papers, heavy-eyed. When my eyes were about to close altogether, I sat down at the desk, remembering that at 10 a.m. next Friday I had to enter the recording studio and close the soundproof door behind me; the tall gray-haired man would switch on the introduction—"This is Radio Liberty"—and I would be left alone with the microphone.

For three years millions of people in Russia have been listening to my program, *Our Daily Bread.* This program disturbs and wounds everyone there—Russians, Ukrainians, Jews, Kazakhs, Latvians—for my subject is why a great nation, a superpower with the largest area of arable land on the planet (twice that of the United States), is unable to feed its own people. And why, in a country where five times as many work on the land as do in America, people cannot walk into a store and buy meat, or fish, or chicken, or milk, or potatoes.

But with every passing month my program gives me less and less satisfaction. Sometimes I get an oppressive feeling that even here the Soviet jammers have somehow secretly penetrated the editorial offices and the recording studio. And this was not some mental aberration of mine.

"Don't you think it would be better to avoid your personal opinions? Especially since they're always negative," the patronizing, lordly baritone advised; it was the era of détente.

That screenwriter who had so recently been on the other side of the Wall, a mere listener to this very same radio station, if he had been told that, when he arrived here, his new superiors, just like his old ones, would admonish him—at times, indeed, pressure him—not to blurt out over the airwaves the whole truth about that closed society, gathered crumb by crumb, he would never have believed it. It was quite enough to tell half the truth, and a quarter was even more commendable. My superiors "played" at détente as enthusiastically as I "played" at driving a taxi; and the overseer did not fail to drop the occasional hint that, in the final analysis, willfulness could cost me a job.

It was all so familiar, so much the same; but in my present position as an émigré there was a fresh nuance. My employers knew that my Russian program was my only real means of livelihood; that here, in America, I was good for nothing else.

That is why in the last few weeks I have been feeling so much better, and why my heart grows lighter at sunrise as my yellow cab crosses the Queensboro Bridge into the city, where I am invariably greeted by a living symbol of New York, the tipsy "traffic lady."

In one hand the traffic lady holds a bottle wrapped in a paper bag, with the other she directs the flow of cars. *Stop!* she signals when the light is red, and waves energetically *Go! Go!* when it turns green. It makes her happy that the cars obey her. Young, fair-haired, she is always smiling, always in good spirits. I think the two of us must be the happiest people in all New York.

Observing Mr. Forman's chief commandment—a New York cabbie is always in motion!—I barrel northward far up into the East Nineties, until I pick up a passenger. Having mastered this tactic, one day I turned south for a change, drove for half a mile through the still empty canyons

37

of the streets, and began to cruise around Midtown, when I suddenly came upon a long yellow snake whose head lay alongside the entrance to the Madison Hotel.

What were the drivers of all these parked cabs doing here? Why were they not taking part in the morning race?

As I pulled up, the revolving door ejected the standard guest of a decent hotel, carrying a light-colored raincoat and an attaché case.

The man looked around, took a deep breath of the exhaust-saturated air, glanced at his watch, and headed for the taxis drawn up at the entrance.

The driver of the first cab was reclining on the hood of his Ford, one hand crooked, swanlike, under his cheek. Noticing the approaching customer, he warded off any possible fare with a theatrical gesture.

"I'm not going anywhere. I'm on my break."

"My car's taken," said another cabbie.

When my Checker got a bit nearer, the man was entreating the next driver:

"Please, take me to the Port Authority. I'm in a hurry, I would be *so* grateful."

"Sorry, mister. We only cater to foreign tourists."

The passenger turned to me. "How about you? Who do you cater to?"

"Everyone," I said meekly.

―――――

At the Port Authority bus terminal five black teenagers, going as it happened to the Madison Hotel, were waiting for a "big cab"; in New York only Checkers were allowed to carry five passengers. The boys and girls were sleepy and rumpled after their night bus ride, except for one tall, wide-mouthed girl, who looked as if she had just gotten dressed up to go dancing. Her blouse was dazzling, her skirt gorgeous. Life was a party!

Her girlfriends looked at her askance, but this princess, ignoring the bags that everyone was putting into the trunk, climbed into the front seat and "danced" even as she sat. Her shoulders swayed, her hands fluttered. "Where's your radio?"

Trying not to look a complete fool—you could not help being charmed by her—I put on a grim air.

"There aren't any radios in fleet cabs," I said.

"How can you live without music?"

The girls were openly furious: the boys could not take their eyes off her.

"Which disco do you go to?" (She was flirting with the cabbie!)

"Taxi drivers don't hang out in discos," I muttered through my unreliable temporary teeth. "We work too hard."

The impish look vanished; stifling a deliberate yawn, and in quite another tone, as if dozing off from the unspeakable boredom I produced in her, she switched to the one and only topic that a drip of a cab driver was capable of holding a conversation about:

"So, how's Lucy?"

"Who's Lucy?"

"Your wife!" And, as if I had already answered her: "How're the kids?"

"Just terrible!" I said. "You can imagine—they're pretty much like you."

She grinned from ear to ear; then, syllable by syllable, read the blue ID card mounted on the platform.

"Vla-di-mir? Is that your first or last name?"

"First."

"Nice. I can't stand all these Toms, Cliffs, Sams. Bor-*ing!*" She peeked in the rearview mirror, checking the boys' reaction, and fidgeted again; what was she going to come up with next?

"Are you from Russia?"

"Uh-huh."

"Jewish?"

"Uh-huh."

"Listen, are Jews the only people who live in Russia?"

I choked.

"Sir!" The boys were alarmed. "She didn't mean it like that!"

"Last time we came to New York, sir, the cab driver who brought us in from the airport was a Jew from Russia, too."

Realizing that they were not mocking me, I answered in a conciliatory tone.

"I don't know. I haven't met any Russian taxi drivers in New York."

The line of yellow cabs outside the Madison Hotel had not budged during my absence. The same driver reclined on the hood of the front cab in the same languid pose. Two others were leaning against the wall, smoking. In front of them stood two middle-aged women listening respectfully.

"All the cabs outside this hotel are specially ordered." One of them, in a flat cap, was explaining.

"Over there" — he pointed toward the corner — "you can always get a cab."

The ladies thanked their benefactor for the explanation and plodded drearily off to the corner.

"Why didn't you take them?" I asked.

"Because I've already been waiting more than an hour," the cabbie answered irritably.

"What for?"

There was no reply. Another Checker rolled up to the hotel entrance, and a strapping black man in a red shirt and sky-blue pants (his colorful clothes betrayed his island origins — Jamaica? Trinidad? Haiti?) began to unload suitcases with the help of the doorman. The passenger, a stoop-shouldered hasid, paid him and minced off toward the entrance.

Looking after him, the black man stooped, and twirled his index fingers beside his chocolate cheeks as if he were winding locks of hair around them and had grown invisible payesses. He produced a green bill, and proceeded to put on an entire pantomime: How a greedy Jew settles up with a taxi driver.

The lone bill, folded in half, which he kept counting and re-counting over and over again, became a fat wad; the "Jew," frightened by the impudent stranger's outstretched hands, was protecting his riches from them; passersby stopped and laughed, it was such a talented act! Meanwhile the "Jew" kept on withholding, and haggling and suffering, so painful was it for him to part with the money; and, finally, tore it away from himself like a piece of his soul, paid up — and became his original self again.

The black man held the twenty-dollar bill over his head for everyone to see, gave President Jackson a smacking kiss, and in front of the whole of Madison Avenue proclaimed the reason why he had left his wonderful Caribbean island and ended up here, in America:

"I LOVE MONEY!"

Enjoying the effect, he ran to his Checker. Reversing to the end of the block, he took up his place at the tail of the line. "Kennedy," sighed the driver in the flat cap.

"What are you all doing here outside the hotel?" I asked, turning to Flatcap and the guy with him, who wore his gray hair in a crewcut, but they were silent.

"This is disgusting! How come you don't answer when someone talks to you?" I said indignantly, and started when a voice spoke in Russian.

"If you wanted to talk to me, why are you speaking English?" Flatcap said reproachfully.

"How could I know you were Russian?"

"I'm not Russian."

His accent was Georgian, his cap too.

"You're Georgian?"

"I'm Jewish."

"He thinks he looks just like an American," the driver sprawled on the hood observed about me, and it was clear from *his* accent that he was from Odessa.

"What are you getting at the guy for?" Crewcut stood up for me. He was a Muscovite, born and bred.

"Putz!" someone bellowed behind me. It was the black man. I was probably wearing a very silly expression, because everyone started laughing.

The black man slapped me on the shoulder, and, as if introducing me to my countrymen, translated the Yiddish swear word: "Rooskyprick!"

His audience was growing.

The hilarity had not died down when a quarrel flared up. The Odessan and the Georgian were each bent on proving that it was he who had taught the Haitian his Russian obscenities.

"Not a smart guy," the Georgian complained to me, confidingly. "When I started teaching this monkey, *he* was still in Odessa!"

"It's obvious," I said, "your comrade arrived after you'd done all the groundwork."

The Georgian nodded gravely.

41

A girl carrying a holdall emerged from the revolving door. The doorman asked the girl something, relieved her of the holdall adroitly, and announced:

"First cab!"

The driver got off the hood (he turned out to be very tall), stretched and yawned, and tried to slip the doorman a dollar. But the doorman pushed his hand away, and an injured look appeared on his haughty face. The lanky cabbie was by no means taken aback. On the contrary, he was happy about something, and got out another dollar. In a moment the yellow Ford, carrying the girl with the holdall, disappeared around the corner. Crewcut followed it with a sad gaze.

"Why did he give the doorman money?" I asked, but the Georgian in the cap spoke as if he hadn't heard the question:

"Now I'm first. Park your cab in front of mine."

Everything that had happened in front of the hotel was shrouded in mystery.

"Aren't you going to take the next job?" I said, unable to let it drop.

"We'll see," the Georgian said significantly.

———

It was annoying that my fellow "Russians" were stringing me along, turning some nonsense into a professional secret. But their behavior was more funny than offensive. After all, I was not going to become one of them, a "chief" who twists anyone he meets around his little finger. I did not need to know their secrets. Even if I made less money and had to endure my temporary bridges coming loose from their bearings. An extra month—what was so terrible about that?

Meantime, the Haitian did not stand still for a moment. Now he was playing basketball. Every passerby was his opponent! He dribbled an invisible ball low and swiftly along the edge of the sidewalk, overtook a policeman, went around two lesbians walking with their arms around each other, swerved sharply toward the sideline, dodged past me, almost collided with a mother pushing a stroller, and ended with a triple jump at an invisible backboard.

"The idiot can run like that all day," the Georgian said, and called to the black man: "Hey!"

The Haitian came over.

"Repeat after me!" With elaborate precision, the Georgian pronounced the new linguistic pearl.

"F-f-fak!" the black man articulated with effort.

"Say it goud!" The Georgian was aiming for perfect pronunciation.

"F-f-fak-yo-muzzair!"

I thought he did pretty well, but the professor was inordinately demanding. "Stoopid!" He shamed the student.

A cart piled with suitcases rolled out the door of the hotel onto the sidewalk, followed by the passengers.

"Japanese!" gasped Crewcut. "How many?"

"Six!" the doorman muttered conspiratorially out of the corner of his mouth.

The Georgian cackled with pleasure and opened the trunk of his car.

"How are you going to squeeze the luggage and six people into your Peugeot?" whispered Crewcut.

"Gimme *ten* of 'em!" said the Georgian, and Crewcut began rushing around, torn between the Japanese men, whom he smiled at, and the suitcases, which he could not help smiling at, and the doorman, whom he implored, "Two cabs! Tell them they need *two* cabs!"

A Checker, coasting along from the end of the block, zoomed up to the entrance, and in the next moment the mighty figure of the Haitian rose up between the Georgian and the suitcases. The black man evidently had some plan and was full of determination.

"Show me your money!" he ordered the Japanese, and one of them ingenuously opened his wallet. The black "chief" touched the bills delicately and pulled out a five by one corner.

"This is the tip," he explained to the passenger. "Good Japanese give doorman a tip, and for that good doorman calls a *big* cab."

"Sankyu!" The Japanese nodded, while the black man, presented the doorman with the money.

"They need a Checker," the doorman said to the drivers.

"*What* are these bastards doing?" Crewcut howled, trying to shoulder his way into the group, but the Haitian merely threw his athletic torso backward, and Crewcut yelped: a back of stone was pressing him into the body of the car.

The Japanese stood there, frightened and pale; they probably would have run away if the paid-off doorman had not already loaded all the suitcases into the Haitian's Checker. The Georgian gesticulated hope-lessly. Almost crying from hurt and spite, he hurled at the Haitian all the Russian words he had taught him so painstakingly.

The black man released the subdued Crewcut, by now pretty bat-tered, and returned the wallet to its owner.

"Sanka-bury-match!" the Japanese squeaked out, quite happy, while his five fellow travelers began to bow all at once: to the doorman in his top hat, and the big cab, and the whole of the hospitable Madison Hotel. An invisible curtain fell, the scene was over, and new suitcases appeared on the stage.

The Georgian and Crewcut got so carried away discussing their plan of revenge on the "goddamn hustler" who had cheekily swiped the meek Japanese that they failed to notice these new suitcases in front of the hotel. The doorman flung open the door of *my* Checker. Somewhere, deep in the recesses of my consciousness, stirred a previously unknown excitement: maybe I might sneak a Kennedy, too!

Two old ladies in blue wigs got in decorously; I waited with bated breath.

"Ship terminal!"

But I felt no disappointment. Why was a trip to the ship terminal worse than a trip to the airport? Everything fascinated me. Perhaps the famous *Queen Elizabeth 2* would be moored there today.

The walk takes about thirty minutes, the ride lasts only five. The diamond-district shop windows on Forty-seventh Street, heaped with gold and precious stones, gave way rapidly to the skyscrapers of Rocke-feller Center, followed by the theaters of Broadway. Then squads of prostitutes, crummy movie houses with Xs on their signs, and cheap joints where, fliers promised, satisfaction was guaranteed for seven dollars. Past houses whose windows were boarded up with plywood, catching occasional glimpses of ruins that looked like bomb sites. The white faces vanished. And then a stunning white girl stands in the middle of the sidewalk, shirt unbuttoned, breasts bared. She lifts her elegant skirt, and, squatting down, urinates. Two men bustle around her, one with a camera, the other with a reflector.

The cheap joints disappeared; ahead lay only the run-down West Side highway and the *Queen Elizabeth 2*. I dropped off my passengers. Before I even had time to take a look at the ship terminal, into the car jumped a black man in a short leather jacket worn over his naked tattooed chest. Calling me "Hey-man," he asked permission to smoke, and filled the cab with marijuana fumes.

So it was through these fumes that I saw the reverse panorama, the rebirth of New York, as we returned from a neighborhood of slums to the magnificence of the city center. Around Times Square, a girl, with a bob like a boy's, surfaced out of the human maelstrom right in front of the Checker's hood. Flaxen hair and worn jeans. She had probably smoked herself into a stupor; she waved at me, not noticing I had a passenger inside. But maybe that was exactly why she was clambering into my cab—because there was a client in it! A brazen little underage hooker. I could distinguish between New Yorkers pretty well by now. I indicated that the cab was taken, but "Hey-man" rolled the window down, calling "Get in!" and she was already in the backseat.

"Sorry, miss, I'm not allowed to take a second passenger until I've dropped off the first one."

"But I'm late!"

"For what?" I poured a gallon of sarcasm into this pintsized phrase. I did not like the way things were going at all, and I certainly had no desire to leave them together on the backseat. Cars were honking behind me, but I would not budge.

"Take another cab, miss."

"Hey, man, cut the crap, okay?" The black guy got out, slamming the door loudly.

"What about my money?" I jumped out, but what could I do? Run after the bastard and leave the car? The drivers behind me, swearing, were going around my Checker.

"He left the money!" the prostitute shouted through the window. When I got back, she pointed to the crumpled bills in the change cup and, as if nothing had happened, said:

"Can we make it to NYU by ten o'clock?"

"It's already five past."

Now I was even more upset because I did not know exactly where the university was. I had to ask and then ask again. But, as it turned out, all we had to do was get to Fifth Avenue and drive down to the very end, to the archway in Washington Square Park.

"I can walk from the Arch, it's right around there," my passenger, who had only been in New York since yesterday, explained to me, the cab driver.

The girl's from Michigan. Wants to study here. She has an appointment with the dean at ten. Being late doesn't matter, though. She's already late by a few months anyway; her scholarship application should have been sent last spring. But that is not important either. The main thing is that she knows quite definitely that she wants to be an actress.

"Listen, Miss Future Celebrity," I said, somewhat embarrassed that I still could not read every passenger at first glance. "Do you realize who that man was?"

"Who?"

"A dangerous guy. Especially for you."

"You only say that because he's black!"

"Not true. You saw how he was dressed."

"He didn't do anything bad to me!"

"Maybe he just didn't have time. He told you to get into the cab, and you got in. He'd only just been smoking hashish," I said, with slight exaggeration.

"Really?" she exclaimed with unfeigned interest.

"If he had asked you to go to a bar—"

"Please, stop it," the girl requested. She slid over to the jumpseat, poked her head through the partition, and stuck out her tongue. I melted, of course.

"Ah," I said, "you little minx!"

She noticed the blue card.

"Why did you leave Russia? After all, it's the country where everything belongs to everybody."

"And who told you about Russia?"

"My history teacher."

I could see him now: an enlightened person, a Marxist intellectual, the idol of his upperclassmen.

"What will you do if the university doesn't accept you?"

"I'll stay a while. I like it here."

"But where will you 'stay a while'?"

"With my girlfriend. She has a studio on Sutton Place."

"And will your mother let you stay in New York?"

"Mom doesn't have too much time for me now. She's expecting a baby, getting married, you know."

I looked into the fathomless blue of her eyes and my heart turned over. If someone offered her a drink, she would drink it; if someone offered her cocaine, she would snort it. She would go with anyone who would treat her as a pal, an equal; and the only thing her present convictions would not let her do was torture animals. What sort of ordeals would this tender, trusting child go through?

But driving a taxi is not conducive to profound thoughts; it's a kaleidoscope. You look into it and see a bright, unique picture. A moment later there is another magical design. Twirl the toy in your hands and ask yourself which image has etched itself on your memory. None. Only a phantasmagoria remains. Your impressions change every time the meter clicks on. Before half an hour had passed, I had already made friends with a hefty albino.

A clinking sound came from behind me, and my new passenger, whom I had not yet caught a glimpse of, exclaimed:

"Sir, someone left something here!"

I stuck my head through the partition and saw a soaked paper package oozing blood and disintegrating before my eyes. I leaped out of the cab, banging my head on the doorframe—ouch!—and, clutching the bump, opened the rear door. My passenger was wiping his bloody hands on a corner of the wrapping paper. On the floor lay a bottle of whiskey and a bottle of wine. Pieces of meat were spilling out of the ripped package.

The package had been left by a gay couple, one young, one young-looking. They were kissing on the way to Columbia University, I complained to my passenger.

"Back where I'm from in Oklahoma," said the albino, "they wouldn't dare behave that way!"

"I'll have to go back to Columbia," I said, vexed.

"Forget it!" the passenger shouted at me. "Back in Oklahoma those jerks would have been chucked out of the cab and had the daylights beaten out of them!"

"What am I going to do with the meat? Throw it away?"

"How could you? These are terrific steaks."

"But they'll go off. It's sweltering out. And I have a long day ahead. Take them if you want."

"Wait a minute!" And my passenger vanished into a grocery store. What was he thinking of? Why the hell did I have to wait for him? But he soon came back, looking preoccupied. He had brought some empty paper bags and a plastic bag of ice cubes. He wrapped everything up again deftly and handed me the tidy bundle with an air of quiet triumph.

"Now you can drive around in the heat all day!"

Need I describe what sincere friends we parted a quarter of an hour later? But the albino had hardly blended into the crowd when my meter clicked again, and I made yet another friend. A rabbi from Tel Aviv. He laughed till he cried when I told him how the Southern gentleman had urged me to appropriate the steaks and booze in order to teach the gay men a lesson.

When he could laugh no more, the rabbi unlocked his old-fashioned traveling bag and extracted from it a skullcap, which he held out to me. In this crazy city, this Babylon, a Jew who forgets he's a Jew will come to a bad end. . . . Realizing that this threat had no effect on me, the rabbi assumed a pitiful expression and said:

"What does it cost you? Put it on, just for a minute, until we get to the Hilton. Please, just give me the pleasure."

I put on the skullcap and started singing the Sabbath hymn. *"Eliahu, ha navi!"*

"Eliahu, ha girgashi!" the rabbi intoned.

I felt so good again! And the rabbi could not get enough of me.

"If only you knew how that skullcap suited you, you'd never take it off!"

On the way to the Hilton we had to stop off on Forty-seventh Street; to pick something up, the rabbi said.

Shortly after he got out, some handsome fellow appeared beside the Checker. Dark-haired, brilliantined, he kept glancing at me. I felt silly and took off the skullcap. But he still did not take his eyes off me, and I began to look at him too. At last he said:

"My friend's going to the Hilton with you."

"So?"

"So nothing. He just asked me to keep an eye on his things."

Normally quick to take offense, somehow I did not feel the least offended. Perhaps because I had already made a coup that day: someone else's bottles were clinking gently at my feet. Joking apart, the package was worth at least forty dollars . . . What was happening to me? Was I losing my sense of dignity? Was I becoming a *cabbie?*

"Tee-hee!"

There was a short chuckle behind me. Not just any chuckle, but like a ripple of jingle bells. A woman of about fifty was giggling.

"Tee-hee, I'm in such a hurry. Today's my doggie's birthday."

How on earth had she gotten into the cab? I had not heard the door open.

"I'm going to the West Village. It's been such a crazy day, I didn't bring any money with me, tee-hee, not even enough for the subway."

I sobered up immediately.

"I can't take you if you don't have any money."

"Oh, my goodness, tee-hee, aren't you impossible. Don't worry. The doorman will pay you. Only please let's go, or I'll get home after the guests. That would be awkward, tee-hee, turn left—"

"You told me too late."

"Never mind. Take the next left. Pierre loves company so much, but—turn right—he loves going to the bank even more. When I say, 'Pierre, shall we go to the bank today?' he's so happy, and when we get there, he runs straight to the manager and scratches the desk."

"What desk?"

"The one where the manager keeps biscuits for Pierre. And I say, 'Pierre, today we'll take out *your* money.'"

"Tee-hee!" It was my turn to giggle. "Lady, I don't quite understand who you're talking about exactly. Who's this Pierre, your son? Or is it your husband who behaves this way?"

"Pierre is my dog," the lady pronounced sternly.

"Do you mean to say that your dog has his own savings?"

"Pierre has a checking account."

"And is there a lot of money in it?"

"Tee-hee, a good deal more than in mine," the passenger replied, and she proffered an ordinary Citibank ID card with a photo of a white

49

poodle on it. I began to realize that our queer conversation had not just come about by chance. It was a well-rehearsed comic routine, with carefully polished cues, calculated to astound new acquaintances of the owner of Pierre, the hero of a children's TV series. Pierre had been in movies many times and with unvarying success. He had taken part in four feature films and eleven commercials.

"How did your Pierre make this career for himself?"

"My boss saw him one day."

"And who's your boss?"

"The owner of a TV station."

"So you work in television?"

"No, I clean my boss's apartment and look after his three dogs."

The routine she had worked up ran dry and the conversation stumbled along on the rocks of my questions. Before Pierre's owner got her present job, another woman used to clean the apartment.

"Why did she quit?"

"It just happened that way."

"She helped herself to something?"

"Oh, no! Why would you think that?"

What had happened to her predecessor who looked after the boss's dogs was an entirely different story. She fell in love with the charming millionaire. One evening when her boss was going to bed, he found a letter under his pillow. He read it, got upset, and fired the enamored domestic.

My customer disappeared into her building and soon returned with the money and an old, ailing poodle in her arms. Pierre was not making movies anymore; today was his sixteenth birthday. Poodles rarely live that long. If you compared Pierre's age with a human's, he was already over one hundred years old. His decrepit eyes watered; out of his mouth hung a hypertrophied tongue, blackened at the tip.

It was already noon, and my bookings still had not hit twenty-five dollars. Damn it all, I hadn't made anything—yet again!

————

Getting out of the labyrinthine West Village is easy only for those who know the neighborhood. Turning from one alleyway into another, I wandered around in search of a familiar thoroughfare and could not find either Sixth or Seventh Avenue, both of which were somewhere quite close by, when suddenly I saw—suitcases! Two black and two brown ones.

A very short time before I would have paid no attention whatever to these commonplace objects, standing by the curb. But now my heart jumped and fluttered; dangling from their handles were labels bearing the bright letters JFK. Had my hour really come at last?

The owner of the suitcases bent down and asked through the window, "Will you go to Kennedy?"

As I was opening the trunk I noticed two more passengers, nicely dressed little girls who stood to one side, hugging their dolls. The girls' father passed me the suitcases one by one, and I asked, very cautiously, in an artificially casual tone, so as not to unnerve my customer:

"You'll tell me the way?"

He studied me carefully.

"I live in Los Angeles. Don't you know where the airport is?"

"More or less," I mumbled.

Meanwhile, the trunk—containing *three* suitcases, which, due to their square shape, we had barely managed to stuff in—had been slammed shut; the girls were already in the cab, and the passenger, who must have been wondering whether he ought to find some other taxi to the airport, had still not taken away the cabbie's profitable trip, but had left it to me to decide the matter for myself.

"We've got an hour and a half. Can you make it?"

Nothing ventured, nothing gained.

"We'll make it!" I said. "We'll find it!"

The blood pounded in my temples. I heard the door slam and took off toward the intersection. Oh, how I cursed my thoughtlessness now! After all, I could have asked the drivers at the Madison Hotel today for detailed instructions on how to get from Manhattan to Kennedy. But then, why Kennedy and not, say, Yankee Stadium? And up to now my passengers had quite spoiled me; almost every one of them had known his route.

By some miracle, in a minute I found myself on Sixth Avenue, and as soon as a red light barred my way, I leaped out of the car and dashed over to the taxi standing next to mine.

"How do I get to Kennedy?"

Both the driver and his passenger burst out laughing. What a cabbie!
There was no time to wait until they finished laughing, and I was
about to rush over to another yellow cab when the taxi driver got a grip
on himself and said:

"Don't worry, it's simple. Go up to Forty-sixth Street, turn right, get
on the FDR Drive and keep straight on, across the Triborough Bridge.
Follow the signs and you'll get to Kennedy. You can't miss it!"

The light turned green and horns were blasting behind us, but the
cabbie grabbed my arm.

"Repeat it!"

"Forty-sixth and turn right, Forty-sixth and turn right!"

I drove like a bat out of hell. I heard children's voices behind me but
did not look round. I was ashamed of meeting the eyes of the man who
had trusted me and now saw me so flustered. The little girls' voices were
barely audible, but I gathered that they were saying the same thing over
and over again. ". . . hereourdaddyisnthereourdaddyisnthere . . ."

I listened harder.

"Our daddy isn't here."

I looked round and my head swam. On the backseat two terrified kids
were clinging to each other. On the floor bumped the *fourth* suitcase.
Daddy was not in the cab!

The moment I saw the accursed suitcase, I realized what had happened.
The girls' father had put it in and slammed the door in order to go
around behind the Checker and get in from the other side, and at that
instant I had stepped on the gas. But as soon as the picture became clear,
another chilling thought flooded my brain. *Where?* What street had all
this happened on? Where had I left him? I could not remember
anything!

The girls were very frightened, but they did not lose their presence of
mind as much as I had.

"We left Daddy behind at Grandma's house," said the younger one.

But I no longer had the strength to look for "Grandma's house." I was
glad that at least the little mites were not howling.

"Children," I said, in a voice as nice as the wolf's in *Little Red Riding
Hood,* "we're going to the police, and they'll tell us where Grandma's
house is."

"Mister Driver!" said the older one, who was barely five years old. "We have to go straight to Burger King and turn left. That's where Grandma's house is."

I got to Burger King and turned left, and we saw Daddy.

"Daddy! Daddy!" cheeped the girls.

What had that man gone through, when some suspicious-looking guy, passing himself off as a taxi driver and not knowing the way to the airport, not to mention his broken English, had torn off in a car with his children? How had he brought up his little ones? What sort of upbringing had he received himself, if, when he saw me, he did not curse me out and take the job away from me—after all that? Obviously he was still ignorant of the trials his kindness would be rewarded with en route from Greenwich Village to the TWA terminal.

———

Kennedy airport! Half of the soul, half of the life of a New York cabbie belongs here, in this inexhaustible well of fabulous driving dollars. Not for nothing does an old hack like to brag about his thorough knowledge of Kennedy; he can drive it blindfold, he says, whether it be to the cargo center or the customs section of any of the airlines, whose branches are scattered all over the enormous area; he knows by heart the approach routes to every one of the hotels, every short- and long-term parking lot. But no cabbie would ever think of mentioning, even in passing, that he knows all nine main airline terminals—Pan Am, Northwest, Eastern, United, American, British Airways, National, TWA, International Arrivals. You'd have to be a total fool not to know the *terminals!* And yet *I* did not know them.

I had been told TWA, and one really did not have to know anything to find it. Just take the main road and watch for the colored signs. See the brown one? What's the number on it? Four? And what letters do you see on the sign? TWA? Well, aren't you smart!

And here, right in front of your nose, above the same main road, are numbers on colored signs: 1, 2, 3, and a brown 4. Which route do you take to get to TWA? The brown one? The fourth one? Hey, buddy, a guy with a brain like yours shouldn't be driving a taxi.

You can laugh. You hadn't left Daddy behind at Grandma's house. His look of loathing wasn't boring into the back of your head. But when

I saw all the signs and numbers, the tangle of overpasses and under-passes, I was so dumbfounded that I immediately lost the main road and found myself on a narrow, deserted lane with no cars or signs at all. Clearly, I was going in quite the wrong direction, but I could not admit it to my passenger, who was about to miss his plane. What was I hoping for? Nothing, of course. This was probably how a condemned man feels going to his execution.

Off the road, above a tall, windowless building, I saw the legend "TWA," some high, open gates, and a plane with the same three letters on its tail.

"Here it is," I said, without looking round, and for some reason without turning off the road. "There's TWA."

"That's a hangar," said Daddy in a voice now filled with despair. "But I, strange as it may seem, need the passenger terminal."

A taxi was coming along the road toward us. In a total daze, incapable of grasping anything by this time, I attempted to make a U turn. There was a sharp screech of brakes, a rumble of choice obscenities, and I saw close to my face a distorted mask of hatred and heard my own voice:

"For God's sake, how do I get to TWA?"

The storm subsided, the taxi driver got his breath back and muttered, "Follow me."

And so, thanks to yet another good Samaritan, my passengers did not miss their plane after all; and, having mumbled my pathetic excuses once again, I followed another cab that had just dropped someone off and soon found myself in a big parking lot: a kind of stockyard, where, behind a chain-link fence, at least a hundred yellow cabs had accumu-lated, and where a hundred drivers were smoking, chatting, and tinker-ing with overheated engines; and over all this hung an inescapable stench.

Having parked my Checker in the row the drivers indicated, I in-stantly felt myself overcome by the same desire that every cabbie experiences on arriving at an airport lot after rattling around the city all day.

"Where's the toilet here?" I asked a driver whose eye I happened to catch.

The man shrugged his shoulders and turned away.

"Where's the toilet?" I addressed another, and, with an ironical gesture of welcome, he pointed downward.

The asphalt surface of the stockyard for the yellow herd, I now made out, was stained with damp patches; the potholes were filled with greenish puddles evidently mixed with antifreeze, but nobody except me paid any attention to this revolting sight: the cabbies were chewing on sandwiches, drinking soda and coffee. "Animals!" I thought, repelled by my comrades.

I looked at my hands; they were black.

"Hey!" I shouted to the driver who had just invited me not to be shy. "Can I at least wash my hands somewhere?" But this time I did not even merit a reply.

"Pigs!" I thought, infuriated, shoving my way along the narrow alley without knowing where or why, only treading gingerly. Not a single human face. I listened to what the taxi drivers were saying as they crowded around the coffee van, which was doing a brisk trade in rolls, cigarettes, and soda.

An Arab emitted guttural sounds; "*Rakhat akharam LaGardia,*" while the Arabs gathered around him strained their ears.

"*Feeoot feeoot Jei-ef-kei,*" chirped a Chinese, surrounded by more Chinese.

"*Ora-tora-aeropuerto,*" gibbered a bunch of Puerto Ricans.

Suddenly I realized what I was looking for. In this foul cloaca I could neither eat nor drink. So as not to stoop to the level of the rabble around me, I had suppressed my need to relieve myself; but there burned in me all the stronger the *third,* unquenchable desire of every taxi driver who has just parked his cab. I could no longer hold inside me everything that had happened to me that day. I had to tell it all to somebody: how I had just come to Kennedy for the first time, and how I had taken my passenger to the hangar, and how the rabbi had offended me, actually, and about my unusual trophies, the steaks and the whiskey. But if my longed-for listener had come along just then, my adventures probably would have served only as an excuse for the most shameless bragging — about my reckless cabbie daring, my acumen, and all the rest of my prowess. Heavens, what I could tell about *this!* I wanted to so desperately.

Yet I did not frighten them off with all the stories that seethed and bubbled in my breast; instead, I listened to theirs.

I went back to my Checker, took the pen I used to write on my trip sheet, found a scrap of paper, and settled myself more comfortably, already thinking: *Notes of a Taxi Driver.* I did not get a chance to concentrate: the door of my cab opened, and Crewcut looked in. Without waiting for an invitation, he flopped down on the seat next to me and said:

"Boy, do I hate this country!"

Part Two

A PROFESSION FOR LOSERS

Chapter Four

A BREAK WITH
THE RUSSIANS

The yellow cab has entered my dreams. I see the white Dnieper river in the predawn mist that thickens along the banks. We are sailing in an antediluvian paddle steamer from the days of my youth, to the village where my Ukrainian nanny was born. I am standing at the helm, and I have made a mistake; the mouth of the Desna has slipped past.

We have to go back. But it is impossible to turn the steamer around in the narrow river. We should go back in *reverse*, and I do not know how. The steamer disobeys me in just the same way as my Checker, which always misbehaves in this maneuver. I am terrified that the crew, who have been eyeing me suspiciously ever since I took the helm, have now guessed that I do not really know how to steer a ship. There: a fierce-looking sailor has guessed, he is coming toward me; terror seizes me by the throat—

A piercing ring explodes the vision. I jump up, and, groping on the nightstand, try to silence the old alarm clock brought from Russia. Still asleep, I do not immediately recollect that I am in my bedroom; I do not remember where the window is, or the door.

Early in the morning, when I leave the garage, I no longer head for a still sleeping Manhattan. There is nothing much I can do in the city at this hour. I am quite capable of winning the "race" twice or even three times before the rush hour starts, but it drains too much effort for too little money. That is why, on reaching Queens Boulevard, I turn away from the bridge and drive toward the sun rising above Long Island; I am going to Kennedy.

The twenty-dollar bill the forgotten daddy gave me was so much to my liking that, having found out from the cab drivers when the first plane comes in, I set off to meet it every morning.

The wind blows the pages of yesterday's papers along the sidewalks. I am wearing only a T-shirt, and I am still not cool, but I know that in Manhattan it is already hot, and the scorching engine blasts its heat in a driver's face. So my anticipation of a rest in the open, breezy expanses of the airport is especially pleasant. I will reach the Manhattan oven a couple of hours later, and, what is more, not empty-handed.

I drive along Queens Boulevard, thinking of all the blessings the yellow cab has heaped on me. The thought of losing my job at the radio station does not scare me anymore; my family will not starve. With every week my driving gets better; and my insomnia is forgotten. Only one thing bothers me: I am still not making any money.

I have developed a foolish habit, which holds down my earnings day after day. I pick up passengers other drivers will not take. A passerby raises his hand, and a cab with its off-duty light on stops. I should drive right past, but I slow down. Maybe the driver is returning to the garage and this customer is not going his way. The cabman opens the window, asks something — and drives away.

Conscious of how insulting it is for someone bending down to the window of a cab to hear that unpardonable, "Where to?" from the cabbie lounging in the front seat, I never allow myself to interrogate passengers. First of all I invite people to get in.

"Thank you very much indeed," the passenger says. "I've been hanging around here for half an hour. Nobody wants to take me. Will you go to Brooklyn Heights?"

We get there about seventeen minutes later; the meter shows $3.65. You might think that's nothing to sneeze at. But I have to go back to Manhattan empty, and if I have ended up in Brooklyn in the rush hour, when the roads leading to the city are jammed, I will hardly make anything else in this futile hour.

An invalid is waving from his wheelchair. The cabbies are not stopping. This is not because every last one of them is a jerk. The wheelchair will not fit in a Ford or a Dodge or any other cab except a Checker.

The invalid has rolled up to the open door, but he cannot get out of the chair. He needs help. I stand behind him, grasp him under the arms, and try to nudge his leaden body forward. My muscles are strained to the limit. Only when my strength gives out completely do I realize that I am getting in the poor man's way rather than helping him. It turns out that I have to stand facing the invalid, bend down so he can catch hold of my neck with both hands, and back up into the cab, dragging the helpless carcass with me.

For my pains the invalid, of his own accord, pays me double the fare. But we have traveled only a mile or so. Getting out, with the aid of the unskilled assistant, is even more complicated than getting in, and we part displeased with each other: he hurt his leg because of me, I wasted time because of him.

On Delancey Street, at the Big Apple's most famous discount market, where the lure of the chase entices people hunting for fashion bargains, one often see Jews in long black coats, with eyes sad as twilight in Williamsburg, standing over a pile of cardboard boxes at the curb and trying to hail a cab.

They stand there interminably. Neither goyishe nor Jewish drivers want to be bothered with boxes. Why the hell do I pull over? So I can hear, "You're a good man. You understand Yiddish?"

We have loaded all the cartons that were standing on the sidewalk. But they keep coming out of the miserable boutique underneath the ramshackle sign. The wife of the unlucky merchant waddles along on her elephantine legs, and a boy with a sickly, strained face comes puffing up, while behind him a limping black man rolls up yet another mountain of goods on a dolly.

"It'll all go in," my customer assures me. "Only don't turn the meter on while we're still here. Better my money should go to your family instead of 'them.' You get me?"

Although the customer turns out to be right and we manage to cram all the boxes in, my Checker is piled up from floor to ceiling. I cannot see out the back and have to drive very slowly, with my warning lights on.

After twisting through the wretched streets beyond the Williamsburg Bridge, we stop at another dusty, cracked plateglass window. The meter reads $3.05. I help unload, in order to be done with it more quickly. Finally the businessman, struck by the happy thought that in *this* shop his goods will sell like hotcakes, produces the money. He counts out a second, a third, a *fourth* dollar, and waits for my thanks, proud of his generosity. But in some mysterious way all the sadness in the eyes of the Orthodox matron with her shaven head, in the eyes of her scrawny child and the lame black man, has flowed into mine. I looked for a passenger for ten minutes. We drove for ten minutes. We carted the boxes back and forth for ten minutes. I will not get back to Manhattan in less than ten minutes. So how much can I make in this hour?

Stopping at a wagon selling hot pretzels, I swallow the tasteless dough — it hurts to chew. Ten yards away from me, an old, corpulent black woman is trying to stop a cab. Empty taxis fly by. Black drivers, white drivers — they look right through an old black woman.

"Hey, lady, get in the cab!" I shout. "We'll go in a minute."

Frowning, the old woman waddles toward the car, and mutters — as if to herself, but so I can hear — "What a smart aleck showed up! He wants the customers to wait while he eats his lunch."

What possessed me to call her? As soon as she sank into the backseat and the meter clicked she went crazy.

"Take off that sixty-five cents right now! He hasn't even started the motor and I owe him money. I'm not paying that. You fixed it!"

"Fixed what? The meter goes on automatically."

"Will you look at him — 'automatically'! I have a nephew in the police force, he'll show you!"

It would not be hard to teach the old woman a lesson. I could call people over, shame her, reduce her to tears. What was more, she deserved it. But how much would it wear *me* down? Wouldn't it be better to turn the whole thing into a joke?

"Lady, please, don't complain about me to the police!"

"They'll take away your license, then you'll know!" Head held high, she gets out and walks off.

Was it funny? Not really.

I stopped for a pretzel not because I was awfully hungry (I certainly could have waited), but because I had not been able to get a fare for fifteen minutes. I ate for about three minutes, while the episode with the old woman took another two. Sixty-five cents to pay again. If the next passenger gets in my cab in ten minutes, how much will I make in this hour?

Still, arguments with passengers did not occur more than once a week. Is there any job where one in a hundred of the people you deal with does not give you problems? Not to mention the fact that I was to blame for much of it. How many times had I said to myself: don't pick up people other taxi drivers won't take. They know better, after all. I have promised to quit, and made vows about it, but some demon keeps prodding me. If someone treats a person unfairly, ignores him, must you really do the same?

But let's not exaggerate either our troubles or our virtues. The passengers whom I should not have allowed in my cab did not take up that much of my time—not more than an hour in a day. So why could I not recoup the loss in the remaining time? Whatever it took, I had to find out how a cabman made money. That was why I drove out to Kennedy at dawn. There, in the parking lots, I mixed with other cab drivers, and I learned.

––––––

As with any place where we are used to seeing throngs of people, the first sight of a deserted airport, like a deserted subway station, provokes a faint sense of unease. After driving past several empty, darkened terminals, past empty taxi stands and lots, I found myself in front of a small stockyard, its outlines reminiscent of a half moon. It was filled with yellow cabs. I turned into it and stopped behind a car whose lights were flashing. In a taxi queue this means, "I'm the last in line."

Getting out of the Checker and looking around, I felt a little conspicuous: all the cabbies in this parking lot were black. But I decided to behave as if it meant nothing, and walked up to a group of drivers who were conversing loudly in some unknown language. When I approached, they squeezed together and made room for me in the circle. I greeted them and they responded, while the man who was speaking switched to English.

The conversation was about what happens to taxi drivers at Kennedy when, returning to New York after a vacation, they become passengers themselves and the quarry of their fellows in the business. It appeared that the most enjoyable adventure a cabbie-customer could have was to end up in the car of a cabbie-crook.

"We get into the terminal," the young Puerto Rican was saying, "and I warn my wife: not a word in English! It's night. No dispatcher, no police. A hustler's already managed to grab my wife's suitcase. I ask him, in Spanish, '*Señor*, can you take us to Astoria, in the county of Queens?'"

As he said the last phrase, the storyteller hunched his head into his shoulders and extinguished the gleam of wit in his eyes; his face took on a dumb, insolent expression.

"Queens county? That's quite a trip. But for forty dollars, all right, I'll take you."

Another hustler dashes up and snatches away the second suitcase.

"*Amigo*, I'll take you for thirty!"

"No, *señor*. Your price is better, of course, but this *señor* offered his assistance first."

The trip from Kennedy to Astoria costs about ten dollars. The rogue drives the "tourists" halfway around New York. $37.55! The cabbie-customer paid him ten dollars.

"If you'd ripped me off for another ten bucks, pal, I wouldn't have said a word, but you went too far."

Unfortunately each of the listeners was so eager to tell his own story that the end of the tale was ruined. The baton passed to a gray-haired black man, about sixty years old. Again it was night, again at Kennedy, a flight just in from Atlanta. A black guy approached the cabbie with his wife.

"Where to, brother?"

"I'm going to Harlem, sir. Do you know the way?"

"Yeah, I know the way, but it's far. Across the river."

"How much will we owe you, sir?"

"Depends which bridge we take. If you want the fastest way—"

"I'd prefer the shortest."

"Well, if you'd like the shortest, it's $59.75."

"We get in," the black man went on, "and my old woman gets out her glasses and a pen."

"What's wrong, lady? Are you going to take my number?"

"Don't worry," the passenger says reassuringly. "She's a little strange. Her husband's been driving a cab in New York for thirty years, you know."

"Hey, brother, why didn't you say so right away?"

"I'll show you $59.75!" the cabbie's wife explodes. "I'll teach you a lesson, 'brother'!"

"You just didn't understand me." The eel wriggles on the hook. "I said that if we take the Fifty-ninth Street bridge, you'll save the seventy-five cents for the toll."

I thought about those stories all day. If a cabbie's qualifications really consisted in seeking out trusting people and swindling them, then I was indeed not cut out to be a taxi driver.

Although the black and Spanish drivers had accepted me willingly and were quite friendly, the next morning, all the same, I drove past American Airlines and made a circuit of the deserted airport. After passing several empty lots, I saw a yellow tail emerging from a concrete tunnel that led somewhere underground and the flashing lights of the last cab in the line. I soon found out that I was at the arrivals level for British Airways, where a plane from South Africa would be landing in less than an hour. A minute later I realized I had also come upon a sort of symposium of top-class cab drivers. These were aces!

The day before, one of them had driven to Connecticut for a hundred and fifty dollars; another had landed a trip to Philadelphia and brought home two hundred.

"Who cares about your Philadelphias?" said a third driver with a stern, manly face. "I made more in the city."

"More?" I was amazed.

"That's right—two hundred and eighty-seven bucks!" the cabbie replied, and he looked even more manly.

"How many hours did you work?" put in a black fellow, whom I had met and chatted with once at Penn Station. A native of the British colonies, he had lived in London, where he had been a kind of leader of a colored workers' union; now, for some reason, he had ended up in a yellow cab in New York.

"I never work more than ten hours," said this champion of cabbies. "So how did you make three hundred?"

"Two eighty-seven."

I was not the only one interested in how to rake in such fabulous sums. The champ drew a crowd. However, modesty did not permit him to brag about his exceptional skill in front of other drivers. He had made so much yesterday simply because he had had a huge piece of luck! He had picked up a drunk. The drunk paid twenty dollars in advance, and, when they arrived, forgot about it and gave him another twenty. But it did not end there! Scrambling out of the cab, the drunk asked the driver to see him to the elevator—another twenty!

The audience was in raptures. How they rejoiced for this cabbie! My acquaintance and I were shoved aside, while the champion was interrupted by a driver who, just an hour ago, had taken an incredibly lavish family to Mill Basin—father, mother, their daughter and her husband. The father gave him sixteen, the mother eighteen, the daughter twenty, and her husband twenty-five.

"Why are they lying?" I asked quietly.

"It makes life easier. At least someone will envy them," remarked the man from London, while the liar kept holding forth: "Was I ever lucky!"

"I don't think so," the Londoner said loudly.

All the cabbies stared at him with hostility, but he was not abashed.

"People who are lucky don't drive yellow cabs. People who are lucky are still sleeping now. They'll wake up when we go back to the city and drive them to their offices to sell apartment buildings . . . oil . . . arms. There are lucky businessmen, lucky actors, lucky lawyers, but there are no lucky cabbies. Everyone here is a loser."

Nobody said a word. I, too, felt ill-at-ease. Little by little I sidled away and went down the alley between the yellow cabs into the windy concrete tunnel.

———

This tunnel led me to the front of the terminal, where more cab drivers were gathered at the entrance. They were standing around two men. One, who had stainless-steel teeth, was sitting on the granite ledge of the wall. Above him towered a giant of a man whose mouth glittered with gold like Aladdin's cave. It was by these very teeth—gold and steel—that I recognized them as my compatriots.

Aladdin was jabbing the cabbie sitting in front of him in the cheek with the point of a pin.

"Here and here, does it feel the same?"

The medical examination in such unusual surroundings was accompanied by an even more unusual exchange between doctor and patient.

"You're an idiot!" the doctor kept saying, tapping the patient on the knee with a small wrench, while the patient's leg jerked and he snapped: "So make me smart!"

"Who can do that? Read my lips: you shouldn't be working."

"And who's going to pay for me?"

"You'll croak!"

The Georgian in the flat cap who plied his trade outside the Madison Hotel walked up to me.

"The plane's already landed, we'll be going soon."

A professorial finger was raised level with our faces.

"Don't forget, comrades, it's an *international* flight: the passengers have to go through customs."

A driver appeared in a gabardine macintosh, albeit fraying at the cuffs, and a velour hat that had also seen better days, but had once been chosen to match the coat.

"Do you know him?" I asked, pointing to the neuropathologist with the gold teeth.

The eyelids drooped slightly, which probably meant yes.

"Is he a doctor?"

An imperceptible nod. Evidently Gabardine Macintosh was used to people around him guessing at his answers and opinions.

"So why does he drive a cab?"

"And what else can an educated man do in this stinking America?"

Stinking?

I did not risk contradicting him aloud, but neither did I express any agreement with such a categorical judgment. This was taken to be impertinence. An abrasive look sized me up.

"When did you come here?"

"Three years ago."

"And you still don't understand anything!" Gabardine Macintosh thrust his sleeves behind his back and strode away; the Georgian shook his head in disapproval.

"Who's that?" I said curiously.

"A big man!" the Georgian replied sadly, and steered the flow of conversation back to its abandoned channel. "My friend, I didn't see through these Americans right away, either."

And he launched into a scrupulous, detailed explanation of the difference between the deceptive first impression that Americans make on a trusting immigrant and what they really are.

The industrious Georgian had started driving a yellow cab the day after he arrived, although he did not understand a word of English, and, of course, knew nothing about New York.

"The passengers, you know what they're like: they laugh, they tell you the way, they give good tips. But I was still stupid then, I thought, 'What good, kind people!'"

The Georgian wised up in about a week, when he and his wife were invited to dinner by a couple of volunteers who helped newcomers from Russia.

An ordinary dinner. Soup out of a can, frozen turkey. The Georgians could not eat it. They had a little jelly, drank some tea, thanked their hosts, and off they all went to the synagogue.

However, it was certainly not the dinner, whether modest or a failure, that wounded the Georgian's self-esteem, but the fact that after the service, when the Jews crowded onto the temple steps—and here I believed my acquaintance wholeheartedly—the volunteers began to brag about their hospitality: "Get to know each other. This is a family of Jews from Soviet Georgia; we just had them over to dinner."

The story was accompanied by much winking and whispering: you can imagine what a dinner it was, and how our guests, God bless them, gobbled up our American goodies! And at that moment the Georgian's eyes were opened and he realized that America stank, and the people who lived here stank, too.

"We get home. I say to the wife, 'Tomorrow you set a table!'"

"What table?"

"'An ordinary table!'" The Georgian glared at me. "You ever seen a Georgian dinner table?"

I said I had, and he continued:

"The next day I call these volunteers. 'Come on over! . . . Why do we need a holiday? We'll just eat together. Yesterday we ate at your place, today you eat at our place. Only please call all your friends and invite them, too.'

" 'Which friends do we invite?'

" 'Whichever you want! Invite ten people, twenty people — fifty would be even better!'

" 'We don't have that many friends,' the volunteers say, amazed.

" 'So, call your neighbors. Call your children. Children you have, neighbors you have — call them all!' "

The volunteers brought neither children nor neighbors, but they did come themselves. They walked in and gasped: "You must be having a wedding. Why didn't you tell us, we would have brought presents." But the Georgian's wife, who had spent a good fifteen hours in the kitchen, roared with laughter.

"What wedding? We eat like this every day."

"And what's left over" — the eyes of the Georgian glittered — "we throw in the garbage!"

Another Caucasian joined us.

"It's hard for them to understand the way we lived."

By "them" he did not mean the volunteers, or Americans in general. He meant me. Unlike the other émigrés, the Caucasians did not consider themselves Russians. "We're not from the Soviet Union. We're from the FRG," they would joke. "The Federal Republic of Georgia."

"Here's a little example," said the Georgian who had interrupted us, clarifying his remark. "Suppose I go to the barber. They've shaved me, given me a hot compress. I get up, I don't pay anything. They say:

" 'Thank you, sir. Any time, sir.'

"In a couple of days I come again, they do a manicure, a facial massage. I get up, I say, 'Thanks.' They answer: 'You're quite welcome, sir.' "

"And you still don't pay?"

"Not a penny! I go a third time. They've cut my hair, styled it. I toss 'em a hundred rubles, casually. The barber says:

" 'Thank you very much, sir. You're always welcome!' "

I probably should have taken advantage of this friendly chat to ask the drivers what they had earned the day before and find out in more detail how a cabman really makes money, but for some reason I said instead:

"I don't know what kind of salary you used to get, but I couldn't pay barbers a hundred rubles out of mine. My family had to live about ten days on a hundred rubles."

The Georgians' faces blossomed into smiles; my words gave them such pleasure.

"May my mama live to a hundred and fifty," swore the barber's favorite. "I never got a salary in my life!"

"So how did you live?"

"I lived good. Beautiful."

"I mean, what did you do?"

"I was a sculptor," the Georgian answered bitterly. "Understand? A sculptor."

But I did not understand. "So why are you driving a cab?"

"And what else can a sculptor do in this filthy America?"

The sleepy terminal had suddenly woken up. The glass doors of the building opened, five or six engines revved simultaneously, the cabbies hurried to their cars. The driver with the steel teeth flashed past; he was running, with his left hand clamped to his chest as if it were wounded.

It's quiet and breezy in the airport at dawn. There are five or six of us drowsy Russian drivers today. Having locked the cars—some of the guys stick their electronic meters under their arms, so nobody can lift them—the whole bunch heads for the snack bar to get a cup of coffee. Along the way the cabbies' stories start. Want to hear one? For instance, "How the Doctor Got His First Dollar Tip."

He had just failed the medical exam, and his better half told him either to get a job or get the hell out of the house. An acquaintance, with whom the Doctor had worked in Odessa at a taxi depot, bought him a license for a hundred dollars, and yesterday's physician became a cabbie. In his new role, wherever the Doctor went—airports, hotels, repair shops—he heard, "Fak-yu! Fak-yu!" He asked his buddy what it meant. His buddy explained:

"It's slang. Instead of 'thank you,' New York cab drivers usually say 'fuck you.'"

"But why do they say it that way?"

"It's their idea of a joke."

Well, the Doctor had always loved a joke—but for a joke to be appropriate, you need an occasion. One day, an old woman from Borough Park, in a fit of generosity—it was Sabbath eve—left the *yiddishe driver* a dollar tip!

"Fak-yu!" the Doctor said, grinning.

"You ought to be ashamed of yourself?! I'm an old woman—"

"You're not so old as all that," replied the Doctor gallantly.

"Shut your dirty mouth!" shrieked the old woman. "Where's your gratitude? Is that any way to talk to a lady who gives you a dolla?"

"Sha, sha!" said the Doctor. "If that's not enough for you, I can say more: *I fak-yu very mach!*"

It's good to be among your own people. I already know all the Russians who meet the early planes at Kennedy. There is Alik-the-Birthmark, a former waiter at the Intourist Hotel in Leningrad. Cute-looking, with a strawberry mark on his cheek, he used to wink at foreigners and quietly suggest they pay in hard currency. He exchanged the money at the official Soviet rate of seventy kopeks to the dollar and sold the dollars on the black market for five times that. Alik-the-Birthmark had been a well-to-do man.

"How come they didn't pull you in?" I inquired, since hard currency speculation in the Soviet Union carries a jail sentence of up to five years.

"What are you talking about? I worked for eight years. Did I ever see a cloud over my head?"

"Ah, so you were *useful.*"

"Don't talk garbage!"

"But that's the way it works."

"You don't know everything!" snorted Alik. "I never turned anybody in. But if they asked me—"

"What did they ask you?"

"Well . . . they might tell me to keep people at the table while they went through their luggage. So I brought the main dish half an hour later. Big-dil!"

"And that's all?"

"Well, they might tell me to put a plate with a microphone on the table. Big-dil!"

Alik made no more revelations. And anyway, what was the point of

71

trying to extract his confessions? Here Alik could not get a job as a waiter in a decent restaurant, and he did not want to start as a busboy. His professional pride would not permit it.

"I waited at diplomatic receptions—fourteen dishes to a course! I don't care if I rot in this yellow cage, I won't clear dirty crocks off tables!"

The earliest to arrive at the parking lot was always Tomato or Valet, who were partners. They had bought half shares in a taxi and took turns driving it every other day. Tomato was rotund and ruddy, while the other derived his nickname from the title of the company printed on the door of the cab: Valet Taxi Corp.

First-class metalworkers, they were broke when they arrived and had to iron clothes in a dry cleaner for pennies. Suddenly work found them. A small Brooklyn contractor had gotten his hands on a rush job: installing the plumbing in a Park Avenue penthouse.

"'Can you do it?' 'You bet!'" The boss rolled out the red carpet, ordered food for the guys from a Chinese restaurant—just get it done! They worked day and night. But before the job was done, he fired them.

The plumbers knew how to read blueprints, but not English. They had hooked the hot water up to the toilet bowls.

Around the time we first met, Valet and Tomato had formed their definitive opinion of America. "A faggot language and a faggot country!"

Another morning habitué of the lot was Long Marik, perpetually reclining on the hood of his Ford. In clear weather the Odessan took off his shirt to sunbathe, and from his nostalgic chest a sad-looking Lenin would gaze up at the American sky.

Long Marik did not despise America, however. He was disappointed. He had spent his whole life hacking meat at Privoz, the biggest market in Odessa.

"Is it really impossible to get a job as a butcher in Brighton Beach?" I asked.

"Putz!" Marik replied. "What do you mean, 'impossible'? You think butchery is a calling? Like a movie star? In Odessa I did deals."

"And here?"

"Here all I can do is doody!"

The only person whom I heard say something sensible on this subject was Crewcut.

"Have you ever noticed how they build houses?"

"How?"

"Have you seen the private homes in Forest Hills? Pretty exteriors, nice balconies on the second floor. But a window opens onto the balcony instead of a door."

"So?"

"You can't use the balcony."

"What does that tell me?"

"Listen! They're putting up a big building at Lincoln Center. Two hundred apartments. Each one costs over a quarter of a million, but they don't have balconies."

"You've flipped. What's all this about balconies, a fixation?"

"Don't you understand? It's a fuck-you architecture, a fuck-you philosophy!"

"What gives you the right to judge such things?"

"'Right'? I'm an architect! My wife and I made a special trip to look at those apartments. No soundproofing, crummy layouts—they're holes, not rooms. Just so they can say 'three bedrooms'! A marble sill at the front door—just so they can say 'luxury apartment'—and hand over all your money!"

"Total nonsense," I snapped. "They built a hundred good houses and ten bad ones. So what? If you want to talk seriously, tell me: why are you, an architect, driving a cab?"

"But what else can I do? Who needs architects here?"

I said, "It would sound quite different if you didn't distort it. It's hard for any architect to find a job at the moment. Who's to blame for the fact that you came without knowing the language? That's why it's twice as hard for you now."

Crewcut blew up. "You can go to—"

He doubtless had not told the whole story. A lot of émigré engineers worked in New York without knowing the language. They earned less; they had technicians' jobs. Why had he not made a start as an ordinary draftsman? What did this hatred, this despair, spring from?

The only person who could answer these questions was Crewcut himself, but, now that he had abused me, he would not say hello anymore. I was not angry with him, but I did not lose any sleep over his fate either.

———

It is nice when you know everybody, and even nicer when everybody knows you! They don't call me "Hey, Checker!" anymore. My nickname is Bagel. If I am too lazy to trudge over to the snack bar, anyone who is going says:

"Bagel, want us to bring you a coffee? With milk?"

Even Macintosh singles me out: the rest of the drivers get a general nod, while he shakes hands with me. The Doctor is my best friend:

"I'm going after that bitch with an ax!"

"What's the matter?"

"I didn't make any money yesterday, I had to fix the cab. I get home — she won't give me anything to eat."

"Are you serious?"

"No, I'm kidding," he said facetiously. "She took a pot of hot borscht off the stove and said, 'If you open the refrigerator, you'll get this borscht over your head!'"

"But your daughter — didn't she say something?"

"I have no daughter!" he snaps.

Not wanting to rub salt in his wounds, I say nothing, but he needs to get it off his chest.

"I sit down in front of the TV. I need to calm down, I'm all shook up. And that little piece of trash stands in front of me and blocks the screen!"

"Why?"

"'You didn't buy it, you don't watch it!'"

"How old is she?"

"Sixteen. A grown-up, developed person."

The eyes behind the glasses are moist.

"Doc, buddy, forget it! To hell with them! You're still young, you're a great guy. Just think how many lonely émigrées here — kind, wonderful women — would be happy —"

He got angry.

"Cut the crap! What am I, a playboy? A bridegroom? They're my family. They're my cross, my shame, but I can't live without them."

There had been a change in the arrival schedule that nobody knew about. The glass doors of the terminal opened suddenly, but what came as an even greater surprise was that the crowd pouring out toward our cabs was black.

The flight was domestic instead of international. And domestic night flights, with their lower rates, are generally booked by black people, who have less money.

One after another the cabs were leaving the parking lot and speeding *past* the crowd of blacks. The Doctor, Crewcut, Macintosh, all left empty. Two of my acquaintances, a Czech and a Pole, took off too. A funny fat boy, Itzhak-Schpitzhak, who was shy about urinating on the asphalt and carried with him a jar with a lid, also took off. After coming to the airport empty, hanging around waiting for a plane for an hour and a half, the drivers did not want to let black people in their cabs. Were they really so afraid of them?

———

I stayed and got a fare. It was not a twenty-dollar job, but around ten — Jamaica. I had to take a soldier on leave and his stereo in a cardboard box.

The box was unwieldy, and would not fit inside the cab; the soldier and I had a hard time with it until we hit on the idea of letting it stick out of the open trunk.

The soldier turned out to be such a good lad, so free and easy! He had bought the stereo by chance, yesterday in Chicago, right on the street where his girlfriend lived. A classy thing, brand-new, and only a hundred dollars!

Stolen, I thought, but I did not tax the soldier with it. He had flown in from Europe to see his girl, decided to spring a surprise on her, and a present had turned up right under his nose. He made a deal with the sellers to help him get the stereo up to the fourth floor for the same price. They carried it up and rang the bell.

"Who is it?" the soldier heard his honey's voice.

"Delivery! From Sears."

"What's that? Who ordered it? Oh!" the door chain tinkled as it stretched, the soldier's heart was pounding. Now she would entwine him in her arms, delirious with joy, warm from sleep. But no such luck. A male torso draped in a sheet loomed up behind her.

From Chicago the soldier had flown to New York, where his mom, his dad, and his little sisters were always glad to see him. It was to them that we were now taking the ill-starred stereo.

The soldier talked about the army, too; respectfully and seriously. He had become a different man in the army: he had shed the habit of killing time pointlessly. In one year they had made him into a top-notch auto mechanic. In fact he had learned a heap of really useful stuff now; he could tackle anything that might come up.

"Like what?"

The soldier searched for an example, and gave one that could not have been more interesting to me: how an American paratrooper ought to behave if he were captured by Russians.

First of all, you had to try to escape. Even if there was no hope of success.

"So why try?"

"They would pursue me, and that would divert the enemy's resources."

"Well, and if you did manage to escape, what would you, a black man, do on Soviet territory? Where would you hide?"

"With a priest or a prostitute."

"But you might be caught. They'd start interrogating—"

"At interrogations you play dumb. If they ask how many men in your regiment, you say, 'A lot, I couldn't count them.' You say, 'I did poorly in school.' If they ask how many tanks in your division, you say, 'A whole bunch. About five thousand!'"

"Would they believe you?"

The soldier winked: who cared if they believed him or not?

The whole family met the soldier on the porch. His young mother shrieked and hung on his neck. Father and son embraced warmly, the little sisters squealed when presented with silver dollars. Together, I and the dad, who was all ready for the office in his tie and waistcoat, heaved the stereo onto the porch.

Tearing himself away from his sisters, the soldier pulled out a wallet. "How much?"

"It's $7.75 on the meter," I answered diplomatically.

The soldier counted out eight dollars; I gave him a quarter back. The coin disappeared into a pocket of his uniform. There was a dramatic pause.

"Why did you pay like that?" I asked.

"Hey, I'm not rich."

"But I'm not supposed to lug your stereo."

"We didn't ask you to," the mother, still glowing with happiness, objected politely.

I had already heard black customers as a rule do not tip, but I never thought it could be so insulting.

––––––––––

My new position among the Russian drivers, which I was very proud of, had been achieved unintentionally. Arriving at the parking lot one day, I got in line behind the frail "Uzbek" with the steel teeth, whom I had already seen the Doctor examine a couple of times. Uzbek was smoking, screwing up his eyes against the smoke without taking the cigarette out of his mouth, while his right hand nursed the left one. "It hurts!"

"Want an aspirin?"

"What good will it do?"

"It takes the pain away."

He washed a tablet down with my Coca-Cola and walked away without a word. But in ten minutes he was back: "It's better!" With visible satisfaction he clenched and unclenched his fingers.

"What's the matter with your hand?"

"How would I know?"

"What's your blood pressure?"

"Two-ten."

"You shouldn't be working."

"And who's going to pay my bills—you?"

Uzbek, a Jew from Samarkand, had bought a medallion the year before. He did not have enough money for the downpayment and had borrowed it from loan sharks. How could he have known that he would get sick? And what was there to be done about it now?

Like many taxi drivers, Uzbek carried with him a framed photograph on the dashboard—the wife and kids. This seemed odd to me; I had not yet realized that cabbies seldom see their families.

"Is it hard to sell a medallion?" I asked.

It wasn't at all hard. But you couldn't buy a medallion one day and sell it the next. A poor man always loses between buying and selling. If he,

Uzbek, were to flog his medallion now, there wouldn't even be enough to pay off his loans.

"How many hours a day do you work?"

"Sometimes fifteen, sometimes more."

"How many days a week?"

"Seven. Goddamn this America!"

Crewcut butted in, ignoring me. "We've told you a hundred times: of course you have to keep paying the loan sharks, but you can always miss a couple of payments to the bank."

"But they'll take my cab away!"

"They won't say a word. Just write them a letter. Tell them you're sick and you're short of money this month. Tell them about your blood pressure. If you'd only stay home for a few days and take some medicine, you'd feel better."

"Sounds good, but who can write that kind of letter?"

"I'll write it," I said, "if you want."

"In English?"

"There'll be mistakes, but the meaning will be clear."

The cab drivers gathered around while I wrote. The Sculptor peeked over my shoulder and praised me in the tone of an expert. "I like your style, Bagel!"

"*Mister* Bagel!" Gabardine Macintosh corrected him.

The Doctor lamented aloud, "A cultured man has to take such trouble over this pig! If he mails the letter, may I die before tomorrow."

"And why not?" Uzbek shrugged. "You think I grudge the stamp?"

Nobody ever knew whether Uzbek mailed the letter or not; but he continued to work seven days a week, and nurse his sick hand, and ask me for aspirins. However, my social status had risen three hundred percent! Macintosh, who felt lonely among the taxi drivers, decided that it was not demeaning to socialize with a man who could write in English, and almost yanked me out of the group.

"What can you talk about with these hucksters?"

"Why do you say that?" I protested feebly. "Givi's a sculptor, for instance."

"That's what *he* says! Sculptor! He used to carve inscriptions on gravestones."

"What about the architect?"

"You really are very naïve," Macintosh remarked condescendingly. "When the lapdogs emigrate, they all pretend they used to be Saint Bernards. He just had a part-time architect's salary, at a *racetrack*. The boss would tell him to put another ticket office here, or make an awning for that grandstand there."

"He was a laborer?"

"Not really. He wrote down the orders for the laborers. Personally, I wouldn't hire that apology for an architect even at a measly hundred rubles a month."

"And what did you do?" I asked—and I realized how Macintosh had been aching for this very question!

With a dramatic, well-rehearsed gesture, he threw open the gabardine folds and pulled out of the breast pocket of his old suit jacket a dark red ID booklet, the proof of his former might. For a second or two an inscription embossed in gold flashed before my eyes: COUNCIL OF MINISTERS OF THE ABKHAZIAN A.S.S.R.

Here, in the taxicab parking lot, to which we had both hurried at dawn without enough sleep, this pretension, this booklet, could elicit nothing but ridicule. All the same, I put out my hand for the document. I wanted to read what was written there with my own eyes. Abkhazia was a tiny ethnic and administrative subdivision in Georgia. Had Gabardine Macintosh really been what he insisted on presenting himself as—a government big shot?

A seal, some flourishing signatures. Aha, there it was: "Deputy Head of Board of Construction."

"I was the *first* deputy," Macintosh corrected, but it was not true. Had he really been the first, he would have made sure they wrote exactly that. His rank was certainly not equivalent to a general's, nor did it warrant all the mannerisms: the half-closed eyelids, the barely perceptible nods, his questions—"How's your health? How's the family? How's work?"—which he was in the habit of asking me without pausing for the answers.

Now I understood why I had recognized the Big Boss in him, literally from the first minute. Copying someone whom he had once pandered to, this provincial "deputy" had assumed this farcical image, this caricature. It was not hard to guess, however, that his official position had enabled him to steal cement (which was in short supply) and sell bathtubs and wash basins on the black market.

"Rolling in it, were you?" I winked.

He showed no embarrassment whatever at being identified as a Big Crook rather than a Big Boss.

"You better believe it!" he said, animatedly. "I never knew how much money I had."

He buried his millions in the cellar, lowered packets of hundred-ruble bills in sealed jelly jars into the muck of the backyard outhouse, and lived in constant fear. If he had been caught he would have been sentenced to death. That was the reason why he left.

I had lived all my life in Russia, but I had never known my country. Didn't these working stiffs, these drivers, salesclerks, waiters, and the Doctor, who treated them all (and who was convinced that mushrooms become poisonous when a poisonous snake slithers over them), and the Boss, whose authority they acknowledged—didn't these human individuals go to make up what we call the *Soviet nation?* Moreover, the people with whom fate had brought me together at the taxi parking lot, thousands of leagues from the land where we were born and raised, certainly were not the worst segment of that nation. They were toilers; they were not drunks. If it was raining in the morning, they took their wives to work and their children to school instead of meeting the first plane, although they had to make it up with an extra hour's work at night.

They were Jews when they went to synagogue so as to wheedle secondhand furniture out of the rabbi after the service. They were Georgians when they boasted, "Can you really understand the way we lived?" They were Soviets when, arguing with a passenger, they threatened him: "Just you wait. The Russians are coming!"

The taxi drivers were in no way worse or more stupid than the people with whom I was used to mixing. The only distinction I noticed was that cabbies—white or black, Russian or American—had, if I may put it like this, *a disorganized mode of thinking.*

Any of my passengers could explain the specifics of his business, far more complicated than ours, in a few sentences, for five minutes or ten, depending on the length of the trip. My present pals, the cab drivers, were incapable of this, just as I was incapable of driving in reverse. If I asked what one had to do in order to make more money, they would answer: "Don't try to be smart."

Frowning with the effort—so unintelligible did my question seem to him—a veteran cabbie from Bensonhurst said, "To drive a cab you have to have *mazel*."

"You'll learn by doing!" Alik-the-Birthmark summed up.

The Doctor brought over to me an old hand with whom he had once worked at the taxi depot in Odessa:

"Tell this man how it's done, pig, so he stops busting a gut!"

"What's to tell?" The cabbie nodded his head. "He doesn't make enough because he drives slowly. I've seen the way he drives."

My self-esteem was all the more wounded because the dig was true. I asked:

"How fast did you drive out to Kennedy just now?"

"Seventy."

"But you hang around here for an hour, and no less at the hotel afterward. So what's the point in gaining ten minutes on the highway?"

"It's a habit."

"But isn't it dangerous to belt along that fast?"

"Crashes are an occupational hazard in the transportation business."

Can one make sense of explanations like these?

"Doctor, did you drive a cab back in Odessa, too?" I asked.

"Why would you think that?" The Doctor was miffed.

"I've heard you mention several times that you worked in a taxi depot."

"But I worked there as a doctor." He smiled with pleasure at the memory. "Those years in the pig farm were the best of my life!"

"What exactly did you do there?"

"Nothing special. I stood at the gate and said to each of the pigs, 'Breathe out!' By lunchtime I'd be drunk without taking a drop of vodka."

The "Russians" around us roared with laughter.

"And what did you like so much about this role?"

"'Like'? 'Role'?" the Doctor repeated derisively. "I liked that every pig paid me twenty kopeks!"

I frowned, and the Doctor got mad.

"Look at him! He's so educated, he can even write a letter in English!

What do you know?" The Doctor pecked away at me. "I'm a physician with years of experience. I saw forty patients a day in the clinic and after that I'd go out on house calls. My feet would swell up! I worked like an ox and got a hundred and twenty rubles a month. Have you forgotten what a chicken costs at the market? Ten rubles! Two pounds of potatoes costs one ruble. We were starving!"

He was looking somewhere over my shoulder, as if his most important listener was standing behind me.

"If I went into a house and saw a plate of apples on the table, I would look at that plate instead of the patient until they said, 'Doctor, please have an apple.' Then I would take *two*—and stuff them in my pocket. You think I could buy apples for my child?"

He was looking somewhere beyond me again.

"We lived with my parents in *one* room. My wife turned her face to the wall every night, she was so embarrassed. I stood a month at the taxi depot gate and we came back to life! We had food to eat. In a year we bought a co-op!"

The Doctor's words made no impression on the Russians. Physicians were not the only ones who lived in poverty there. They say about anyone who does not know how to be on the take that he doesn't know how to live, poor thing. The topic was of no interest to anybody, and it would have died if I had not turned around and seen where the Doctor was looking. Behind me stood the same fat Itzhak who carried a jar around with him. At that point the devil got my tongue.

"Wait," I interrupted the Doctor. "If the Soviet regime degraded you so far that you were obliged to collect twenty kopeks from the workers, then why, when you get to a country of people, rather than 'pigs,' do you curse it?"

"I wish an atom bomb may drop on their heads!" shouted the Doctor, and he threw a quick glance at the boy. Why had the kid become an obsession with both of us?

"A bomb?" I retorted. "For putting your old folks on welfare? For letting your family live in what amounts to a free apartment? For that?"

My incautious words fell like sparks on a dry haystack. All hell broke loose.

"Putz! Putz!" the entire group yelled as one, while the Doctor clutched his head and groaned:

"God almi-ighty! Wha-at a putz!"

"We get what we're entitled to!"

"Entitled!"

Shouting almost the loudest of all, I tried to appear calm. I said, "I think so too. If a guest comes to my house, I should feed him and make him welcome. But if instead of 'thank you' the guest says that he's 'entitled' to it, that my home 'stinks' — "

"He's a 'believer'!" sneered the Doctor. "Run! Run as quick as you can and report me!"

"That's great!" I said with glee. "So you're telling me to inform on you? Terrific idea. But if I went to the FBI and said that you were putting out anti-American propaganda, what would happen? What can they do to you? Take away your food stamps? Move you out of your cheap apartment?"

The answer dawned on the Doctor's face.

"They can kiss my ass!"

"Right," I said. "In this country freedom of speech exists even for people like you. The Constitution protects even your rights."

Why was the sound of bombast ringing stridently in my ears? Was I not saying what I really thought?

"Just a minute!" The disappointed butcher from Odessa raised himself up from his windshield couch. "Comrade Bagel, I beg you earnestly to answer one question. Why does a cow make pies, while a goat makes nuts?"

Long Marik seemed to be talking some kind of nonsense, but they were all listening attentively.

Marik looked at the asphalt as if he could really see cowpies on his left and goat "nuts" on his right, and had come to a standstill before the insoluble riddle. The drivers giggled nervously, tickled with rapture.

I was obliged to say something and, smirking sarcastically, I growled, "Leave me alone, I don't know." But that was exactly the answer Long Marik was waiting for. He spread his hands wide to emphasize my hollowness.

"So if you don't even know from shit, how can you debate the American Constitution?"

The fat boy laughed along with the others; I was choked with helpless rage. But I knew it was impossible to win an argument against everyone, and I went for the Doctor again.

"How many times did you fail the test?"

"Four, I guess."

"Why couldn't you pass it?"

"Who can pass their test anyway? It's a mafia."

"What did you say?"

"The medical mafia. You think they would let anyone near their trough?"

"But I know at least three doctors who passed it on the first try."

"That means they paid somebody off."

"They're penniless émigrés just like you."

In an effort to attract the cabbies' attention, I took some money out of my pocket.

"Doctor, for every correct answer I'll pay you five bucks. Of course you know what the English for this is," I said, slapping my thigh.

"Leg!" said the simple-hearted Doctor. "Give me the dough."

"No. You'll get five dollars if you tell me the name of the bone inside. Well? What are you thinking about?"

"Let's say I've forgotten."

"Okay."

I curled back my upper lip and pointed to the smarting tissue beneath one of the temporary bridges. "What's this called?"

"Gum!" the Doctor answered victoriously.

"Great! But you'll have your five dollars if you tell me the name of the bone inside."

An uncomfortable pause ensued.

"What are you getting at?" said the Doctor.

"I want to prove to you that you drive a yellow cab not because the 'mafia' won't let you near their trough, but because you don't know anything."

"Fool! I treated people for twenty years."

"Not people," I said. "'Pigs.'"

He pretended he had not heard.

"I need English like I need a hole in the head! I can treat émigrés."

"No, you can't," I said. "You shouldn't be allowed anywhere near sick people. You don't know American medicines, you don't know how to use the reference books. It isn't the first time we've talked about this stuff: you aren't capable of explaining the mechanics of a heart attack. You haven't read a single book since you left medical school."

"And who do you think you are?" The Doctor advanced on me; he was on the verge of beating me up. "Everyone laughs at you. You're not even good enough to be a cab driver!"

"Quite true," I said. "You're as good a doctor as I am a cab driver." The boy had moved away some time ago and was smoking a joint with another youngster. To him the Doctor and I were equally contemptible. But I plunged on.

"There's at least one advantage for all of you in this 'stinking' America: nobody keeps you here against your will!"

They were saying, "Do you think there's a single stone in Kishinev that I wouldn't get down and kiss?" "I would crawl back on my hands and knees!" "I'd be willing to spend ten years in jail!" But—they would not let them back in.

I spat on the ground.

"You're filthy scumbags! The dregs!" I jumped into the Checker. The front exit out of the lot was blocked with cabs. I reversed away so violently that the poor Sculptor barely managed to get out from under the wheels.

———

I drove round and round the empty airport. But my hands were trembling; I could not pull myself together. How stupid! I had lost the place I had had in the line since half past five—and for what? I had been convincing these unfortunates, crushed by emigration, that in fact they had it good. Or maybe I was trying to convince myself?

Among the notes I made during that first cab-driving autumn is a grubby pad with the heading "Morning: Kennedy" and a list of the cast of characters: the architect Balcony, the Georgian Dinner, the plate with the bug, the Sculptor, the vanished Uzbek. Below the list is the heavily underscored conclusion that struck me as a discovery: ÉMIGRÉS HATE AMERICA. This entry is followed by two pages, written in tiny script, entitled "Fried Potatoes."

The notes, in minute handwriting, recalled an odd fare I had picked up.

"Number 830 Fifth Avenue, on the corner of Sixty-sixth Street. Repeat it, please," he had said.

"Why?"

"I like to be sure the driver knows the address."

The strange passenger was right: misunderstandings over confused or misheard addresses did sometimes occur. I repeated it the cabbie's way, "Sixty-six and Five," and, catching the soft *l* in the word "please," I asked, "Are you from England?"

"From East Africa."

The reply was pronounced with irreproachable correctness. A gentleman was talking to another gentleman.

"And what do you do?" I asked—the question I was in the habit of feeling out my passengers with.

"What can I say? I read books, I collect stamps."

"If you don't mind, I meant what do you do for a living?"

"Oh, in that sense? Nothing. Nothing at all."

After the war he had had to spend several years here in the States. But since that time he and his children had been freed forever from the necessity of working. And again I did not catch the whole meaning of his words.

"Do you come here often?" I asked. "Do you like America?"

"*Like?*" He was slightly more surprised than his reserve permitted. "And what exactly is there to like here?"

My shoulder blades shivered as if a drop of cold water had run down my collar.

"But of course you're right. It can't be that there's nothing to like. Hmm. What do I like here? Let me think. Aha! The fried potatoes. Yes, that's it. In America I like the fried potatoes."

"Bastard!" I thought, but aloud I said, "Sir, this country has benefited both you, personally, and the whole world so much that your witty answer sounds cynical."

"Well, I can't help it."

We drove in silence for a minute, but it was not just I who found it hard to refrain from continuing.

He said, "My personal circumstances in the postwar years certainly did change here, in America; but that was more the result of certain shortcomings than of any merits of this country."

In his answer he used none of the words which, had he uttered them, would have sounded vulgar: "got rich," "made a fortune," "loads of money."

"Do you like the country where you live?"

"Indeed I do! And I like Switzerland too. And France, after a fashion." He did not mention England.

"What about Russia? Have you ever been to Russia?"

"Oh, yes! Twice in '41 and once in '42."

(*Inappropriately precise reply,* I decipher with difficulty from my old record in the notepad.)

"You were a diplomat?"

"I was a sailor. We were escorting convoys to Archangel."

My Checker turned onto Fifth Avenue and stopped twenty yards from the entrance to the building so that the doorman would not interrupt us.

Convoys to Archangel! In 1941, Russia, gravely wounded, could be saved only by direct, vein-to-vein transfusion. That summer she had lost a great part of her European territories and, along with it, much industry. America extended the donor's arm, but the actual infusion—of artillery, tanks, trucks, planes, strategic raw materials, food supplies—was carried out by British sailors. The Germans knew the wounded giant might get up off its knees and therefore positioned a crack North Sea squadron in the way of the convoys. The British sailors who escorted the marine caravans to Archangel were essentially suicide squads. To get through, past the German battleship *Tirpitz*, was equivalent to playing Russian roulette.

We had been talking for at least a quarter of an hour.

"Do you think anything will change in Russia?" I asked.

"Possibly. There are still more Christians than communists there, you know," he said.

"That's a legend dreamed up by Western journalists," I said. "There are very few people in Russia who really believe in God."

"But then nobody at all 'believes' in communism," he riposted, and in a corner of my mind I suspected that I was drawn to this man by an ignoble feeling, which was nothing but envy. I envied him not only his wealth, his elegance, his manners; he was more *intelligent* than I. And because of this I was looking for a weak point in him. I was waiting to see if he would stumble, make some gaffe; and then, with complete satisfaction, I would be able to glance at my watch and "remember" that I had to work. And stumble he did.

There is so much cruelty and blood in the history of any country that it takes little to wound anyone's national pride. I should like to think, however, that I did not do so on purpose, but, inasmuch as we were already talking about everything under the sun, that I mentioned the extraditions *accidentally*.

I asked him where he was serving in 1945–46, when the British delivered the Russians in Europe into Stalin's hands. Not only those Russians who joined the Wehrmacht, but also the hundreds of thousands of girls and youths whom the Germans had sent into slavery. The valiant British ("closing ranks" with the Americans), with weapons in their hands, beating women with gunstocks, had driven them— liberated from Fascist bondage only yesterday—straight to Soviet concentration camps in Siberia and certain death.

He said, "Yes, it was terrible, but then we knew nothing. It was Anthony Eden who did it."

How could this refined man say such a thing about events that were spread over two years; about actions that whole regiments took part in. *We knew nothing?*

The members of parliament did not know that hundreds of women wrote them hundreds of despairing letters. The generals did not know that their subordinates, privates and officers, undertook sham marriages with these women to save them from the "return to the motherland," from execution or death by starvation in Kolyma. They did not know.

But even this egregious absurdity, which had escaped my companion's lips, did not make me feel a shadow of superiority over him. Only he who loves a woman will call her sordid act a mistake. He *loved* his England, this intelligent snob; Russia he pitied, America he despised.

For what?

We shook hands in parting. He smiled, and in his smile I read (probably because I wanted to) respect, and sympathy, and wishes for luck. I was as proud of his handshake as if the King of Sweden were awarding me the Nobel Prize for my incredible achievements in the taxi business; for the fact that I had at last learned to drive my Checker in reverse.

Chapter Five

- - - - - - - -

ENOUGH'S ENOUGH

I had gotten behind the wheel only three months ago, but what a lot I already knew about taxis!

Hordes of motley cabs dart around New York: blue and red, green and brown, you name it. If you get the urge to ply your trade as a carrier, if you have no choice, you daub the word TAXI in magic marker on a piece of cardboard, place your art work in your windshield, and sally forth. Whatever money you manage to scrape together is all yours. You are already a "cab driver."

However, when a person who needs a cab sees all of these white ones and blue ones and black ones, he will not get in any of them. As a rule, even New Yorkers, visiting businessmen, and tourists from overseas, will stand and wait for a *yellow* cab. A yellow cab means, above all, security; and travelers warn one another on the plane that only drivers of yellow cabs are checked up on.

My license with its photograph, affixed to the dashboard, is a guarantee of the exceptionally important fact for passengers that I have had my fingerprints taken, and that the city authorities have ascertained from a thorough police check that I am not a criminal. My past is not marred by murders, burglaries, or rapes. True, I have yet to hear that any taxi driver, checked or unchecked, has ever attacked a passenger, although the reverse happens every day, but the public is firmly convinced that one can expect anything of a New York cabbie, and it is not up to me to combat their prejudice.

It is impossible to determine the number of these self-styled "gypsy" cabs in New York. The papers say fifty thousand, the authorities estimate the number at seventy thousand; nobody knows the exact figure. But the number of yellow cabs like mine is 11,787. No more, no less.

Only we, the drivers of yellow cabs, were allowed to pick up passengers on the streets. Our many-hued competitors had the right only to the customer who called a cab by phone. We were the "yellow kings," the law protected our privileges. (In 1986 this law was changed and nonmedallion cabs were allowed to pick up passengers in every borough except in the principal area of Manhattan south of Ninety-sixth Street.)

The hood of every yellow cab is graced with a special metal ornament, one of the 11,787 medallions—the permits to hack—which, in 1937, Mayor Fiorello LaGuardia sold off to individual drivers for a hundred dollars each, while garages paid ten apiece. Yes: garages officially paid ten bucks for a taxi medallion. And although this dubious sale had occurred in a different era, neither I nor my passengers could comprehend why today this piece of tinplate, the size of a can lid, should cost as much as a cozy townhouse in Brighton Beach.

I found it especially difficult to grasp that the ornament fixed to the hood of my Checker was a valuable property in itself, without the car. That any bank would loan thousands for this bit of tin. That the owner of this trashy bauble could rent it out, do nothing, and collect money. But, frankly, no hackman would ever talk that way about a medallion: "piece of tinplate," "ornament." That's just my glibness speaking. The word *medallion* always has a solid ring to it on the lips of any cabbie, like *interest, property,* or *deposit,* whatever the context or tone in which it is uttered.

Enviously: "See that Greek? He's got four medallions!"

Painfully: "I could have bought a medallion for ten thousand. In those days . . ."

Those fabulous days will never come again, and your whole cab-driving life has been flushed down the drain. I could not buy a medallion for thirty thousand in 1975. Currently a medallion costs about $145,000.

I was thinking about all this on a dank morning on the last Friday in September, as I was returning to Manhattan from distant Whitestone. A heavy fog blanketed the highway. The road was slippery, and I drove slowly. The mauled corpse of a dog shuddered beneath the wheels of a car passing my Checker.

I was reminded by the smoothness of my carefully shaven cheeks, by my good jacket folded neatly on the front seat, and by the envelope on top of the jacket containing the script of my radio show that today was Friday. My taping session was on Fridays, at ten o'clock. Since I had started driving a taxi on the side, I did not have to jolt across the city on the subway to get to the radio station. An hour before taping time I would leave the cab at a taxi stand at Grand Central Station, put on my jacket, and run across the street to 30 East Forty-second, and there, on the third floor—

Blast! Carried away by idle thoughts, I had missed the main thoroughfare into Manhattan, and now I would have to go all the way down Northern Boulevard to get to the city.

"As if driving empty weren't bad enough," I fumed, "I have to go through a hundred traffic lights as well!"

But a cabbie never knows when he will win and when he will lose. No sooner had I turned off the highway onto Northern Boulevard than I saw a huge figure on the curb clumsily brandishing a crutch. I was being asked to stop.

"Manhattan!" The springs of the cab creaked under the weight as the invalid lowered his bulk onto the backseat. "Take the Queensboro Bridge," the man-mountain said.

Glad though I was that the unexpected passenger was going exactly where I had to go, it did not escape my notice that for some reason my customer had not given a precise address.

"Manhattan's a big place," I remarked to myself, but as the meter ticked away my thoughts carried me a long, long way off to the foot of a fantastic construction which I had glimpsed several times that autumn in snatches of conversation among drivers, and of which I had seen, as if through a haze or smoke, first an edge, then the top—but which I now suddenly saw whole! It was a PYRAMID, the real thing, resembling those the Egyptians built. Not the mightiest, perhaps, but undoubtedly the *last* of all the pyramids erected on earth: the result of the laborious, antlike efforts of several generations of New York cabbies.

The concept of this pyramid constructed by professional failures—who not only had not become brothers in their hapless lot but, on the contrary, were divided into a multitude of closed castes—consisted in yet another reminder to the world of a primordial truth: *All men are not created equal.*

The top of the pyramid, which dismissed all that primitive talk about the equality of cab drivers—"If you're a hack and I'm a hack, what's the difference between us?"—was occupied by the medallion owners, who formed something like an estate of nobility. Naturally they looked down on the proletarian hacks, but the truly remarkable thing was that not all the taxi "nobles" were equal within their caste, either. And not because all medallion owners were arrogant to a man. Far from it; they were very ordinary people, but the medallions they owned were different. Some were individual medallions, while others were "minis" (as in a taxi corporation consisting of two cabs). I will probably never be able to tell the difference. One owns a yellow cab and the other owns a yellow cab. But if the price of a minifleet medallion had recently risen to thirty-five thousand, an individual medallion had soared to forty. And therefore the owners on top looked down on the owners in the second rank.

The step below the owners was assigned to those who say, "The cab's mine, I just lease the medallion." A hackman who buys a vehicle (and signs a lease on a medallion) may hire a co-driver to work for him. Nobody is capable of driving twenty-four hours around the clock. Why let your old buggy sit idle? Why not give up your seat for the night to some sad sack who is even poorer than you are? A hired hand is sure profit.

But not every cabman can sell his labor to a private owner. You have to have money to become a co-driver on a relief shift, as much as five hundred dollars, which is a lot for a cabbie. Who knows what tricks a lumpen cabbie might get up to: he could bang up the car and say it was like that before he had it. So a security deposit is a must. Without a deposit you cannot lease either a medallion or a cab.

The next step down on the pyramid, therefore, was assigned to those who had managed to raise this initial five hundred dollars, while its very foundation, the dust underfoot, consisted of the fleet drivers, the "barge haulers" like myself. But it would have been wrong to view even our position as hopeless. Cabbies of every rank had diligently erected their pyramid because in this way even the very last, bottommost hack, in total unanimity with an owner of six medallions, was granted the miraculous right to *despise* all those red, green, brown, and other raggle-taggle "gypsies."

Yes, raggle-taggle—how could we view them otherwise?

How could we view them otherwise as they continually flouted the law by grabbing passengers on almost every corner, stealing jobs from us, the yellow kings, the rightful masters of the streets of New York?

Column on the bridge, halt! the traffic lady ordered with a commanding gesture.

"Turn right onto Third Avenue," my passenger said.

Why did he not want to tell the driver where he was going?

"Now, go straight on!"

We passed Seventy-second Street.

"Straight!"

Eighty-sixth.

"Straight!"

I realized that this white man was going to Harlem.

"Where's the big secret?" I thought, having been to Harlem a few times already.

We finally turned off Third Avenue onto 120-something Street and ventured onto the territory of a housing project consisting of several high, unwelcoming buildings exactly like the one I lived in. Except that the children playing in this courtyard were black, and there were no flowers here, no grass, no trees. This yard was bare asphalt.

The little ruffians chasing around the yard had turned on a fire hydrant and were spraying each other, although it was not hot; there were shrieks, laughter—and suddenly I was blinded!

An icy stream hit me right in the face; I braked instinctively, and at that moment the little devils were all over my cab, like ants on a wasp. They clambered up on the hood, flung open the doors, and crowded onto the front and back seats as if neither I nor the passenger was in the car. Hands ransacked the glove compartment and the pockets of my "good" jacket; then, as if on command, all of them were held out to me at once.

They were grimacing and shouting angrily. They had become aggressive.

"Dollar!"

"Gimme a dollar!"

I still remember how struck I was by the behavior of my passenger. Scrambling out of the cab with difficulty, the muscular mountain did not shove aside any of the boys entangled under his feet and crutches; he was afraid of them.

"Gimme a dollar!"

"Dollar!"

I gave two or three of them some change and would have moved off, but they would not let me go. The smallest kids stood fearlessly in the way of the car, pushing against the radiator with their hands, while those inside swiped absolutely everything within reach. One grabbed the drenched pack of cigarettes, another the receipt book (what did they want with receipts?). A third ripped the sunglasses off my nose, but instead of taking to his heels he stood next to the cab, teasing me with the stolen goods.

Another stream of water hit me in the face. I closed the window; a stone banged on the roof. Now I was really scared; the cripple had disappeared.

I leaned over to the other window, where they could not spray me with water, and flung a fistful of coins onto the asphalt. With a whoop, the whole gang rushed to pick them up, and the way was clear!

The kids jumped out of the car as it was going; the rear doors, still open, flapped back and forth, but I drove and drove until I heard a shot, which hurled me sideways and to which my "tank," breaking out of the trap, instantly responded with a thunderous salvo—*tra-ta-ta!* The gas pedal had become the trigger of a machine gun; the injured Checker shook, and pulled sideways, but sped along and went on shooting.

———

The racket ceased when my cab had crossed the boundaries of Harlem. As soon as I put my foot on the brake, the machine gun fell silent. I got out of the car and saw that the right front tire had burst; the metal wheel rim was resting on the pavement.

My clean shirt, trousers, socks, shoes—everything was soaked. The meter showed eleven dollars; I had forgotten to turn it off, and the cripple had sneaked off in the commotion without paying. Maybe he had been afraid to produce the money? Or maybe he had stuffed it in the change cup? I felt around—no money. The kids might have taken it.

I would have to inform the dispatcher about the money right away; otherwise, when I turned in the takings at the end of the shift, I would have to make up the deficit from my earnings.

DON'T PASS UP THE CHANCE TO MAKE $600 PER WEEK!

It was all lies, bait. In three months of slave labor I had saved just over a thousand dollars.

However, it was not merely the stolen money I had to phone the dispatcher about. I was a fleet cabbie, after all, whom the manager would not trust with a jack or a spare wheel. A fleet cabbie is supposed to call his garage for road service when he gets a flat. I plodded across the street to a phone booth, leaving wet footmarks on the asphalt.

"Where are you?" the dispatcher asked.

"Park Avenue and—" only now did I take a good look around—"and Ninety-second."

"Wait there! Don't leave the cab."

The dispatcher hung up; he had not given me the chance to tell him about the money.

Ninety-second Street! I had driven like a mad thing for a good mile with the rear doors swinging. I tasted blood in my mouth. One of my temporary bridges had come loose from its moorings. At least I had not swallowed it. Water had gotten into my watch, which had been a true and faithful servant for many years, and it had stopped, fixing the time of the incident—7:43.

TAXI DRIVER, BE YOUR OWN BOSS!

Lies again. Every passenger was my boss. I had to go wherever he told me, whether to Harlem or to hell in a handbasket. The dispatcher had ordered me to stay with the cab, and, wet and shivering, I would have to hang around and wait.

I took off my shoes and put them on the hot hood to dry, I hung my jacket on the door. How could I show up at the radio station in this state?

And what would I explain, and to whom? I had not told my colleagues that I was driving a yellow cab. And how much longer would I have to endure in this damn taxi? Six months? A year? I sat on the curb, as cab drivers do. The street is our living room, our home. None of the passersby paid any attention to me.

———

A yellow Ford, shiny as a new penny, bowling down Park Avenue, slowed sharply and swerved toward me. The cab driver, who was about thirty-five, looked like a weight-lifter, and exuded an air of great good humor. He came over.

"Hey, what are you sitting around here for?"

I pointed silently to the flat tire.

"Waiting for them to come from the garage?"

This guy was clearly no rookie. But he was too well-pressed and Brylcreemed. An owner. Your cabbie aristocrat.

"Buddy, you're soaking!"

I told him what had happened, and he began to laugh.

"Very funny," I snarled, but he did not reply in kind.

"Don't get mad. You got off lightly. It could have been much worse. You think they wanted your wet cigarettes? Your receipts?"

"Why did they take them, then?"

"They wanted you to chase after one of the kids."

"What for?" I asked, although I was vaguely beginning to get the picture.

"They wanted you to get out of the cab and threw a stone at the car when they saw you weren't going to get out. If it had worked, you'd have gotten a rock thrown at your head, and they would have gotten more money."

"In broad daylight?"

"Are you nuts? That's Harlem, get it? Harlem! How come you went there, anyway?"

This windbag was annoying me. "Don't you ever go there?" I said.

"No way! Remember: a black passenger should never be in your cab. You'll come to a bad end."

He looked inside the cab. "Working a couple of months?"

"And how do you know so much?"

"I looked at your license."

My hack number had told him I was a novice. The cheerful nosy parker picked up my trip sheet next.

"Jeez, you really don't have a clue, do you?"

What did he mean? I already knew at least three routes to Kennedy! And the day before yesterday I had made the garage's quota, hadn't I? And I could draw a map of the main roads through Central Park right there on the asphalt, without making a single mistake! None of that counted?

"Not one of the passengers you took today," the cabbie observed pontifically, "should have been picked up."

"And what do you think I should have done?"

"Taken different ones."

I had never met such a blowhard in my life.

"You picked up your first passenger," he lectured me, "at Second and Fifty-eighth. That means you'd only just come off the Queensboro Bridge and didn't even take a look at what was going on at the Regency or the Pierre. You were right by the Plaza. It's Friday today, airport day, everyone's checking out. But you took a customer to Sixth Avenue for $1.55. Dumb. Next, you didn't drive two blocks over to the Hilton. Dumb again. You might have gotten a Kennedy, but you went to Whitestone instead. You can't get a fare back to the city in Whitestone. How come you went there?"

"A woman got in the cab."

"And why did you let her? You drive with your doors unlocked?"

According to the rules, the passenger doors must always be unlocked, but the cabbie aristocrat was of a different opinion.

"All four doors of your cab should be locked!"

He was at least half right. If even the front doors of the Checker had been locked, the black kids could not have gotten into the front seat, and it would have been easier for me to get out of the rumpus.

"And how come you picked up a black in Flushing?"

"He was white."

"All the same, you shouldn't go into the jungles."

"He was a cripple!"

"That's none of your business. A cripple can take a gypsy cab to Harlem quite comfortably. If you wanted to be so nice, you should've pulled over with your doors locked and asked, 'Where are you going, sir?'"

"Asking is prohibited," I reminded this know-all, but he threw this argument out like an empty beer can.

"Get this into your thick skull: the more you're afraid of the rules, the police, the passengers, the less money you make. A cabbie's got to think about just one thing: how to make money. One hundred bucks. Every single day."

He had touched a sore point, and I admitted that I had never even gotten near seventy. It was not easy admitting such things, and my self-appointed teacher probably understood that. With unexpected sympathy he said:

"Money's hard to come by in the mornings. Why do you go out on the day shift?"

I had guessed the advantages of the night shift myself, having observed that the influx of passengers began in the afternoon, just when it was time for me to go back to the garage. But I lived in Brooklyn, while the garage was in Queens. How could I switch to the night shift?

"How often do you take the subway at three o'clock in the morning?" I asked.

"I never go on the subway," he replied.

"There you are!"

What I had mastered best of all while driving a cab was the art of explaining my failures. I did this so convincingly that my wife and son always agreed with me. However, for some reason this harsh cabbie, from whom I had heard more unpleasant things in the last ten minutes than I had for the preceding three months, argued the matter quite differently. His logic ignored the labyrinth of my circumstances and simply hacked open an exit in the most unexpected place.

"There's no point working for a garage at all."

"So who should I work for?"

"Lease a cab."

There is a very appropriate response to this kind of smarty-pants: *Talk is cheap.*

"How can I lease a cab and pay the owner sixty dollars a day, and buy gas as well, if I make less than that?"

"Hold it!" The cabbie reined me in. "You only think you don't pay for gas at the garage. In fact you pay for everything. If I turn on the meter, I get sixty-five cents—you get forty. The union takes a quarter from you every drop. And that road service you've been waiting an hour for, to do a wheel change that takes five minutes, you pay for *it*, too. Sure, leasing a cab costs a lot. You'd have to bust your ass more, but then you can start and finish your day at the best hours. Plus you won't pay taxes, you won't take vacations—that's how you raise the money for the downpayment."

"What downpayment?"

"For a medallion!"

"But I'm not going to buy a medallion. I'll only be driving a cab for a few more months."

He shook his head.

"It doesn't happen that way. Either you drive a cab for two weeks and quit, or . . . When I came here I thought I'd just give it a try, but I've slogged away for eight years."

"Where do you come from?" I said, putting on my wet shoes.

"Albania."

For politeness' sake I ought to have asked a question or two, and wondered, say, if my new acquaintance had a family. But he had preached to me too much already.

"Look," I said. "I must call the dispatcher, or I'll have to kick my heels here all day."

I did not even ask him to keep an eye on the Checker, although it is easy to get a ticket on Park Avenue. I wished he would go away.

———

"The car's on its way to you from Brooklyn." I heard the dispatcher's voice, annoyed as usual.

"But I've been waiting at least an hour. Why are you sending a car from Queens to Brooklyn and then to Manhattan?"

"Listen, 866, you're not the only one. The other guy called before you."

Now I was pleased that the Albanian had stayed. As long as I had to wait anyway, it was better to have company. But still, when I got back I asked him, "Do you know how long we've been talking? Don't you have to work?"

"No!" He smirked smugly and pulled a wad of hundred-dollar bills out of his jacket pocket. "I've got money coming out of my ears! From now on the only way I go in a taxi is in the backseat. Other guys will work for me. Come on, take a look at my car. Forty miles on the clock!"

The brand-new cab, with the fresh lettering on the door—TIRANA TAXI CORPORATION—really was magnificent. The gentleman cabbie stroked his beauty.

"I'd lease it to you, but I've already promised it to another fellow, an Albanian."

It turned out that he had bought not one medallion but two, a whole corporation! And paid for the lot in cash. No loans, no monthly payments. Two medallions and two cars had to cost close to ninety thousand dollars. Where did a cab driver get that kind of money?

"Did you save for several years?"

"You won't save ninety thousand in a lifetime driving a cab. I made it"—he snapped his fingers—"like that!"

"How?"

"You couldn't do it even if I told you."

Had he found a bagful of money in his cab? Such things happened, I had already heard; and I had read in the papers, for example, about a cabman who had returned a case of diamond samples to a jeweler. Probably this Albanian had also found something and had not returned it. The massive gold watch on his wrist said 9:15. I might be late for the taping session. I ought to phone right away, either to make my excuses to the radio station or to remind the garage of my existence. As I ran across the street I noticed that my shoes had dried and were no longer leaving wet footprints.

"It's 866 again. I've been hanging around for an hour and a half. I can't wait anymore!"

"Don't you dare leave the cab!" the dispatcher bellowed. "Or you'll have to look for another garage!"

I hung up.

"You're too jumpy!" remarked the Albanian. As a counterweight to his riches, I boasted that I had another job and must be there by ten.

The Albanian launched into another lesson.

"If you work one day a week and make a hundred and ninety dollars, what are you doing in a taxi? If you don't have enough money, take some classes, learn something, but forget about yellow cabs. Hacking is only for people who are no good at anything else. It's a dirty job, it makes you dumb; you keep counting and counting someone else's money, but you hold it in your hands and think it's yours. Driving a cab isn't a profession, it's a bad habit. You get used to handling a bit of fresh money every day and it sucks you in, like dope, and then you're hooked."

It was not hard to convince me, wet and miserable as I was, and the Albanian sensed it.

"Throw the keys in the trunk and don't go near this heap ever again!"

I recalled that I still had to explain about the eleven dollars to the dispatcher.

"But how will they get the Checker back to the garage?"

"That's not your problem!"

"What about the bookings?"

"What about them?"

"You're absolutely right," I said.

The Albanian still did not believe I would have the guts to leave the car on Park Avenue, and he followed me to the Checker. I chucked the keys in the trunk and slammed it shut.

"Well done!" the Albanian said approvingly. "Let's go! I'll take you."

We got in the Ford. It was twenty to ten.

"Where would you like to go, sir?" He beamed, one cabbie to another. I gave the address of the radio station and said, raising my voice, "Listen, pal, if you want to get your quarter, move it. I'm in a hurry!"

"Yes, sir! Thanks a lot, sir! You're so generous, sir!" And we sped away.

I was happy again: the game was over. The Albanian was also in seventh heaven; we had both said farewell to our yellow cabs: I after three months, he after eight years.

"Never again!" I said. "I didn't come to America to drive a cab."

"Never!" echoed the Albanian, as if it were an oath.

Chapter Six

"OUR DAILY BREAD"

The tall gray-haired man was waiting for me at the entrance to the studio and glancing at his watch to underline his displeasure. I usually arrived an hour early, and we would spend the time working together. Today, crumpled, in a lather, I showed up at two minutes to ten, greeted him on the run, and scuttled inside. But as soon as the soundproof door closed behind me all of it vanished—the fog on the highway, the mauled corpse of the dog, the jet of water in my face, and the Albanian cabbie with his mysterious riches.

A shiver of excitement ran over me; the red light flashed, the recorded announcement came on.

"This is Radio Liberty."

Here began *my* nine and a half minutes.

"You are listening to the weekly program 'Our Daily Bread.'"

Nine and a half minutes of the truth.

As the saying goes, bread is the staff of life. Bread is the marvelous, treasured creation of man and nature. By bread we measure the wealth of our nation.

These are the words of a perennial member of the Politburo for the last quarter-century, but any Western sovietologist, anticommunist or leftist, would willingly subscribe to them. They convey an extremely profound and precise axiom: the wealth of Russia is indeed measured in bread. Such is the economic peculiarity of this superpower.

Nature has given us a rich land. Nowhere else in the world do such vast, fertile black-earth zones as ours exist. Nowhere else in the world is there a sea of wheat covering 150 million acres.

One can find pronouncements like these in any Soviet paper almost every day; but they are true nonetheless.

Displayed behind glass in the museums of Kiev, in the famous Crypt monastery, one can see heavy gold trenchers, dishes, chalices, goblets, jugs. "The ancestors of the Ruthenians," say the tour guides, "did not obtain these inestimable treasures by war or pillage. The ancient Athenians and Romans paid with this gold for wheat grown on the steppes of Taurida, the Azov uplands, and the lower Dnieper."

For Russians this is beyond comprehension: why are they now bringing millions and millions of tons of wheat to these very steppes — from America? What inhuman efforts had to be exerted to break a thousand-year-old tradition of arable farming and leave Russia, the most lavish granary on the globe, breadless?

It was these inhuman efforts that I discussed on every one of my programs.

———

Imagine a sleepy town in the Russian provinces, where they still bring out the bride's bloodied shift for the wedding guests to see; where children, when they greet their parents in the morning, still kiss the hand of their father, the provider. An embankment of the Volga, spattered with sunflower seeds, 1916.

Imagine all this as well as you can, and then consider what could be more boring than a lecture on private farming in an agricultural school in the sticks of Saratov. Only, perhaps, the prolixity of some academic upstart, a lecturer who dazzles the local maidens with such dicta as that civilization on our planet began at the moment when some unknown genius among our forebears gathered a handful of wild wheat seed and, instead of eating it, scattered it on the earth.

"Tell me," the upstart lecturer asked his audience. "Do you think that *white* cornflowers exist?"

Bewilderment and silence. Every child knows there are no white cornflowers. They are blue; their color is even called cornflower blue. "What about red lilies-of-the-valley?"

The students laughed.

"Few have seen them! They are rare, like many precious stones. But they do exist."

The lecturer on private farming was quite certain that somewhere on earth white cornflowers and red lilies-of-the-valley must be growing, so that the gaps in the "color groups" in the periodic table of plants he had invented could be filled in. This absurd idea was, in its own way, in tune with the times, however: a revolution was raging, received notions about all sorts of things were being overturned. The lecturer's mustache was quite charming, his young lady students adored him, and one of his devotees even published a note in the local rag saying that here in Saratov was a marvelous enthusiast who could predict the properties of plants as yet unknown to science. White cornflowers; the Mendeleev of botany.

His renowned colleagues inquired skeptically:

"But where should we look for your red lilies-of-the-valley?"

Of course the upstart did not know, and so he answered, vaguely, "At their birthplace. Where they first sprang up."

Some articles in foreign journals completely turned the poor man's head, and he acquired an eccentric new theory: the entire vegetable kingdom, in all its diversity, had "erupted" onto the earth's surface out of a single "crater."

How do you like that? Out of what "crater"? Where was it?

The young professor did not know the answer to that either, but, odd though it may seem, he was a dreamer of a practical disposition. He lost no sleep over cornflowers or lilies-of-the-valley, and fell in love with none of his female graduate students (by now they were in Leningrad) as deeply as he had fallen in love, in the days of his youth, with the queen of five continents, *Triticum*. He conceived the idea of searching the planet for *her* birthplace! In the prospect of this discovery he saw the purpose of his life.

The botanical reference books list over twenty thousand species of wheat. While analyzing them, he described an ideal strain, one that had never existed and which he dreamed of creating. Not himself—he was a theoretician. He knew that the realization of this dream would devour the lives of thousands upon thousands of crack scientific troops. His mission was to show them the way.

The birthplace of wheat, as he understood it, was what he called a storehouse of genes, a "genecenter." Every gene contains a characteristic: the size of the grain; the heaviness of the ear; the resilience of the husks that hold the grain; the sturdiness of the stalk that bears the ear; the capacity of the root system that waters and feeds the plant. From fifty desirable characteristics of different wheats he wanted to synthesize an Ideal. But until the "genecenter" was found, until the exact geographical location of the "crater" from which the present vegetable kingdom had "erupted" onto the earth's surface was established, all the successes and failures of the breeders, the "plant designers," could be nothing but a series of accidents.

By now head of a prominent research center, he made the young botanists, who idolized him, study roots—of dead languages.

It was to old folios, to ancient farming implements, hoes, sickles, and millstones, to inscriptions on clay tablets and to numismatic collections that his disciples turned in their search for the birthplace of cereals, copying the depictions of ears of grain from semiobliterated coins.

Might not an Assyrian chronicle have preserved, along with a story of military campaigns, some half-forgotten lines about wheat's mysterious past? Might not a deciphered cuneiform tablet reveal the secret of rye? Might not cave paintings name the motherland of oats?

"But where is this celebrated center of the origin of plants?" the government bigwigs would ask him.

He did not know.

"You have wasted millions. You have been looking for ten years now. Give us a firm date!"

He could not; he answered that unfortunately the research method he had chosen had turned out to be wrong.

"We have collected thousands of facts, but they are all untrustworthy."

Yet the all-powerful masters of the country, to whom he was answerable, could not accept such explanations, for they knew full well that *Soviet* science could NEVER be wrong.

However, a few years later, this scholar, fallen out of favor in his own country, won worldwide renown: sitting in his herbariums, he could now indicate, to within a hundred miles, the point on the globe where dozens of cultivated plants had originated. It was unimaginable; almost unreal. He pointed to a spot on the map of the western hemisphere and declared that this was the birthplace of corn. He equipped an expedition and sent one of his followers across the ocean; in a couple of years the future prominent scientist Bukasov brought back to Leningrad 1,183 species of corn. Many were previously unknown.

Sometimes an idea of his, casually dropped, was enough to send science in a new direction. The entire world, the planet: this was the only scale on which he thought. His favorite expression was "straddling the globe." But his inconsistency shocked party leaders, his conduct knew no bounds. If it had only been his love affairs!

The devil was constantly bearing him off, through Africa one year, Australia the next. Over caravan routes—on horseback, over desert dunes and mountain paths, across ravines—he wandered through fifty-two countries and corresponded in twenty languages at a time when in his own country one miserable letter to a great-aunt in Rumania or Poland could often cost its writer ten years in prison. He did not just hire Jews for important positions, he sought out the most pernicious Jews of all, those who had studied Hebrew, and sent them to examine the fields in Palestine.

The ministers were afraid to let him in their offices; he was always begging for money. Hardly anything: only a four-year expedition to Tibet and Mongolia. There, in the Gobi Desert—where snow evaporates in the winter drought before it can melt; where, in summer, animal carcasses dry out instead of decomposing—there must be a wild wheat growing with roots that went a hundred feet deep! If that gene could be transferred to cultivated cereals, the world could forget about droughts and famine.

He did not get the money, but he was optimistic: "We'll manage somehow. Let's flog my gold watch for a start."

What need had he of a gold watch when in the storerooms of his research center the earth's greatest treasure, its "plant capital," was gradually being concentrated?

In an old Leningrad palace, which housed his main research center, along a squeaking wooden gallery stretched rows and rows of racks containing thousands and thousands of drawers, each with a label marked HOLLAND, or MOUNTAINOUS CHINA, or EGYPT, or PERU, or ALGERIA, or MESOPOTAMIA, or AUSTRALIA, or BORNEO, or JAPAN.

In each drawer lay grain. The living grain from every kind of ear that grows on the planet. It was one of the wonders of the world, a global collection of cereals.

Many and many of them were first discovered by his disciples or himself.

Triticum Zhukovski ... Triticum Yakubtzinner ... Triticum Vavilovi.

They arrested him literally in the field. That day he had discovered yet another species of wheat, and it was to be his last.

In the New York Public Library I was leafing through the files of the international scientific journal *Heredity*. The cover of this highly respected publication has not changed for several decades: a gray background with a column of five names, the greatest in the entire history of biology:

Linnaeus

Mendel

Morgan

Mechnikov

And the last name——Vavilov.

There is none greater in twentieth-century biology.

He died of starvation in a Saratov prison, in the very town where, as a young man, he had written his first work—now a classic—on the law of homologic ranks.

WHY DID THEY KILL HIM?

It is difficult to pose a more senseless question.

Why did the ovens of Auschwitz burn?

———

As I speak into the microphone, as the huge reels turn on the recording equipment, I follow the expression on the tall gray-haired man's face. If he looks alert and his eyes glitter, everything is fine; my tone is unsullied by pathos, and at least one listener is moved by my words.

If you could glance with me through the glass wall, you might perhaps recognize the man I am talking about. He is Nick S., an American actor who appears from time to time in TV series and commercials, and who has been in charge of the recording department at Radio Liberty's New York branch since the station was founded. His parents brought him over from Russia fifty years ago, when he was a child, but he has remained a small part of that country, living a Russian life to this day.

Nikita Nikolaevich (as he is called in Russian) knows the name of every street and square in Moscow, Yaroslavl, or Ryazan. He can remember last month's premieres at the Bolshoi theater and at the Kirov. In American movies Nik Nik plays affable bishops, charming generals, and good-hearted businessmen, but this is merely a cinematic snare and a delusion. Heavens, what a difficult man fate had thrown me together with. In the recording studio he is a despot. He interrupts me at almost every word.

"The more emotional a commentator sounds, the less I believe in his sincerity. The more horrible your facts, the more neutral your voice must be."

I trust this man deeply. I owe him a great deal. I love him. We sweat blood over every broadcast: he teaches me to speak into the microphone naturally, without sounding stilted. And that is the hardest of all.

"Stop! Who's that spiteful demagogue I hear yowling? I don't have the slightest desire to listen to him. One more time, from 'They arrested him right in the field . . .'"

For over three years I had talked into the microphone. But if you knew how hard it is to speak month after month into a void, with no response from those you are addressing. . . . The only response to my program was that they tried to find out who the person concealed behind the pseudonym was. News reached me that former neighbors in my old apartment building were being questioned; I was afraid for my father. But suddenly they blundered. The KGB officer conducting the investigation made a mistake. He had probably been misled by an unscrupulous informer.

Glancing through the *Moscow Evening News*, I came across an article about the "ideological saboteurs" of Radio Liberty, which said that a traitor going under the pseudonym Lobas was slandering the Soviet Union, and his name was Alexander Katz.

Alik Katz is a real person: an actor, poet, artist, and playwright who had failed in every one of these capacities on both sides of the ocean. Having emigrated to the U.S., he wrote me an indignant letter from Los Angeles: why were the KGB muddling us? What could I reply? That the muddle had offended me, too?

Unfortunately, my direct supervisor, the editor, and I had nothing like the relationship I had with Nikita, though he too was a perfectly intelligent man, whose manners would not permit him to make a wry face when I came to see him in the murky little office that overlooked an airshaft. He would rise gallantly to greet me, but every time I appeared his features were stamped with such oppressive anguish that he felt he had to offer some decent explanation for it.

"It's dreadful!" he exclaimed. "This mixture of daylight and electricity is simply dreadful, you know. And it's extremely bad for the eyes."

With that he switched off the desk lamp. A minute passed; neither of us spoke. I had not come of my own accord, but my supervisor had certainly not summoned me because he was in the mood for a chat.

He looked at my shabby suit with barely perceptible perplexity. He could easily and willingly have spared me from going on with the "taxi epic," could have offered me a salary of twenty thousand or so a year, given me health insurance, moved my family out of our Brooklyn paradise to a nice house somewhere in the green suburbs of New York or Munich; but was it his fault that my broadcasts were biased when, after all, we were at the height of détente?

It would seem that we had nothing to discuss; but the editor had been told to talk to me one more time. This unpleasant mission forced him to begin, as usual, almost enigmatically.

"Let me put it this way: the other day a certain influential American requested your last script for review."

And since we could both guess that a certain influential American could have nothing good to say about my script, the editor took me to task with a mixture of sympathy and irritation:

"Why do you always write about the same thing? Bread, bread, bread.

The way you do it, it's always so gloomy, always painted so black. And, well . . . it's so dull!"

When I chucked the keys in the trunk of the fleet cab, I had thrown away my newfound independence, and now, having heard the editor's advice, I would probably have tried to redesign my program about Soviet agriculture to suit the bosses. But I did not get the chance to figure out how to do this. Into the stuffy little cubicle burst a tornado.

"Excuse me for barging in like this!" the tornado roared, knocking the editor's hat off the stand lurking by the door.

It was Dr. Kukin, the head of the news department, a professor of political science and the most tireless veteran of Radio Liberty. He hastened to pick up the hat and overturned the desk lamp. But the editor was on his guard. He grabbed the lamp deftly and reached over to retrieve his headgear.

"A thousand pardons!" Kukin thundered, not letting go of the editor's hat. "Allow me to kidnap our worthy author!"

And all three of us were glad. The professor because he had found me, the editor because he had got rid of me. And I was more pleased than either of them: Kukin could have need of me for only one purpose, "doing the news."

"Doing the news" meant translating information from *The New York Times* into Russian and reading it into the microphone. The job took a couple of hours and was well paid; and I had become accustomed to making a little extra between the regular checks for $190.

"Today you'll have some fun!" Kukin bellowed. Putting his arm imperiously around my waist, he bore me off down the hallway, and I noticed with surprise that we were not walking but running.

"Today I'm giving you *two* pieces, and you can choose *yourself* which one we should air!" With this Kukin held out to me two newspaper clips: "Soviet Gold Dumped on International Markets" and "Conflict Between Peru and Bolivia Over Off-Shore Fishing Zone."

"This is very interesting," I said. "They need hard currency to buy more grain."

Kukin was delighted.

"I knew it," he said, "I knew you would want to do the one about gold!

110

You see? You've only been working here three years and you've already decided that you can select the stuff we should broadcast."

It appeared that the professor had wanted to test me to see how I had matured as a radio journalist. I had not lived up to his expectations, but he was pleased about that.

"Moscow wasn't built in a day," he said consolingly. "When you've worked as long as I have, you'll learn. Until then I would like you to prepare 'Fishing Zone.' Immediately."

Well, that'll be a real sensation for Soviet listeners! I thought. Are they sitting up night after night, over the howl jamming their transistors, so as not to miss a word about the latest diplomatic note from Peru to Bolivia?

It was not so long since I myself had sat for hours over my old radio, trying to pick up any Western station, and then, after hearing this sort of gibberish, I had not gone near the thing for a week.

But Kukin would pay fifty dollars for "Fishing Zone," and I followed him obediently to the news department.

Chapter Seven

— — — — — — — — —

ANOTHER LIFE

E ven in our most sincere impulses, our most resolute acts, there is
always an element of posturing.

Yes, I had had a hard time since the dentist had put in my "free"
temporary prostheses. Every bite of an apple or crust of bread, every
spoonful of hot soup was painful. And yes, to feel myself a whole man
again, I needed money. But it was not really a question of survival, after
all. It had been clear from the outset that driving a yellow cab was an
inappropriate, overdramatic method of paying a dentist's bill. And now,
with a thousand dollars in my bank account, there was no real need for
me to go back to hacking. Brighton Beach was seething with émigré
dentists who, like my friend the Doctor, had not yet surmounted the
hurdle of the American professional tests, and any one of whom would
have been glad to put in my teeth for two thousand dollars rather than
five and to receive this modest fee in installments to boot. My wife
and I had discussed this alternative. A Russian moonlighter would
undoubtedly do an inferior job, but then our previous experience had
hardly taught us to seek only the best in goods and services. All the same,
I was in no hurry to part with the money that had been so laboriously
come by.

Like the prodigal son to his father's hearth, I returned to my Russian "pocket." When I was working for the garage I had had neither time nor energy to stroll along the boardwalk after sunset among the crowds of émigrés. Now old friendships were renewed. Misha, the future millionaire, was still selling hot dogs, but his ardor had cooled and he was no longer raring to mint gold medals. He had become a serious man: he was looking for a fish store.

"He doesn't even know himself what he wants. He's a laughingstock!" Misha's wife was choked with envy. "Volodya, am I right?"

"Who's laughing at him?"

"These kikes! While he's thinking his deep thoughts, people are doing business!"

A month earlier, Brighton Beach had seen the opening, with much pomp and circumstance, of a new store, Gifts of the Ocean, behind whose windows lazy carp swam in tanks; since then Misha's life had become a nightmare.

"A nothing!" Rosa picked away at it like a scab. "From now on, Volodya, I'm going to call him 'My nothing'!"

Misha looked at his wife, deliberating whether to punch her face now or later. Without waiting for the decision, Rosa beat a rapid retreat.

The stripe of surf, hissing on the sand, crept toward the boardwalk; Misha and I were left alone on a bench.

"She'll come running back and say, 'Oy, you were right: they burned out!'" Misha prophesied, looking after his spouse as she receded into the distance.

"What are you talking about? Who's going to burn out?"

"Gifts of the Ocean. They'll close down the same way they opened up."

An invisible wave broke quietly in the darkness.

"You know what, Volodya. You've got to buy a fish store in a black neighborhood."

"Why does it have to be black?"

"They buy a lot of cheap fish." Misha's lips trembled. "I've found a store!"

But there was suffering, not triumph, in his voice.

"Are they asking too much?" I said.

"That's not the problem. The owner wants twenty thousand under the table."

"Is this guy to be trusted? What sort of a person is he?"

"A Hitler. He robbed his own eighty-year-old brother. Took the shirt off the old man's back."

"So how can you give him twenty thousand on trust?"

Misha threw back his head and looked at the sky.

"That's exactly what my lawyer says."

The stars of Brooklyn glowed above our heads.

"But I'm going to give him the money, Volodya! Let her scream that I'm crazy. Listen—this could be my big break!"

In this Russian corner I felt like a fish out of water. I missed my yellow cab. Thus do ex-convicts miss their jail. It happens now and then in our complex world that events occurring far from the places where we live, events we have taken no part in, directly or indirectly, suddenly turn out to have a much stronger influence on our destiny than our most pains-taking efforts to obtain or make something out of life. A remote wave of precisely this type of event—one that had nothing to do with me—pushed me, too, off the path I was treading. This transpired about two years after the day in Moscow when, at the apartment of a Soviet dissident—a former general, long since deprived by the government of his rank, his wartime decorations and pension—an unknown visitor appeared.

"I am a Ukrainian writer from Kiev," he introduced himself, giving his name, which meant nothing to his hosts. "I don't have any recom-mendations. I thought that if I came to you just as I am, you wouldn't throw me out."

"There was such charm and simplicity in his words," the dissident's wife remembered afterward, "that we trusted the stranger instantly. We sat and talked for a while."

The guest had brought a present: the manuscript of his book. But the present was not the only reason for the visit; he also had a request. His hosts pricked up their ears.

The writer from Kiev was clear-eyed and fair-haired; there was urgency in his voice when he requested that they arrange for him to meet with foreign journalists, to whom he intended to speak about the political situation in the country, and the old general, who had driven thousands upon thousands of just such clear-eyed, fair-haired soldiers into battle, toward death, suddenly felt a pang of pity and said that he would not help him with this.

"The consequences of such a deed are unpredictable."

These were the words of a man who had already been through arrests, jails, and years of torture in psychiatric prisons, where doctors had "treated" him with mind-destroying drugs.

"Go back to Kiev," advised the dissident's wife, softening the refusal. "Try to think about your decision. Talk it over with people you trust. Who knows, perhaps someday you'll be grateful for the answer you got today."

With that the guest left, but the manuscript remained.

The craggy general, whose appearance even the General Staff Academy had not purged of the traces of a peasant son, was reading the copy he had been given, and his obstinate shaved head hung ever lower.

I did not immediately decide to hand over the manuscript of this book for publication abroad. There were two alternatives. The first was to leave for the West myself (a real possibility), and to publish the book when I got there. The second was to stay in my country and send the manuscript abroad.

If I stayed, I knew, going on evidence derived from experience of the conduct of the authorities in my fatherland, that I would be arrested and convicted.

But I choose the second alternative: I am staying. Reader, I ask you, when you hear I am on trial, do not fret for more information. Know now that I told the court exactly what you are about to read.

And here is what I "told" — will tell! — the court:

"Citizen judges, I sent my manuscript to the West because when a writer has written something he wants to hold the fruits of his hard-earned labor in his hands in the form of a book, published in many copies, which may reach many readers. In my own country I could not publish my book. But I wrote it and considered it necessary that people read it."

That is what I would say in court.

But perhaps it will never get to court. Even a closed session. They may simply take me away, and I will disappear.

The general's wife also read these lines, and—I permit myself to conjecture—she cried. In her understanding heart, which had suffered much grief, she knew that the writer from Kiev would return, and then she and her husband would have to grant his request to help him destroy himself, finally and irrevocably.

And return he did.

———

The year in which these events took place was dubbed by Soviet newspapers "the Year of the Constitution," since Brezhnev's new code of fundamental laws was due to come into effect that December. For several months the press and television had been talking about the unprecedented enthusiasm of working people, who had forgotten even to think about such temporary hardships as the usual lack of flour or potatoes or sugar or milk in the stores, and who only rejoiced that the wise Party had thought up a new Constitution for them. And so, when the general and his wife—who had not even tried this time to dissuade the visiting author of the book (by now published abroad)—notified foreign correspondents that on a certain day, at a certain time, in their apartment, a certain Soviet citizen, a writer, intended to express his critical observations regarding the Constitution then, risking expulsion from the country, as no fewer than twenty foreign reporters hastened to the unauthorized press conference.

Months or years later, back home again—in an editor's office, a press hangout, or their own bedrooms—the journalists would try to explain how much courage it sometimes took simply to walk through the entrance of an ordinary Moscow apartment building, and would sense bitterly that the story sounded clumsy and somehow unbelievable. Because—well, how can one put it?—the point was not that "they" might have punched your face in, taken away your tape recorder, or stomped on your camera. Life in Moscow differed so much from an ordinary one because in broad daylight on the streets of this wonderful city you could be suddenly enveloped in terror, in the knowledge that at any moment something unknown—anything—might happen to you. A brick off a roof? An attack by "hooligans"? An arrest on charges of espionage?

All excited, they entered the dissidents' apartment, feeling proud that they were carrying out their duty as reporters. A man of about fifty, the person whose opinions they were going to hear (twenty pens jotted down his name in block letters on twenty notepads so as not to get it wrong: G-H-E-L-Y S-N-E-G-I-R-E-V), a former member of the Communist Party, a former member of the Soviet Writers' Union, former member of the Cinematographers' Union—got up from his chair and read aloud the following:

"With this declaration I renounce my Soviet citizenship. I have made this decision at a time when the government is conducting discussions of a new constitution. In the newspapers, on the radio, at mass meetings they scream of unanimous, rapturous approval. Very soon the draft will become law amid a general thunder of hurrahs.

"Your constitution is a lie from beginning to end. It is a lie that your state voices the will and interests of the people. . . . Your electoral system, mocked by your own people, is a lie and a disgrace, as is your national emblem, the hammer and sickle encircled by ears of wheat which you have to import from the United States."

In the room all was quiet.

Even the foreigners understood what had happened. This man, who was clearly responsible for his actions, had quite deliberately crossed an invisible, fateful line, as surely as if he had stepped into a radioactive zone.

There was no outburst, not a sound. Head, arms, legs—everything was there. But the man was doomed. And one could not predict what might happen to him. Perhaps he would be run over by a car tomorrow. Perhaps "muggers" would shove him out of a moving train. Perhaps he would be declared mentally ill. I, of course, had been completely unaware of these events, taking place thousands of leagues from where I lived, until the New York office of Radio Liberty received from our Munich headquarters a "Declaration of Renunciation of Soviet Citizenship," and a thorough librarian photocopied the document and, just in case, put one of the copies in the pigeonhole marked LOBAS, for the freelance commentator.

Thus some very special Fridays entered my wretched life. Now I left the recording studio fired up, and none of the editor's warnings seemed worth any attention. Tomorrow, in the long, angry lines at the empty counters in the grocery stores, people would whisper to each other the last words of my show.

Your hammer and sickle, encircled by ears of wheat which you have to import from the United States, are a lie and a disgrace.

Did *I* have an ending today! I knew these words by heart, they burned in me. They were *my* words and *my* thoughts! Long before I left, had I not intended a thousand times to say just that, in just that way, openly? And yet dared not. And my excuse was that millions of others, who had swarmed alongside me in that other, Soviet, life, yearned to say the very same thing—and dared not either.

Even here, in quiet backwaters, living in New York, Washington, Munich, many of us, who worked for radio stations that transmitted to the Soviet Union, broadcast our programs under pseudonyms, as I did. It is always sensible to be circumspect with regard to the KGB. But this man, who had hurled in their face his "I DO NOT WANT TO BE A CITIZEN OF THE USSR!", this writer, whom I was merely quoting, was on the other side of the Wall and was not hiding behind a pseudonym. He signed his open letter to the Soviet government with his full name and gave his address: 8 Tarasovskaya Street, Apt. 6, Kiev. He had overcome the fear.

Radio Liberty's political department, which strictly forbade any anti-Soviet pronouncements, did broadcast Ghely Snegirev's political writings. The gentlemen of détente could still respect another's courage; they knew what awaited this author. And I envied him the more, because it was not a contest of wits between the two of us. It seemed we were made of different stuff. For I did not feel free here, in America, while he was boundlessly free even there, in Russia.

Besides, for me his name was not an abstract symbol, as were the names of Sakharov or Grigorenko, whom I had never seen. Snegirev I knew and remembered. He and I had rubbed shoulders for many years, and I had been used to calling him not by his last name, nor, of course, by the Russian name-and-patronymic formula, Ghely Ivanovich, but by the nickname commonly used by his friends, Gavrila.

We were not really close friends. We knew each other to the extent that he also worked in movies, as a screenwriter and director, and even, at one time, as head of a scriptwriting department. He lived in the center of town, in a better apartment than mine; he had connections I could only dream of, and, all in all, was the sort of person of whom one says, Well, what more can he want? Once he surprised everyone: an elite literary journal, then quite unattainable for a mediocre writer, published a story of his. It was genuine literature, and after I read it, I stopped sneering to myself about this universal favorite, so inferior to me as a screenwriter. He was inferior because he drank too much and chased girls even more.

His head was constantly buzzing not with scriptwriting ploys, angles, or contrived situations, but with women: he was always falling in love. One day, at some booze-up in the home of mutual friends, Gavrila took me aside.

"Can you do me a favor?"

I was puzzled: Gavrila had plenty of friends, much closer to him and much more influential than I, of whom he could have asked a favor.

"The bastards slapped me with a Group Four!"

I could not help laughing. A special evaluation committee categorizes every Soviet film in a "Quality Group," somewhat similar to the stars awarded by film critics. The director is paid according to this evaluation. As a rule, only the most unabashed hack work can get you a Group Four. My productions seldom made the premier group, but then they almost never got a Group Two, either. If a picture was awarded a Group Four, the director did not get a penny, and justly so. People work in movies because it is a vocation; producing hack work is disgraceful.

However, Soviet standards of behavior do not allow one to judge whether a friend's request is fair or not. There is only one rule: if you can help, you help. As usual, Ghely was in love, this time with a college student, tall as a basketball player. I asked him what he wanted of me.

"Write an article."

"What about?"

The straight, fair hair hung down over his forehead, sweaty from all the vodka; his bleary eyes danced.

"About a director's right to experiment."

I finally grasped what he was requesting. While running after his "basketball player," Gavrila had (not for the first time) cobbled together the movie with one left foot; however, if it were mentioned in the press that the film was the result of an unusual and original concept, and that failure had befallen the director in his search for "new approaches," then should the failure not be considered an "honorable defeat"? The evaluation committee could not ignore the opinion of the press; it was likely that after the review appeared, they would change the Quality Group from Four to Three, and Gavrila would receive at least half his fee.

I called a high-up friend of mine, a member of the editorial board, and explained the problem: a nice guy, very much in love, and short of money, like all of us.

"Tut-tut-tut!" the member of the editorial board said.

"It's got to be done," I whined insincerely. I had no desire at all to write a stupid article about some dreadful movie I had not seen.

"Papa!" said the newspaperman, who called all his male friends "papa," and all the female ones "mama." "Tell me honestly: if you haven't seen the movie, have you at least seen the girl? Is she worth the effort?"

"She's worth it," I said truthfully. "A cute blonde co-ed." And I could not resist a dig. "Definitely better than any of his movies!"

I heard his chuckle down the receiver.

"Papa, directors of his stature undoubtedly have the right to make experiments and mistakes. Absolutely! It's mistakes like those that make life worth living. Your article's scheduled for Monday. Take care!" He hung up.

After the article appeared in the party paper they upped the assessment, our friends had a good laugh, and we had a splendid time drinking away my fee, but I had not seen Ghely since then.

We were not close enough for me to seek him out and say goodbye before I left the country. In fact I had completely forgotten him, and only after I had already been living in New York for several years did I suddenly see a face I knew on the cover of a Russian émigré magazine. I thought I was mistaken, but no. The caption said:

A feeling in me is growing, a hope is dawning, that my fate is to be the first swallow, the one that will proclaim the Spring of Freedom to my Motherland.
GHELY SNEGIREV.

I froze. This was *that* Ghely? Gavrila? The boozer, the member of the Soviet Writers' Union? The party member?

I larded my broadcasts with excerpts from his open letters, essays, and stories, which kept on coming to the West by unknown routes—and again and again I asked myself: so this is the same Ghely?

Only yesterday he had been a zero, an ordinary Soviet man who could have been sent to rot in a concentration camp or destroyed in a psychiatric "hospital." Who would have put in a word for him? But Ghely had already taken a giant step. His name was mentioned daily on the BBC World Service, the Voice of America, the Deutschewelle, and Radio Free Europe. YOUR CONSTITUTION IS A LIE FROM BEGINNING TO END! Neither Solzhenitsyn, nor Grigorenko, nor anybody else had ever dared talk to "them" in such a way while they were still there.

The Gestapo were evidently perplexed: Ghely was still free. Clearly they did not know what to do with him. I sometimes thought that perhaps they would not lock him up after all. Perhaps they would declare him to be Jewish—Ghely IVANOVICH? But was a purely Russian patronymic any obstacle to them? They would pronounce him "Isaakovich" and kick him out to Israel.

Perhaps that would have happened, but his latest letter was addressed to the General Secretary personally. *"You are a political figure of the 1937 vintage . . ."* He who dares touch the person of the Führer cannot be expelled to Israel.

Georgy Markov, a writer and a political exile from Bulgaria working in London for the BBC, made a guest appearance at Radio Liberty where, since I had been there, "they" had not laid a finger on a single employee. The chief target of Markov's broadcasts was the Bulgarian General Secretary, Todor Zhivkov. On September 7, 1978, soon after Markov's return to London (it was Zhivkov's birthday and evidently a present to him from a friend of state security), a "casual bystander" stuck him with an umbrella in the hurly-burly of the Waterloo Bridge subway station. The writer gasped in surprise: something had pricked him in the thigh.

He died on the fourth day. When his upper thigh was exposed at autopsy, they found a tiny metal ampule, 1.7 millimeters in diameter, that contained ricin, a virulently poisonous protein.

Vladimir Kostov, a journalist who had also written about his leader, was strolling along the Champs Elysees in Paris when he felt a sudden jab in his back. They managed to save him. The gelatin plug on the ricin ampule, removed by a surgeon and shown on TV in a good dozen democratic countries, turned out to be defective. It had not dissolved fully at body temperature, as it was supposed to (and as did happen with Markov), so Kostov received an insignificant amount of poison.

I read the letter addressed to Brezhnev—*Your career began in blood . . . Your hands are steeped in blood*—and wanted to cry, No, Ghely, this one you should not have written!

But did I really live constantly thinking of Ghely? I lived my own life, had my own cares and squabbles. I would yell at my son for his C in chemistry: "You live in a family of immigrants and you MUST be a brilliant student! Do you want to end up driving a cab?"

When word came that Ghely had been arrested, I took it as we usually take such news that, for example, a friend of ours who is incurably ill has gone into the hospital, from which he will apparently never get out. It's a pity, of course, but then it could not really be helped.

Underestimating our state security, I thought they would beat Ghely up during interrogation. But apart from the fact that he had been arrested, we knew nothing. We did not know that his cell had a shining parquet floor, that they fed him copiously, that the warders were invariably polite, and that a special medical team had been assigned to watch over the prisoner's health.

Nor did we know this detail: from the tenth to the twenty-seventh day of his hunger strike the prisoner was not force fed, and when, finally, they fed him according to all the house rules—with the arm-twisting, the handcuffing, the crunch of teeth shattering—he felt in his neck a *needle*, and later, bedridden, already tossing in delirium, he shouted, "Syringe! . . . January! . . . Japanese injection!" while the paralysis slowly crept along his legs, higher and higher.

The radio station broadcast Ghely's last open letter.

Secretary Brezhnev, you are an old man. Death is already brushing you with his wings, the doctors never leave your side. You have spent your whole life living a lie. You lied not just in little things, not just to your neighbor and your wife. You lied to your own nation and to the whole world. Will you die as you have lived, with a lie?

But Brezhnev was not ready to die that year, and God did not hear the prayers of Ghely, who was already begging for death.

We knew nothing of this.

The next edition of *Our Daily Bread*, already taped, was not aired. As sometimes happens, events overtook my commentary, and now I had to make changes in it. The teletype tapped out a special message from Munich:

> *The newspaper Literary Ukraine has published over Ghely Snegirev's signature an article which says, in part: "In the process of the investigation I was able to analyze every aspect of my criminal activity, which, as I now realize, inflicted serious damage on my country. Because of certain shortcomings, caused by our society's rapid rates of development, I came to an erroneous conclusion about the bankruptcy of the Soviet system."*
>
> *"Taking into consideration G. I. Snegirev's wholehearted repentance,"* the teletype rattled away, *"the investigation of his case was halted and the prisoner released from custody, since he no longer presents a danger to society."*

So that ambitious man, everybody's favorite, had wanted to be "the first swallow, the one that would proclaim freedom." Thank God he had gotten off lightly. In the old days they really would have killed one for such things. But the times were changing, the regime had softened. Little by little they, too, were leaning toward détente. And here it was: they had disarmed an opponent and released him in peace.

With reflections like these, I headed for the library.

"Ah, there you are! Give me three dollars."

It was a pretty, flirtatious girl from Moscow who worked there as an announcer.

"Aren't you even going to ask me what the money's for?"

"Why should I ask? You can tell me if you like."

"No, seriously. Haven't you heard?"

"Heard what?"

"They fired Nikita. We're giving a party for him."

She had graduated from drama school in Moscow and performed there for a year or two, but it was Nikita who polished her Russian pronunciation, as he did mine.

Of course, the dismissal was not a tragedy for him. He would receive a decent pension; and he had, on the whole, been "retired" for an objective reason: the radio station's budget had been cut again. After all, it was the era of détente.

"These 'objective reasons' won't let you breathe!" said the actress, and only then did I notice that she did not seem quite herself, and that her almost youthful face was touched with an ominous look of an old woman—her mother? Grandmother? Or perhaps it was that very American death, from cocaine, already lying in wait around the corner for her?

"Get out of this cesspool," the actress counseled me.

"Where to?"

"You think I don't know? They've seen you. I was so glad when they told me."

"Why? It's a nasty, demeaning job."

"And this isn't demeaning?"

Coming toward us along the hallway was a certain influential American. It was our boss. I looked at him, thinking that despite the fact that it was not nice, not smart, and altogether not done, I did not have the heart to say hello to him.

Part Three

ONE DAY IN THE LIFE OF A TAXI DRIVER

‑ ‑ ‑ ‑ ‑ ‑ ‑ ‑ ‑

Chapter Eight

MORNING WITH

CHINAMAN:

7 A.M.–10 A.M.

A taxi driver with a thousand dollars in the bank can rent a cab as easily as a cabbie with no money can get a job at a garage. Suitors vied with one another to make me tempting proposals from every side, but, realizing I was suddenly so sought after, I became choosy.

I turned down all eight-cylinder Fords as uneconomical. I told a persistent Dodge, bluntly, that he was too old for me, and I was not attracted by the prospect of making the rounds of the repair shops with him. Neither of the Chevys wooing me had a partition, and I knew from now on there would be many days when I would not return home before dark; anybody might get in my cab.

Having turned all of these down, I wrote a check for five dollars to the Russian émigré daily and placed an ad that was about as truthful as those that had seduced me in my time.

PUT YOUR CAB IN RELIABLE HANDS! PROFESSIONAL TAXI DRIVER, YEARS OF EXPERIENCE IN NEW YORK, WISHES TO LEASE NEW CAR WITH PARTITION.

An early-morning phone call informed me that the ad had appeared. An inappropriately languid female voice purred, "Are you married? Do you have children? How old are you?"

When she heard my replies, the woman said that we were probably well suited, and suggested we meet in Brighton Beach at the entrance to the Café Dream. However, there had been no misunderstanding; the questions were entirely businesslike. The point was that young bachelors, the group with the best prospects at marriage bureaus, are quoted at a very low price on the taxi labor exchange, due to their unpredictable behavior. It's easy for a young fellow to go on a bender, get pickled, and smash up the car. While a dejected type like me, burdened with a family, is the most desirable candidate there can be for a cab owner. This sort of guy may lie about having driven a taxi all his life, but at least he won't get behind the wheel drunk.

We met. The middle-aged owner of the Checker-with-partition, her lips painted scarlet on a withered face, first of all made it clear that we were "people of different stations in life." (It was some time before I understood why this was so important to her.) Her husband was a "Moscow architect," and she herself was a Muscovite and a theatergoer. Hence the unusual name of the corporation on her cab's door, taken from a popular theater of the 60s and 70s.

This name, TAGANKA TAXI CORPORATION, I had seen before, on the door of the cab that Crewcut drove, but I was not about to tell the woman I knew her husband.

The Checker she was offering me had about thirty thousand miles on the clock, and it remained only to agree on a price and to decide where I would hand the cab over to a co-driver; but then the owner told me she did not want two drivers, who would turn her car into a wreck in a year; and wouldn't I agree to lease the Checker at a discount, $375 for a full week?

This alternative had not occurred to me; I had not been ready to give up my job at the radio station. But for half a week—assuming I leased the cab on a twelve-hour shift—the price was "only" $125 less. The difference seemed insignificant, and offered full possession of the car. With no co-driver there would be no squabbles about who scratched the fender or whose turn it was to change the oil. Work when you want, as much as you want: this was the very freedom which the garage had pledged to me but never given.

The owner and I shook hands on the deal, and for an extra $125 I had bought myself a slew of blessings and indulgences. From now on I would not have to leap out of bed at four o'clock in the morning, head buzzing. Now I could sleep serenely until the nerve-racking early morning race on Manhattan island was over. Nor did I have to drag myself across the city on the subway to the garage and back home again. Nor did my wife have to go grocery-shopping with a cart. Now I took Saturdays off, and, like other couples where the husband drives a cab, my wife and I would set off decorously in "our" Checker for the supermarket.

Unfortunately, leasing a cab also has its negative sides. My trouble was my total responsibility for everything that happened to the car.

One night somebody smashed a side window. The vandal did not even bother to open the door and look inside; under the seat he would have found my changer with about ten dollars in coins, an elegant pen my son had given me, and a carton of cigarettes, but he did not want any of this. He broke the window for the hell of it.

"I'm sorry it happened, but it wasn't my fault," I said to Mme. Crewcut, meaning that it seemed to me I should not have to pay for the glass.

"Well, it's not my fault either," she retorted.

The compromise of splitting the cost of the damages she also rejected. When it came to financial questions, this lady was quite uncompromising. The glass would cost me fifty dollars.

"Is this any way to treat a man who works for you?" I asked. "Your husband drives a cab, so you know how hard it is."

"That's exactly why I do it this way," the owner replied. "If I gave you a break for twenty dollars or whatever it is, my husband would have to work it off. And you'll forgive me if I say that I care about him more than I care about you."

Since we occupied "different stations" in life, the theatergoing lady from Moscow felt no moral obligation toward me.

———

Ever since that memorable incident, each morning, still half asleep, the first thing I do is look out the window. The owner and I have no agreement as to whether she would return my deposit if the Checker got stolen but I would rather we never have the chance to argue about it. Only when I am convinced that the cab, topped by the bright forage cap of its advertisement, is still there, do I head for the bathroom. But all the time I am washing, and gulping hot coffee, my mind is down there, with the Checker. Has anything happened to it during the night? Has a wing mirror been unscrewed? Have the wheels been taken? You cannot distinguish such details from the nineteenth floor.

And so I finally relaxed only when I got down to the cab and examined it carefully. No one had gone near the Checker; everything was fine, and, as usual, I made my first dollar even before I switched on the engine. I was cleaning out the cab, shaking the cigarette butts out of the ashtrays and wiping the windows. Lifting up the back seat, I extracted from the dusty depths a scattering of nickels, two quarters, and a subway token. Was I thinking, while I did all this, about anyone? Hardly. If there was anything I was capable of thinking about after yesterday's fifteen hours' work, it was money: namely, that when I wrenched my head from the pillow, I was already $17.84 in debt to the owner. And of course I was also thinking, as I went down to the car, that another hour had passed and therefore my debt had grown to $20.07.

People who have never leased a yellow cab rarely consider this obvious truth: there are 168 hours in a week. If you divided my $375 rent by 168, the result was that I paid the owner $2.23 an hour, every hour.

When I slept.

When I ate.

When I went grocery shopping with my wife.

And now, when I was gunning along the highway to Manhattan empty.

Of course, I was free to leave the house when I felt like it. I was free not to go to work at all. Nobody was goading me on. But it was not in my power to stop that second meter, the one in the owner's purse, which inexorably, at four cents a minute, $2.23 an hour, kept on swelling my debt. Until that debt was covered and the cost of the day's gas was paid, did I have the right to go home? This was my life: the ratio between the hours of rest and labor was controlled by the dollar.

The Checker sped along the highway. The owner's meter ticked away; when would I switch on mine?

Why did I drive empty? Because in Brooklyn it is pointless to look for passengers going to the city. In the old days I used to cruise around a little in the mornings and go along Brighton Beach Avenue in search of a customer. And customers did stop me sometimes. But since I had gone *back* to driving a taxi, all four doors of my cab were always locked, and before opening them, I would ask the prospective passenger where he was going.

People would get angry, and, frankly, I could understand them; nor was there any need to remind me what the rules of the Taxi and Limousine Commission said. But life goes on obstinately repeating its lesson, over and over again: the more strictly a cabbie observes the rules governing taxi drivers and the more he fears the complaints, the police, and the inspectors, the less money he brings home.

In Manhattan, picking up passengers on short trips is steady work. There are a lot of them: one gets out, another gets in. But in any other borough, taking a "shorty" is a waste of time. The inhabitants of Brighton Beach seldom spent more than five bucks on a taxi. They usually took a cab to reach some corner of Brooklyn where the bus didn't go. Rides like those only took me farther from the highway.

I had never once gotten a morning job from my neighborhood to the city, and the only thing I remembered from all the useless ventures into Brighton Beach was the sinister sight of the Gifts of the Ocean store, burned down in the night. How on earth had my friend managed to predict both the financial ruin and the subsequent gambit of the unfortunate entrepreneurs?

———

The first traffic jam I got into was just before the Brooklyn Bridge. The stream of cars had stopped above the East River, beyond which unfolded the classic view of Wall Street, known even to those who have never been to New York. The bright masses of the skyscrapers swayed in the dark water.

But of all the taxi drivers stuck beside me at the bridge, I was the only one admiring this picture. In the next lane, in another Checker, a fat, stubbly-chinned Arab was frenziedly hammering with his fists on the steering wheel; he was straining to reach Manhattan, while we were barely crawling along.

A middle-aged Italian, his face distorted with rage, who kept leaning on the horn—his yellow Ford had a gaping black hole where one headlight should be—howling like a wounded animal.

And there was a Russian, a neighbor of mine; our cabs often spent the night next to each other. As soon as the lane of traffic on his right or left moved forward, he instantly tried to jump in. Does it make sense? He'll cripple the car, he'll have to fix it, pay for it . . . No, he can't stand it anymore, all he wants is to get to Manhattan . . . Manhattan!

By the time I got stuck at the bridge, my debt had already passed the twenty-one-dollar mark. But I simply would not let myself go like that, and, as I observed the other cabbies, I even experienced a certain feeling of superiority, since none of those hacks could have known what sort of morning he was going to have, while I did.

How ridiculous a cab driver's behavior looks to an outsider. (I was riding a mounting wave of conceit.) Why were they charging into the city when, at that very moment, hundreds of thousands of cars were pouring into Manhattan island over twelve bridges and through four tunnels? Once they finally reached the city, all these cabbies would end up in more traffic snarls; and they would instantly wish, at all costs, to break out of Manhattan again. Where to? Kennedy, of course.

Honest cabbies, like me, roamed the city all day like hungry wolves. We did not disdain any quarry. Down in the mines of the streets and the avenues, we extracted our nickels and dimes, but we never stopped keeping a lascivious eye out for an airport.

———

My trained eye scans the left and right curbs of the avenue for several blocks, registering only the pieces of luggage. Musical instruments, amplifiers, and any kind of electronic equipment in imitation-leather covers, *similar* to suitcases, do not confuse me for a moment. I have quickly learned to identify them. The problem is that the genuine suitcases themselves frequently turn out to be deceptive bait. Seize one and you are caught.

As soon as a little rain drizzles down, the lifeless street—from the cabbie's point of view—suddenly turns into a forest of waving hands. For half an hour before nobody hailed my cab. But as the first drops hit the asphalt, everyone suddenly notices me at once. Now my cab is in great demand. Gorgeous girls knock on the windows, dowagers smile ingratiatingly, aloof gentlemen wink familiarly, promising two or even three bucks over the meter. What should I do in this situation? Which of them should I let in the cab?

Who gave you the right to *choose* your customers? A cab is a form of public transportation. You're obliged to take the first fare that comes along and that's that.

Yeah? Nuts to you! The moment the rain starts I switch on the off-duty light. Now I won't pick up *anybody!*

Will my conscience allow me to refuse that cute girl who's found herself under the weeping sky without a raincoat? Would I really drive past that granny? Look, with wind-blown umbrella inside out.

No one knows where the shoe pinches like the wearer. You think I don't want to be nice? But if I take pity on the granny, who will take pity on me later? When it stops raining, no one will want my cab again. And again I'll be cruising around for twenty minutes in search of a two-dollar fare.

The day will fly by, night will come, New York will go to bed, and I will remain alone on the deserted streets. How can I return home before I have earned $62.50, the daily cost of my lease? And what about the gas? And what about me—must I make a minimum of thirty or forty dollars for myself or not? But in order to make that amount, at seventy cents a mile, a taxi driver has to put a hundred live miles on the clock. Only with taxis scarce as gold dust, only with the forest of upraised hands, comes my chance of grabbing an airport on the street and making twenty bucks at one blow.

———

If you rummage through the dictionaries, if you look in the *OED* as well as Webster, you will find that the word *cab* has a whole range of meanings in English, besides the main one, "a vehicle for hire." Cab is a synonym for "sticky" and "dirty"; it is also a word-for-word translation, the crib by which one cheats on an examination, while the slang verb "to cab" means "to pinch."

Which of these definitions fit me? Did I rob trusting people? Did I tell foreign tourists they *each* had to pay the amount shown on the meter? Did I make that meter run faster? No, never! But going to the airports I did avoid the shortest route over the Queensboro Bridge and tried to head for the Triborough, so I could barrel along wide, swift Grand Central Parkway, which turned my every ride into a holiday. At times, I also allowed myself the luxury of turning on the off-duty light when the cabs within view happened to be taken and I was certain the first suitcase that came along would be mine.

Another minute's patience, a few more pangs of conscience, another malevolent taking my number, and I will be off to JFK!

There it is, the long-awaited and desired one. The old man escorting the suitcase has abandoned all hope of getting a taxi in the increasing downpour. He has flattened himself against a newsstand, doom written all over his face. Poor fellow, how can he know that the only empty cab with its off-duty light on is picking its way down the jam-packed avenue toward him and him alone? That I have spotted his *suitcase?*

I stop the Checker by the newsstand in such a way that no chance passenger can get in, and only then do I release the automatic lock. The suitcase is loaded up, the meter switched on, the car pulls away, and at that moment the old geezer speaks.

"Chelsea!"

I had swallowed the bait. Not only is the trip a three-dollar shorty, but in the crush of cars it will take forever. The suitcase that played such a trick on me was going to the repair shop.

I carped about something, huffing and puffing, but once the old man had warmed up inside my cab, he fought back.

"Don't you get nasty with me! I'm ninety-three years old."

I had to apologize. My father, who had remained behind, in Russia, was seventy-eight. I could not afford to draw down the wrath of God.

———

A Chinese man had showed up in my Checker the day before, toward evening, when, having given up all hope of getting a fare to the airport, which is rare after six o'clock, I had decided to comb Park Avenue one more time and had turned on the off-duty light. The rush hour would be subsiding soon, but dozens of hands were still held out to me, and I was ignoring even the most despairing customers, who practically threw themselves under my wheels. Suddenly, on the opposite side of the avenue, on the corner of Sixty-first Street, I noticed—a suitcase! I glanced furtively around—no police, no oncoming cars—made a U-turn against a one-way sign, leaped out of the Checker, and grabbed the object.

The owner of the suitcase bowed gratefully; but when I turned on the meter, he slugged me in the back of the head.

"Tat!"

All was clearly not well, but a spark of hope still flickered in me. Taxi drivers like incomprehensible words. They bespeak mysterious, remote townships—New Jersey, Connecticut, Westchester—at double-the-meter.

"Tat. Is that a town in Long Island?" I asked at random.

"No lon-ilen. Titi. Tel tat."

Painful though it was, I unfortunately understood. The fiberboard Chinese suitcase could not afford the expensive Regency Hotel, and was evacuating from Park Avenue to somewhat cheaper lodgings on Seventh—the Taft. I was cast down, but nevertheless questioned the man stringently. It was established that he had flown into New York for only a day, and tomorrow would be borne off the devil knew where. From which airport?

When the inquiry was over, it remained only to plant the idea in my client that it was he who urgently needed me, rather than the other way around. I fed him the line that tomorrow Americans would be celebrating President Ford's birthday, and therefore very few buses or cabs would be working. However, since I personally had such respect for the Chinese people, since they were *good* people (more smiles), then, very well, I would take him to Kennedy in the morning, so he would not miss the plane. Besides which, I would come to pick him up for free (more bows), but he had to give me—here the man got really frightened and calmed down only when he realized that I was not asking for money in advance, merely for his business card.

The businessman from Taiwan gave me his card. The next morning, I twirled it in my hands and looked at my watch. Eight-thirty. My cab was at the corner of Houston Street. I had to pick up the Chinese man at nine, and the best way to use the spare time was to wash the cab.

I turned into the car wash, and while the soapy foam and jets of water cleaned the week's grime off the Checker, I worked out that by nine o'clock, when the Chinese man would get into the car, my debt to the owner would have reached $22.30. But that was nothing to fret about. I would drag the man over the Triborough bridge, and (with the tip) would collect the requisite amount.

While I was making these calculations, three Mexicans were wiping the Checker with rags. You could not help sympathizing with them. Always out in the wind, always wet, any of these *illegal* immigrants would have been happy to change places with me, to become the driver of a yellow cab. I threw a quarter in the funnel marked THANKS, and then added another, ashamed of my stinginess. The Chinese man would pay for everything.

I had promised I would come to pick him up for nothing, but he could transport his fiberboard suitcase for free back home in Taiwan. This time I would put a dollar on the bill for the suitcase. I did not have the right? Never mind. The less a cabbie reflects on universal fairness, the more money he makes.

I turned onto Seventh Avenue from Fifty-first Street, parked the Checker outside the Hotel Taft, in front of two cabs waiting for fares, and showed the card to the black doorman.

The doorman nodded as if to say it was all the same to him. Much more important to me now was how the taxi driver who had been first in line would behave. After all, it was he who would have to give up a good fare to the driver who had purposely come for that passenger. The strapping blue-eyed American could quite well lay claim to my fare, if not by right then by muscle. But it was the old-timer parked behind him, a hearing aid sticking out of his ear, who came shuffling up to me to get the full story.

"Why did you park here?"

I showed him the card.

"Appointment," the old man guessed. "Where to?"

"Kennedy, Daddy-o. Kennedy."

The old codger sighed, envying another man's luck, and trudged back again.

"Taxi!" Two black girls came flying out of the hotel.

"I'm on my break," the American driver said.

The black doorman got a whistle out of his pocket; he was in league with the blue-eyed Yankee.

Empty cabs bowled past. White drivers, black drivers; none wanted to take the black girls. Their faces fell at the affront. But the dollar that the black doorman expected from the white cabbie waiting for an airport job was stronger than racial solidarity.

I had seen cab drivers' fights, some of them nasty. I had never seen a spectacle like this one, however. With a muffled roar, the shriveled old man rushed at the younger man, a giant by comparison, and pounded with his fists.

"You don't want to work!" the old guy shouted, and kept hitting him.

The strapping cabbie did not know what to do. He was afraid to react. If he so much as accidentally grazed him, the old man would be pulverized. He turned and ran, but the old man kept after him. A crowd had gathered outside the hotel; people were laughing. The young taxi driver finally had the sense to hide in his cab and lock himself in, while the old man hammered on the roof.

From behind the rubberneckers a policeman appeared. White. He looked at the black girls, sized up the situation, and a heavy nightstick touched the door of the cab. The taxi driver rolled down the window.

"Are you taking the job?"

"Officer!"

"I warn you," the cop interrupted him, "if you say a single word—"

The automatic lock clicked open, and the doorman hastily flung the door wide.

"We're not going with him!" the girls said huffily.

The nightstick touched the hood.

"Clear out!" And the cab disappeared.

"Take the job!" the cop turned to the old man, but the troublemaker stood with his arms akimbo.

"Don't talk to me that way. I'm not afraid of you. In 1931 I took on three guys like you"—the old man began to count, bending down his fingers—"a policeman, a dispatcher, a manager. When the cabbies went back to the garage, they would lie in wait for us so they could take the money. But if all I had in my pocket after a whole day's work was a dollar, I wouldn't give it to them. I had hungry children waiting for me at home!" The old man nodded toward the cowering girls. "Of course I'll take them. Not because you scare me with your nightstick, but because I never refuse a customer."

The old man pointed at me.

"There's another con artist waiting for a Kennedy. He won't go anywhere but Kennedy. Get in, ladies!"

The girls got in the cab, and the cop strode over to me. I proffered the Chinese man's card.

"We'll check right away." The doorman played along, snatching the card from me and vanishing into the lobby.

It was a quarter to ten. Well, Chinaman, brace yourself! The Extraordinary Taxi Tribunal has deliberated and brought in its verdict: for tardiness, sloppiness, and straining the nerves, you are sentenced to the maximum punishment—the Belt Parkway. You, dear sir, will now come with me down the West Side Highway; we will plunge into the Brooklyn Battery Tunnel and head out along the seashore around the whole of Brooklyn. Twenty-six dollars on the meter, guaranteed.

"He left." The doorman interrupted my shameless fantasies.

I could not believe it.

"He checked out at eight this morning and left."

That's an "appointment" for you. Another soap bubble. Only my debt to the owner remained an objective reality.

Patches of sunlight lay on the sidewalks; the rush hour was over. At ten o'clock I pushed off, empty.

Chapter Nine

TREASURE TROVE

ON PARK AVENUE.

10 A.M.–5 P.M.

No fares on the streets. Nor would there be any for another two or three hours. Better not to think about the negative balance. Give me the Bronx, Harlem, Brooklyn—I'll go anywhere! After twenty minutes at Penn Station, I got my first passenger of the day.

"Doral Inn!"

A novice no longer, I knew that while I had been idling at the Taft at least a million cars had been pouring into Manhattan. The biggest concentration of them would be lying in wait for me around Forty-second Street. So I took Thirtieth Street to Park Avenue and plunged into the tunnel that runs toward the Pan Am Building.

A simple job, perhaps, but still I accomplished it perfectly, avoiding the congestion, gaining ten minutes, and saving my customer a dollar. I stopped at the corner of Fiftieth Street: $3.15.

"You'll be better off walking from here. It's only one block."

"Look, just take me to the Doral Inn, please."

"It's jammed over there. We'll waste at least a quarter of an hour."

"Driver!"

To hell with you. I made a right turn and got stuck immediately. The meter ticked away while we sat there: $3.25.

To tell the truth, I had not suggested that my customer take a walk because his money was sacred to me. Fiftieth Street between Park and Lexington is a unique spot for taxi drivers. It is *the* block a cabbie has to drive down empty. Opening onto it is the freight entrance to the Waldorf-Astoria, designated only for guests with luggage—checking in or out—so no piles of suitcases can mar the look of the famous hotel's main doors. And although taxis are forbidden to stand on this block and are constantly chased away by the cops, if you go down Fiftieth Street you will always see a few yellow cabs waiting for airports.

Stuck in the traffic and still fifteen yards from the freight entrance, I saw three yellow cabs, none of which was a Checker. The meter clicked: $3.35. What if, at that very moment, the old-fashioned elevator, with its solid brass handles, was bringing down a group of *five* businessmen hurrying off to Kennedy? They would not fit into any of the cabs guarding the entrance.

The meter ticked away while we sat there: $3.45. The light turned green at Lexington Avenue, but we did not budge: $3.55. A whistle sounded at the entrance, like a dull needle piercing my heart.

"Sir," I said, "why waste your time and money? It's half a minute from here to the Doral Inn."

The young face in the rearview mirror wore a sneering grin. My passenger was not the sort to let some cabbie call the shots. The whistle sounded again, but none of the waiting cabs moved, and I knew what that meant.

It meant that the doorman, without letting the whistle fall, had spread his arms wide. He wanted a "big cab"! I could not see either the doorman or his gesture, but I knew what was happening inside the freight entrance.

"Sir, don't you hear? They're calling for a Checker. Somebody has to catch a plane."

The cars moved off; we were passing the entrance. Last chance! I braked and turned to look at my customer point blank: $3.75. He wouldn't get to the Doral Inn, anyway. He had allowed four dollars for the trip, and now he was delaying on purpose, out of spite, until the meter devoured my tip; even he felt uncomfortable about asking for a quarter back; $3.85. Cars were honking behind me, and I was obliged to go the few yards that had opened up in front.

"Checker!" shouted the doorman, but it was too late. Even if my passenger got out now, I could not get back to the entrance. I was bumper to bumper with the car behind me, locked in.

The meter said $3.95. Money rustled in the change cup.

"I know how to handle people like you," the sardonic young man said in parting. He had had four dollar bills ready; five pennies were clutched in my fist.

"Hey, you forgot the change!" I yelled and flung the coppers on the ground.

Green light. I had to move.

––––––––

The congestion on the streets got heavier and heavier. Even with the meter on there is no pleasure in driving around the city at five miles per hour, and it is even harder to pick your way through the crowds of pedestrians streaming around the cab; but it is unbearable to hang around in traffic jams empty. By noon I had made eighteen bucks and was completely exhausted.

Traveling north along Park Avenue toward Grand Central Station, I turned on the off-duty light. This was foolish, since nobody was trying to assail my cab, but I had decided firmly to get to some greasy spoon for a cup of coffee and a breather. I was about to turn right onto Forty-second Street when someone knocked on the window. God, what do you want from me now?

It was a middle-aged Brooklyn Jew, the kind that loves to "negotiate" with cab drivers. What's to talk about? Look at him, he wants me to open the window, the one on the passenger side, which is unreachable. I had to stretch across the seat to roll the window down.

"What is it?" I asked, still lying full length.

"Can you take me to Kennedy?"

Only then did I—blockhead!—notice that he was carrying a holdall. So much for my professional intuition.

"Sure, sir. I'll take you anywhere!"

"I asked because your off-duty light was on."

"Thanks for reminding me. I forgot to turn it off."

A sly, knowing smile.

"I thought so."

But the holdall was already on the front seat! So why wasn't he getting

141

in the cab, this light of my life, my unexpected savior in shabby pants? It was making me anxious. What if he changed his mind?

"Go around the corner and wait a couple of minutes for me. I'd rather share the meter."

"Share the meter? With whom?"

"With somebody else going to the airport."

Are you out of your mind, you poor sap?

"Where are you going to get them?"

"Right here."

Despite the fact that the customer seemed to be raving, I drove off obediently and stopped around the corner. Sure, flocks of travelers, in a hurry to make their planes, were waiting for some enterprising type, in pants bagging at the knees, to invite them to get together with him and set out for the airport by taxi and split the fare. Was that what he meant?

But I had the holdall. So why did I have to understand what he meant? And time was on my side, too. Let him walk around and ask. The plane wasn't going to wait for this twerp to find co-travelers. Of course, he wouldn't find anyone. He'd come back and off we'd go.

He came back with *two* passengers. If he had pulled a live camel out of his holdall, he could not have made a greater impression on me. But this group-ride organizer addressed me as if nothing out of the ordinary had happened. The gentlemen were going to LaGuardia and would pay five dollars apiece. He would pay another ten. Okay?

I did not reply. I waved them all into the cab, and off we went.

Which way?

Over the Queensboro Bridge, of course.

Through a hundred traffic lights?

But why on earth would I go trailing over the Triborough to put two extra dollars on the meter when I knew nobody was going to pay it? If it's a flat rate, a cabbie always takes the shortest road.

We reached LaGuardia and the two in the backseat got out, nodded farewell to *each other*, and headed off in different directions. I could hardly breathe; my pulse was racing as if I had a fever. My passenger had found each of them *separately*.

If, for some unknown reason, passengers going to the airports really did converge on the southeast corner of Park Avenue and Forty-second Street, then my whole life was going to change!

I wiped off the sweat that had broken out on my forehead and playfully nudged the melancholy Jew sitting next to me.

"Fess up, mister!"

"What?"

"How you found those two LaGuardias!"

"What's so special about it? I always do that."

"You think I was born yesterday?" I snapped, barely containing my fury, but he goggled at me with honest eyes.

"I don't know what you're talking about."

A slippery customer! "Why did those two turn up there?"

"How should I know? I don't live in New York anyway, I'm from Albany. I come through here on trips."

He was fibbing, trying to wriggle out of it.

"Fine. Have it your way. But you yourself, what were you doing on the corner of Park Avenue and Forty-second Street?"

"I was buying a ticket."

"What kind of ticket?"

"A plane ticket to Israel."

Very carefully, as if I were after a butterfly of rarest beauty and was afraid of damaging its delicate wings, I reached for the secret.

"And those two were also buying plane tickets?"

"Everyone buys tickets there."

The wondrous butterfly was fluttering in my closed palms.

"Why are you so excited about it?"

I would be able to work nine or ten hours, like normal people. I could finally have my teeth put in.

"Sorry, mister, but it's really all the same to me who buys tickets or where they do it. I was just making conversation."

Waiting my turn at the International Arrivals lot, I could not stand still. I wandered between the rows of yellow cars, jumping over the puddles and buttonholing almost every driver.

"Where did you get the Kennedy?"

"At the Prince George."

"Did you have to wait long?"

"A couple of hours."

"How are you going to make any money today?"

Concealing the exultation that boiled up in me behind hypocritical sympathy, with a hop and a skip I went on to the next:

Numskulls! They drove for years and didn't know how to make it! It was amusing to look at them, yet pitiful, too. I yearned to bestow on one of these hacks the favor of sharing my discovery. But I did not share it with anyone.

———

Having finally reached the southeast corner of Park Avenue and Forty-second Street, I did not, however, manage to discern the exact location of the ticket office there. My head was spinning.

I did not see the buildings, or the cars, or the hubbub at the entrance to Grand Central Station across the street from where I stood, stricken, in front of a rank of people with suitcases, drawn up next to a wall and stretching for thirty yards!

Trunks.

Garment bags.

Valises.

Traveling bags.

Backpacks.

A whole battalion, drawn up and ready to set off for the airport.

The thrill of the moment consisted not only in the *quantity* of passengers or pieces of luggage, but also in the fact that there was only one cab present. Mine!

With an effort of will I made myself take action. I opened the trunk and strode toward the rank with a spring in my step.

A cool breeze caressed my hot face; I paced up and down the line like a general selecting a group for a reconnaissance mission. Barking out the curt question, "Where to?" I made instant decisions. "Wait! . . . You have to wait, too . . . And you, go over to the cab!"

The majority of the people lined up along the wall were going to LaGuardia; naturally I ignored them and went on looking for Kennedys. But my voice and gestures grew less and less certain with every second; the people's replies to my military-style questions seemed somehow ill-disposed, and they kept glancing at one another; and a cold feeling that I was perpetrating something illicit wormed its way into my heart.

"Where are you going?" I asked the next passenger, but he made no reply, and, looking toward the place where I had left the cab, he snickered in an odd, almost malicious way.

I turned around. Standing in front of my Checker, legs planted wide, was a policeman, who was writing something in a large, long notebook.

"What's up, boss?" I asked, feigning a friendly manner, and trying to conceal the hint of a tremble in my voice.

"Nothing much," the policeman answered in the same manner, without interrupting what he was doing. "Give me your license, please."

"Are you writing me a ticket?" I inquired, somewhat surprised.

"Mm-hm."

"What for?"

Without uttering a word, the cop pointed to the NO STANDING sign.

"But I was right next to the car, you could perfectly well have told me. I just didn't notice that stupid sign."

The policeman tore the sheet out of his notebook and held it out to me. "I saw you pull over. I was watching you carefully. I witnessed everything you did."

Not conscious of being at fault, I raised my voice. "And what *crime* have I committed?"

"Want to play games? Fine!" Now the cop looked really angry, and, without giving me back the license, started writing again. This time in *another* notebook.

"What's this for?" I cried, realizing that I was about to receive—had already received—a *second* ticket.

The policeman mumbled, but what exactly I could not tell.

"What does that mean?" I asked.

He repeated it, but I never heard such a word in English before. It was something that ended in *ing*.

"Why don't you tell me what's going on? I don't understand anything!"

"Don't get so worked up," the policeman soothed me in honeyed tones. "We'll soon see each other again, and then you'll understand everything."

"Where will we see each other?"

"In a certain pleasant establishment. I can guarantee you won't do this sort of thing ever again."

"Won't do *what?*"

"Quit faking!" the policeman bellowed. "And bear this in mind: one more word and you'll get a third ticket."

"What for?"

"For the off-duty light."

Now, finally, I had the sense to shut up. This one I knew about: a cabbie who picks up a passenger with the off-duty light on gets a hundred-dollar fine.

Crushed, devastated, I looked around, and oh, God, what was happening around me! Taxis were rolling up to the curb one after the other, and cabbies, peeking over their shoulders at the policeman, who was *busy*—with me—were rushing up to the people by the wall, grabbing their luggage, and dragging customers to their cabs almost by force. A moment later a bus showed up and the passengers began jumping out of the yellow cabs. Now it was their turn to snatch their belongings away from the cabmen and storm the bus.

The policeman and I were left standing at the intersection. I had indeed found a gold-bearing lode, but mining it was prohibited by some incomprehensible law. The son-of-a-bitch finished his writing.

"Do you want me to explain what to do with these papers?"

"No!" I told my executioner through the pain. "You've done everything that could possibly be done."

"Not everything," the policeman corrected me, meaning that he still had not issued a ticket for the off-duty light. Sure, he was a real pal. He had only given me a *summons*, with, printed across the top like a headline, in bold red lettering.

CRIMINAL COURT OF THE DISTRICT OF MANHATTAN

Chapter Ten

— — — — — — — —

LATE EVENING.

5 P.M.–MIDNIGHT

That dead-and-alive, dim-witted cabbie can forget anything and everything. Once in a blue moon his wife might ask him to bring home "a little something" from Zabar's to lighten the day's drudgery, but it goes in one ear and out the other. If it were only the delicacies, though. Sometimes more important matters slip the cabbie's mind: changing worn-out brakes, or adding water to a cracked radiator. He is well aware of the possible consequences, but there you go—it's his lousy damn memory.

He pushes the lock button, shuts the car door, and groans as if it had slammed on his hand. He cannot get in; he left the keys inside. It's not just the keys, either; that stupid guy would leave his own leg in the cab after twenty fares.

How many times have I frittered away an hour in the line at LaGuardia; the drivers who were in front of me have already loaded up and driven away, and I should move up, but my mind is such a buzzing emptiness that I see and hear nothing.

The guys behind are shouting, "Hey, Checker!" and calling me names, the loud-mouthed dispatcher is going nuts. "Hey, 2V26, are you deaf?" But I am miles away, as if it had nothing to do with me. Somebody has to come and pound on the roof above my head before I remember that there is only one yellow cab in New York with the medallion number 2V26, the one I rent. That 2V26 is none other than I.

Anything. A harried cabbie can forget anything in the world. When did he last eat? When did he last fill the tank? (The gas gauge is broken, of course.) But there is one thing he will never forget. Even if a tire bursts on the highway, even if he plows into a lamppost, or a truck smacks into his car, a cabbie will scramble out from under the burning wreckage, pull the shell-shocked passenger to his feet, and say, "Mister, it was $1.85 on the meter." And only afterward does he deal with the rest of it, the ambulance, the police, who's to blame. That is the way a cabbie's mind works: he cannot forget about the money.

"Why are they like that?" I often wondered about my comrades, observing how the touch of money transformed them: whether receiving a passenger's fare, reluctantly giving change, or counting the bookings for the hundredth time that day. And I swore I would never end up that way! But now, leaving this confounded corner in order to get stuck fifty yards farther down at the turn onto Madison Avenue in the stream of pedestrians flowing around the cab, I felt a noose gently touching my neck. Sixty-two dollars and fifty cents—the cost of the day's rent. I could not forget about the money either. And as I held down the brake pedal to keep the Checker from slicing through the people crossing in front, I recalled not the gold-bearing lode I had discovered and lost, not the big easy money, but the small, hard-won stuff.

Sixty-two fifty for today. How to get it? My only thought.

By the time the traffic light had changed, I had counted all the cash. I had sixty-one dollars, but the No Standing sign was twenty-five bucks. The criminal summons, who knows. What did I have left? The money in my pocket was an illusion. After eight hours of toil, I was faced with starting the work day anew.

I longed to share my woes with somebody. I longed for pity, and for the chance to snort in answer to the comforting words, I'm not the sort you can scare with criminal summonses! The only person who could tolerate this kind of thing was my wife, but I would not even phone her. Whenever I called her from the road, the conversation was the same. She would ask if I were in one piece and if the car were in one piece, whereupon she would say (casually, as it seemed to her), "You know what? Forget the whole thing and come home right away!"

The light in front of me had changed to red, but I completed the turn nonetheless. Where was I going? My heart yearned for my wife and son, for our cozy kitchen, but I was heading toward my enemies, the band of Russian drivers at the Madison Hotel. Who else could tell me plainly what sort of word the cop had written in the summons? Explain what it portended? Advise me what to do?

If anybody knew about such things, it was those rogues. Didn't they brag about their tickets to one another every morning at Kennedy? One of them had copped two the other day, another, three. And it was always the same old tune: "For nothing!" Innocent as lambs! I was not the least fazed that I, myself, had just received a ticket *and* a summons.

———

Although our quarrel was both trivial and long past, I had butterflies in my stomach as I drove up to the Madison: how would they receive me?

Almost the whole gang was there: Odessa Corporation, Taganka Corporation, Tamara Taxi Inc., Padlo Taxi Inc., Tbiliso Corporation . . . I was prepared to march past my ex-friends with an independent air, but they called out to me:

"Bagel!"

"How come you never show up? You quit working?" asked the Boss.

I merely waved a hand in reply. It was quite involuntary: I was copying their gestures.

Alik-the-Birthmark half stood on his bumper, peering at my Checker at the tail of the line.

"You're not plugging away at the garage anymore? Did you buy?"

"He's leasing," said Crewcut. "From my old bag."

"How's the Doctor?" I asked. "He hasn't packed it in yet?"

"Where would he go?"

"What about Uzbek?"

"Uzbek hasn't been around lately."

"For a while now," said Tomato, and they all went quiet.

Long Marik noticed the papers I was holding and broke into a smile. "Bagel, you got a ticket?"

"For nothing," I said.

"Two!" Marik said admiringly.

"For absolutely nothing!"

"'No standing,'" Crewcut observed, somewhat tactlessly.

"Take a look at the second one," I said, pointedly ignoring the "architect" and addressing Long Marik. "Do you understand what it says?"

"'Ing'?" Marik began to work it out from the end. "Ting? Bagel, you were 'off-seat'?" He meant had I been more than fifteen feet away from the cab? I could be fined $50.

"Bagel probably helped himself to a good suitcase," Alik-the-Birthmark hazarded, having discerned which institution the summons invited me to.

The Boss inquired in a matter-of-fact tone, "Bagel, are you a citizen yet?"

"Citizen, schmitizen!" I snapped, but not with great assurance, as I had not gotten my naturalization papers yet.

"The real bandits are the only ones they don't put in jail in this country," the Boss said gallantly. He wanted me to know that, even if I had stolen a suitcase and got jailed for it, it would not change our relationship.

But the more they tried to frighten or tease me with "jails," or "citizenship," the calmer I felt. After all, I was quite certain I had not done anything really bad. And if that was the case, I had nothing to fear! Well, what could they do to me? I would tell the judge everything just the way it was, and he would realize there had been a misunderstanding.

Feeling a kind of peculiar pride in the fact that none of these crooks had ever been given such a summons, I switched on the off-duty light and left.

The digits of the clock over a bank twinkled red: 5:05. Starting the day so late, one could only make money by some improbable stroke of good luck. The line of cabs at the Hilton crawled along incessantly. The early evening rush hour had begun. There did not seem to be any Checkers in front of me. Oh, if only the doorman would ask for a big cab right *now*. A minute had barely passed when a whistle blew and I heard, "Checker!"

I swerved out of the line and up to the entrance. A mountain of suitcases awaited me. Three of us—the doorman, the bellboy, and I—started loading up. The suitcases were enormous, but the labels on them said ALITALIA.

The trunk would only hold three pieces, the backseat four. We loaded the whole Checker up to the roof, but some boxes and bags were still left over. Finally we managed it.

"*Grazie!*" twittered the fidgety, middle-aged junior miss in white stockings, getting in next to me amid her boxes.

The staff of the Hilton are highly trained, but even these performing lackeys had long faces. Five bucks each for the doorman and bellboy on a load like this would not have been overdoing it. But all one of them got was a wry smile, and the other a tender, "*Grazie.*"

What a bitch! I had just time to think, when I heard, "Americana Hotel!"

I couldn't believe it. If she had been joking, I would have told her it wasn't funny in the least. She was not joking. She had to move her stuff to the neighboring hotel. Neither the employees of the Hilton nor those of the Americana were obliged to cart guests' luggage from one hotel to another, and they would never have agreed to do it for less than twenty bucks. In order to save money, the clever signora had hired my Checker to go *one* block.

When we stopped at the Americana, the meter showed eighty-five cents. I started hauling the suitcases out of the back, while the hefty doorman, moaning and groaning, conveyed them one by one to the front step.

The white stockings ran around the cab; the signora was checking that nothing had been forgotten in the front, the backseat, or the trunk.

"*Cuanta?*" she asked.

"*Cinque,*" I indicated, spreading my five fingers.

At this the signora let out a squeal. "Doorman!" she screamed at the top of her lungs.

"Doorman!"

But the doorman was standing next to us, dismayed and neutral. A mauve vein pulsed on the thin neck.

"Police!"

Despairing of anyone's coming to her rescue, the defenseless woman dropped her hands and burst into floods of tears. People crowded around. A black cabbie with a ragged scar across one side of his face pushed his way toward me.

"He's a good guy, I know him," the cabbie said in a worried voice, turning to the audience and putting his arm around me. "Come on, let's get out of here."

I had never seen this driver before; there was a lump in my throat. What could another encounter with the police, my second of the day, promise me beyond new troubles? We left, followed by the indignant rumble of the crowd: "These bastards have gotten so cheeky, they're totally out of hand!" "There's never a cop around when you need one!"

The signora with the white stockings had defeated the extortionist cab driver. She had not even paid me the eighty-five cents.

I drove toward the twilight descending on the city, into a very different New York, beckoning me with the evening glow of the streets. But I entered the neon fairyland of Times Square embittered and gloomy.

"Bloodsuckers!" I muttered under my breath. "Dishing out criminal summonses! Making me carry luggage from the Hilton to the Americana! Well, now it's my turn. I'll show you."

But it was not easy to devise exactly how to avenge myself, and on whom. The only thing that came to mind, and which I was irrevocably resolved on, was that no way would I turn over to "them" the bag of money that the gypsy had once promised me. I could see that bag, stuffed with bundles of bills, more and more distinctly, and, engrossed in this imbecilic dream, I paid no attention to the passengers getting in and out of the cab, made out the addresses among their words automatically, steered the car, and threw the tips—coins, and even dollar bills, which my customers relinquished more and more often—into the "cash register," a cigar box on the seat beside me.

It is not the beauty of the city at night, or the shimmer of its multicolored lights, that enthralls the cab driver. Over twelve bridges and through four tunnels, hundreds of thousands of cars were leaving the island of Manhattan, freeing up the jammed, narrow streets, opening up for me the wide avenues, where the ticking of my meter was now much livelier than in the daytime.

The fewer the cars remaining in the city, the greater grew the number of people who needed a taxi. And the customers who got in my Checker now were different.

For any passenger, a morning taxi ride is the beginning of the day's expenditures: paper, cigarettes, coffee, lunch. After work he has to run to the store or the pharmacy. Indeed, what has a morning customer got to thank me for, when I am dragging him, still half-asleep, into the maelstrom of the day? But in the evening the passenger's attitude toward the driver is quite different. I am taking him away from work and worries, to home and hearth, and the change he leaves me is the last of the day's outlays. And the coins jingle gaily in the cigar box.

"Taxi! Taxi!" they called again and again.

At a floodlit entrance a group of gentlemen in tuxedos helped a haughty old woman in a mink stole into my cab.

"They're all *so* nice to me," she complained the instant we were alone.

"Doesn't seem so bad to me," I responded, thawing by now, and more kindly disposed.

"The receptions they invite me to!" the old woman wept. "The people who care about me!"

The reek of whisky filled the cab.

"At your age, grandma, you ought not to drink so much," I growled, but she kept sobbing inconsolably.

"And nobody—nobody—knows who I *really* am."

At the traffic light I looked back.

"So, who are you, then?"

The old lady took her beringed hands away from her face, and breathed, in an eerie whisper, "I'm a spy!"

I did not doubt for a second that she was telling the truth.

"And who are you working for?"

"'Who for, who for?'" the old woman mimicked me. "For the government! Who else?"

Oh, America! Here watchdogs wag their tails when passersby pet them; here secret agents open their hearts to taxi drivers after a couple of drinks. You ought to be sent off to Moscow for a year or so of advanced training, old girl.

The next passenger was just as strange.

"Move it! Faster!"

I turned around and was confronted with a behind tightly clad in jeans instead of a face.

"Faster, for God's sake!" implored the backside.

Kneeling on the seat, the passenger leaned forward as far as he could into the rear window, checking whether we were being followed.

I stepped on the gas and turned off onto some street.

"Whew!" I heard a sigh of relief.

"Where are you going, anyway?"

A young man was poking money at the glass partition. When had I managed to slam it shut?

"Open up, please," he said.

"Two dollars?"

"It's all I have!"

A hooligan had been pestering a woman on the subway platform. My passenger had gone to help her. The hooligan had left the woman alone but then boarded the same car as her defender. The young man got off the subway at the next stop, the thug followed. It was a good thing my taxi had turned up. I simply did not have time to mull over the adventures of this fellow, who had already gotten out: as the Checker was traversing the wide expanse of Sheridan Square, the red letters on the dashboard were telling me that the last passenger had not closed the door properly.

Seizing the moment, I jumped out to slam it, and some kind of little plastic tube rolled out at my feet. What was it? There was another one like it on the floor mat inside.

"Bay Ridge!"

"I won't go," someone else protested.

"Yes, you will."

"No, I won't!"

The two girls were standing at the curb, while I was in the road on the other side of the cab. A resounding slap made me jump, and the plastic tube, an ordinary hair curler, slipped out of my hand.

I took no part in the fight and it was not I who got slapped. The quarrel had flared up between two stylishly dressed girls, who had appeared next to the cab at the very moment I had made out someone's overturned shopping bag, left on the back seat, out of which curlers were spilling onto the floor.

"You want me to go instead of you?" hissed one of the girls, a forceful-looking brunette whose eyes were blazing with fury. "Then say so. I'll go!"

"Please don't! Please! How could you even think that?" babbled the other, who looked slender and frail.

In the commotion, the shopping bag migrated from the backseat to the front.

"I was upset because you were upset," pleaded the one whose ears had been boxed, by now agreeable to anything as long as she was forgiven. The dark-haired girl put her subdued friend in the cab and kissed her.

"It'll be okay, you'll see," she said, and I felt a shiver of uneasiness at the way her parting words sounded.

As I made my way toward the West Side Highway, I kept glancing at the shopping bag hidden at my feet and thinking that, of course, it had not been left by the young man who had defended the woman on the subway, nor, naturally, by the inebriated lady. When a taxi driver finds an item forgotten in the cab, he can always determine which of his customers left it.

The black bag had been lolling on the floor of the passenger section almost an hour. Neither the girl on roller skates nor the lipstick-smeared ladykiller had noticed it.

The bag must have been left behind by "Honeybunch" and "Snookums," a touching couple whose combined age was about a hundred and fifty. I had loaded their luggage—two suitcases, four cardboard boxes, and a heavy string sack containing oranges—into the cab outside the East Side bus terminal, and had unloaded it again when the meter showed $1.45, in front of one of the best-known apartment buildings in the city, Manhattan House.

While the doorman was lugging the suitcases and I was following him, dragging the sack and tripping over it, Honeybunch had shuffled alongside, saying over and over, "To the elevator, please, to the elevator!" I kept wondering why my passengers had to bring oranges from Florida, and why these exceedingly well-off people had taken the bus from the airport to the city. I finally hauled the sack to the elevator, and we got down to hard cash, and for the whole package—loading up, unloading, and the trip itself—I was tipped only the butt end of the second dollar. Only then did I grasp that in Miami oranges were *cheaper* than in New York.

That shopping bag had been on Honeybunch's knees until the moment she began fumbling in her purse, and then in her jacket pockets, in search of small bills; she could not bring herself to give me a five. For some reason, she was more comfortable paying the exact amount. And then, putting the shopping bag on the floor of the cab, against the backseat, the old woman had run over to her husband, who was making the last trip from the Checker to the elevator, carrying the cardboard boxes. She stuck her hand in his raincoat pocket, lit up with a smile, given me the two dollars, and shut the cab door.

By now we were streaming along the Hudson River, down into the Brooklyn Battery Tunnel, and, as I looked in the mirror at the girl, huddled in a corner, illuminated by the flickering light of the tunnel lamps, I thought: "There's always some dumb good luck working the streets. So why shouldn't it just happen to find me?"

More than once I had discovered, on the backseat of the Checker, signs indicating that Dame Fortune might be flirting with me: an alluringly scented earring; a crumpled green ball that blossomed in my hands into a wonderful twenty-dollar bill; a Rolex watch that now adorns my wife. Underneath the pile of curlers, there had to be some kind of valuable concealed in the bowels of the shopping bag! If not, why would Honeybunch have kept it on her knees?

"We're on Bay Ridge Avenue," I said curtly to the girl over my shoulder as we drove off the highway. "Can you direct me from here?"

Instead of a reply, the girl held out to me a piece of paper with the address on it. She was going to this place for the first time. And at night, too. I found the street whose name was written on the paper, and immediately spotted the house to which I was taking my passenger—a long way down the road that stretched away between two rows of private homes.

A noisy group of Brooklyn boys was waiting for her on the only lighted veranda. Greeting my Checker's appearance on the quiet street with triumphant shouts, and brandishing beer bottles above their heads, they rushed toward the cab in a body. I should have bolted backward and taken the cringing girl away. But life's not like that. I was not a knight or James Bond, I was a taxi driver, conveying customers for the amount shown on the meter, plus tip.

Bowing jestingly amid his friends' laughter, one of the boys flung open the door of the Checker. The girl got out and walked toward the porch. She seemed not to notice the impatient pack, and the bawdy merriment died away. Her footsteps crunched on the gravel. With a sweeping gesture, a second prankster invited this girl, roughly his own age, to pass from the brightly lit porch into the half-dark house. His friends seemed to linger in the doorway—then hastily collected themselves. Giggling and shoving, they poured inside.

"Hey, how much?" The macho-man, standing by my open window—money at the ready—tapped me on the shoulder. "Take it!" He was in a hurry.

I took the money without counting it. I was in a hurry too.

Stopping under a light on the next street, I thrust my hand into the shopping bag, underneath the curlers. My squeamish fingers dodged a sticky jar of cold cream, scratched against a hairbrush, and suddenly felt something metallic and round. You could not tell what it was by the feel. I pulled out my find and saw a gold bracelet!

Somewhere nearby there were voices and footsteps. My Checker sneaked away from the passersby, jogged along the roadway, turned the corner, and stopped under a street lamp again. In front of me, at the foot of a hill up which the humpbacked street wound, somewhere quite close, rumbled the unseen highway. It ran alongside the ocean, drowned in the dark. If I got on the highway now, I would be home in a quarter of an hour. But my impatient hand thrust itself into the bag, plunged to the elbow, and took hold of another mysterious object: narrow, segmented, with no end or beginning. What was it?

Before satisfying my dishonorable curiosity, however, I glanced in the wing mirror, and just in time. A couple was hurrying toward the Checker. It would be inconvenient to pick them up, but not wise to take off. Both tall and elegantly dressed, they were only a few feet from the cab by now, and against my will I was quite entranced by the sight of the woman. She was so beautiful that I still remember the fall of her sheer silk dress, and her demurely coiffed head.

"The city!" said the man, opening the door.

"I'm really on my way back to the garage. I was just counting the bookings," I said. "Oh, all right. You can't imagine the sort of scum I've been driving around all evening. It's nice to have normal people in the car for a change, you know."

"We aren't normal," the man replied in a serious, reserved tone.

"Seventy-fourth and Broadway," the woman added, significantly. Her dark eyes looked straight into mine.

On Seventy-fourth Street between West End Avenue and Broadway some kind of festivity seemed to be underway. The block was jammed with cabs and private cars, while a posh limousine had wormed its way between them. Women were getting out of the cars and primping; efficient parking valets hustled the cars away, but the blockage was not breaking up; the people just kept coming.

The couple whom I had brought got out of the cab before we crawled up to the striped wooden booth that jutted onto the sidewalk. When I finally got abreast of the booth, I saw a steep staircase leading to the basement, down which, behind a black couple and my two from Bay Ridge, a plump lady was descending decorously on the arm of a tall, skinny teenager. Suddenly those entering encountered traffic going the other way: up the stairs came a girl in a silver jumpsuit, prodded from behind by the bouncer, who kept saying, "Come on, please, come on."

"A prostitute!" The excited whisper rustled along the sidewalk.

The striped wooden booth was the entrance to the most popular sex club in New York.

———

Out from under the curlers, which wriggled at my poking arm like a ball of live caterpillars, crawled and lay on my knees a massive gold chain. Mounted at evenly spaced two- or three-inch intervals in the chain were oblong plates studded with green stones. But I had hardly opened my mouth to gasp when at the bottom of the bag my hand grasped and pulled out—more gold!—a tiny, toylike evening bag woven of gold thread, with a finely tooled clasp. What treasures might a golden reticule contain?

My trembling fingers finally got the better of the clasp; I shook out onto my palm some unimaginable marvel of the jeweler's art, created from pearls and pinkish coral—and flinched with disgust. Ugh! It was the old witch's slimy false teeth.

On that dismal evening some irresistible force kept pushing me to go on and on cruising the streets of Manhattan. People would get in my cab, and I would just drive and drive.

A tender parting at the Hotel Navarre. A swanlike hand caressed a bald spot on the back of the man's head and suddenly beckoned to me slyly with one finger.

The finger straightened up, telling me to wait.

"Let's go to the Drake. No, better make it the Roosevelt."

"Maybe the Hilton?" I blurted out.

"Anything but the Hilton!"

"Why?"

"Too many cops!"

Ah.

"How's business?" I said.

"Good!" she replied gaily, moving over to the jumpseat, a bit nearer. Minimal makeup, an elegant blouse.

"What's so good about it?" I said grumpily.

"Well, I like it! A hundred bucks for one hour. He was kind, gentle. I had a nice time with him. Then he bought me a great dinner. Just now he was trying to talk me into going back to the hotel with him."

"And you refused?"

"No, I didn't. But I said it would cost him another fifty dollars."

"You seem to have it easy," I said. "A hundred dollars, fifty dollars. How come pretty young women are offering themselves on street corners for twenty bucks?"

"They're fools."

"But what about the drunks? The weirdos? The diseases?"

"I'm careful about who I go with."

"Have you been working long?"

"Two years."

"And your boyfriend doesn't take your money away? He doesn't beat you?"

"I only have one friend, and that's my dollar."

————

The security guard, snoozing behind the control panel equipped with closed-circuit TV monitors in the empty lobby of Manhattan House, instantly realized who I was when he saw the shopping bag.

"You want to give it to me or call the owners?"

"Call them, of course."

"They're probably asleep by now." The guard hesitated.

"Not likely!" I said meaningfully.

Indeed, Honeybunch did not keep us waiting. In a short, partly buttoned robe, her bare legs knotted with varicose veins, she darted out of the elevator and rushed up to me.

"Oh, I'm so grateful!"

Turning her back on me, the woman rummaged inside the bag, checking its contents. A nasty thought flitted through my mind. However, Honeybunch was satisfied with the results of the inventory and handed me—a buck.

I was dumbstruck. All right, maybe neither the bracelet nor the chain I returned was gold, but what about the teeth? Living in Manhattan House she must pay more rent in a month than I earn in a year—so how much do her teeth cost, for chrissake?

Not one of the dimes left in the change cup offended me quite as much as that dollar reward.

Chapter Eleven

ALL THROUGH
THE NIGHT

From morning till midnight, as I had in the preceding months and as I would in subsequent years, I continually insulted innumerable people merely because they were black.

They would stand, as they stand today, hailing a taxi, at every intersection. Their numbers grew particularly large during the rush hours, but my cab simply drove past them. More than forty passengers took my Checker in the course of fifteen hours. How many of them were black? Not one.

Yet I can say that there was no outright racism in this. Plenty of "colored" cabbies did the same. We were avoiding not dark-skinned people but dangerous trips to Brooklyn, the South Bronx, Alphabet City, and we were avoiding the customers who did not tip.

Is that crudely honest? Undoubtedly. And yet it is not the whole truth.

When I ignored blacks, I remembered the kids who drenched me with water and chucked a stone at my cab; I remembered my trip to Jamaica with the black soldier, and the elegant young woman whom I once took home after a rock concert. When I cautioned her teenage son, who was resting his elbow on the half-open window (he could have damaged the mechanism that raised and lowered it), his mother, who had been dragging on a joint, spat in my face.

She missed. The spittle splattered on the window, but wiping it off afterward was no pleasure. Well, what should I have done? Spat back at her? Oh, no. I punished her churlishness with a vengeance she would recall till the end of her days: I left without getting paid.

But all these memories, with which I fueled the flames of my right-eousness, were still only one side of the truth. Somehow I adroitly managed to banish any thought of the black cabbie who just a few hours before had gotten me out of the brouhaha at the Americana Hotel. Nor did I recall that other black driver, who had said "Follow me!" when I had made a U-turn right in front of his cab near the TWA hangar while the forgotten dad gnashed his teeth. Not a single kind thought about blacks flashed through my mind as I pretended not to notice them, and so it went on, right up to midnight.

But when the clock struck twelve your conscience awakened, right? No. Nothing of the kind. And conscience had nothing to do with it.

As I left Manhattan House, after disposing of the shopping bag, I felt neither crushed nor cheated by fate. I remained what I had always been, in Russia and America: a carefree, cheerful pauper. Stopping at the first phone booth I came to, I pondered whether to call my wife; besides which, I ought to count the money. And at that point a black girl carrying a cello accosted me—please, oh, please, take me home.

"Where?"

"Lexington and 118th."

"I can't," I said. "My shift just finished. I have to go back to Brooklyn."

All I needed was a night ride to East Harlem, the most dangerous part of an already dangerous neighborhood. Every damn day, whether the papers report it or not, bandits rob careless taxi drivers who go to East Harlem. A couple of weeks earlier, at a LaGuardia parking lot, a black cabbie had shown me his finger, mutilated when a nighttime passenger—"a brother"—had wrenched off his signet ring, taking the flesh with it, and then pistol-whipped him because the bookings, surrendered without a word of protest, had come to only twenty-eight dollars.

Fortunately, the girl with the cello was so affronted that I did not have to launch into any explanations. She turned away and looked for a taxi on Third Avenue. I counted my money.

It had not been a lucky day, but still, in fifteen hours I had made an amazing total of one hundred, twenty-seven dollars. I was even with the owner of the Checker, the gas was paid for, and the fine for stopping outside the airline office was covered. Admittedly, I had not made more than two dollars an hour for myself; but I cannot say this weighed on me much. Quite the contrary. One hundred and twenty-seven dollars was a *record* for me! Never had I made such a killing in one day! Moreover, if I avoided the waste of time, effort, and mental energy squandered on the hunt for airport passengers, it was clear I could easily repeat my achievement tomorrow. I had only to break myself of my idiotic urge to seek out suitcases. If I picked up every customer who came along, "swept the streets" as the veterans say, today's record would become the norm.

Not even the thought of the criminal summons could depress me. For, once I had cooled down and reconsidered the whole thing, I had come to the most sensible decision possible: since I was not guilty of anything, I had no reason to show up in court. And that trashy piece of paper I should simply tear up and throw away. Really, what was the worst thing they could do, to a man who had done nothing wrong, for not showing up? Take away his hack license? My wife, for one, would be happy.

———

I put a coin in the slot, but hesitated over whether to dial the number. I should have called earlier; now I did not know if my wife was worrying, pacing the apartment, unable to relax, or if she had gone to sleep. Instead of calming her fears, my call might wake her up.

"Can't you really spare me five minutes of your time?" The black cellist came up to me again.

"No, I can't!" I snapped back. And I drove off to work, while the streets were still empty and the money still flowing.

"Thanks a lot, sir!" the girl shouted in my wake. I did not give a hoot for her sarcasm.

But, strangely, in the space of ten East Side blocks not a single hand went up to stop me. Just a few minutes ago I had not been able to go ten yards in peace. I turned onto Park. It was empty.

The huge city had fallen asleep quite suddenly, like a child worn out with playing. I checked Fifth Avenue: a stream of empty taxis was bowling down it. There were no passengers, white or black. Over by the Public Library I saw the shape of a man—he did not even raise his hand, merely walked toward the curb, and instantly one cab cut across another.

The race is much more dangerous at night than in the morning, but it was as if someone were egging me on. I *had* to get at least one more fare.

Grand Central Station was deserted, Madison Avenue too. My watch said 12:20. I gave myself ten minutes to get a passenger. Whether I found one or not, at 12:30 I would go home.

I traversed Manhattan along Forty-second Street, in vain. The Tudor Hotel had gone to bed too; the discos and restaurants on First Avenue slept.

Just ten minutes more. And this time I really meant it!

————

I was waiting at a red light on the corner of Lexington and Sixty-seventh Street when I noticed a black woman with a child walking toward the intersection. She had not reached the curb yet; maybe she did not want a cab at all.

The shoal of yellow sharks speeding down the avenue was fifty yards away, and I took off without waiting for the light to change, tires screaming.

"Will you go to Brooklyn?" the woman asked. The boy of about five, whom she was holding by the hand, was asleep on his feet.

"Get in!" I growled, as if displeased. There was no need to let her know how well this trip suited me. The city was dead, anyway, and I would be going home with the meter on. But there is always some fly in the ointment. The Brooklyn woman turned out to be shrewish, and we started arguing right away.

"You know how to get to Highland Boulevard?" she asked.

"More or less," I hedged. "Don't you know how to get home?"

"I don't usually go home by car," the woman replied, waspishly.

"Don't worry, we'll make it," I reassured her. I certainly did not want to lose a Brooklyn job after all that. "We'll find your boulevard."

"And you expect me to pay you to go looking for it?" She bristled. "I warn you, you're not getting more than ten dollars."

"All right, all right!" I said. "Ten bucks is okay with me."

No sooner was the woman placated than the child began to whimper. There was a loud smack. The boy howled in earnest.

"What did you hit him for?" I could not restrain myself. "Is it his fault he should have been in bed hours ago?"

"Did you ever hear anything like it?" the woman shrieked, as if there were others in the cab besides ourselves. "This dope wants to teach me how to treat my son."

We were at the southern edge of Manhattan. In front of us reared up a vaulting arch of dim lights, the bridge leading to Brooklyn. I pulled over.

"You can get home from here without me."

"You got no right to dump a woman and child on the street at one o'clock in the morning," the woman said threateningly.

But this was not my intention.

"I'll stop another cab for you," I said.

"There's $4.85 on the meter," she reminded me, implying that she was not going to give me a penny of it.

"Fine. You can pay the lot to the 'dope' who takes you."

I had hardly gotten out of the car and raised my hand when a cab, with its off-duty light on, pulled up level with the Checker.

"Brooklyn!" I pointed to the bridge.

But the driver, who I think was Russian, did not even look at me; he was peering through the dusty window to see who was inside the cab. This done, he took off for the bridge.

The next cabbie did exactly the same: stopped, looked, and left. The third, who was black, entered into negotiations.

"Where's she going?"

"Brooklyn."

"Where in Brooklyn?"

"There's $4.85 on the meter," I said. "She'll pay you the whole thing."

The enticement worked. The black driver got out, opened the back door of my Checker, and asked the woman for the address. But then he went back to his cab.

"Remember!" I shouted. "There's no jobs in the city!"

The cab driver looked around.

"I don't care," he said. "I'm not going to Highland Boulevard. Period."

"At least tell me how to get there!"

"Take Atlantic Avenue all the way down. You'll find it."

———

The bridge seemed as endless as the evening itself. Once over the bridge, I managed to miss Atlantic Avenue, ended up on Fulton Street, and then on something called Marcy Avenue. There wasn't a soul about, but I knew we were in the ghetto from the number of storefronts with the CHECKS CASHED sign.

"Broadway!" my passenger said gladly. "Turn here!"

You should have seen that Brooklyn Broadway! Instead of sky, above us thundered the elevated subway. The pavement was pitted with such potholes that if a wheel had gone down into one of them it would have stayed there forever. Blocks of slums, with boarded-up windows, alternated with blocks of burned-out buildings.

"Bushwick Avenue runs somewhere around here," the woman said. "That's where we have to go. I think it's to the right."

I obeyed, and we lost our way again; the meter already showed fourteen-plus dollars.

All of a sudden, the area came to life. In a wasteland, surrounded by abandoned buildings, fires burned, children gamboled, music throbbed. Groups of raggedly dressed people were talking loudly and laughing around the bonfires. And above this hellish scene reigned the moon, which had come out from behind the clouds and flooded the ruins and the faces with a spectral light.

The seventeenth hour of my long shift was passing, and I caught myself thinking: "They while the night away by the fires because the day hasn't tired them out. They don't go to bed because they don't have to get up in the morning for work. Drivers are wanted at every garage. You can get a hack license in three days. The clientele of the check-cashing offices doesn't *want* to work."

I put my hand out behind me, and the boy, who had been looking through the partition, took it in his hot, damp little fingers.

"Let's take your mama home," I proposed, "and you stay with me. We'll live in my Checker and eat ice cream and hot dogs. Soon you'll grow up and be a cabbie like me. Okay?"

The boy chuckled and gently pushed my hand away. The Great

Tempter. I heard the thump of the jumpseat and looked round. The kid had snuggled up to his mother. She was smiling, our quarrel forgotten; we were driving along Highland Boulevard.

"Here!" she said, and held out the promised ten bucks.

But why had the woman picked such a strange place to stop? On one side was an empty lot, on the other a house with boarded-up windows. The only visible light was about fifty yards in front of us, where a tall apartment building towered above a glassed-in lobby. A few people were gathered around the entrance. They paid no attention to the cab halted nearby. It seemed as if they were dispersing to their homes: some to the right, away from the bright strip cast by my headlights, others to the left. Nobody appeared to be hurrying; nor did I attach any significance to the fact that none of them had gone inside the lobby.

I felt like stretching my legs and giving the boy a goodbye pat. Hardly had I opened the door when the woman, who was carrying the boy in her arms, hissed furiously, "You idiot!"

"Taxi!"

"You fucking idiot, *get out of here!*"

"Taxi!"

The last shout came from two directions at once, and the thud of running feet flared up in the darkness, but I managed to slam the door and push the lock just in time.

Leaping across the last few yards to the Checker, the dark figure had undoubtedly guessed the meaning of my convulsive movements, because the hand, instead of going for the locked door, reached in and shoved down the partly open window. But the Checker was already gathering speed. With incredible agility the shadow pushed itself away from the cab and disappeared into the darkness.

How many minutes later did I come to my senses? Maybe two, maybe ten. All I remember is that the first thing I felt was extraordinarily frivolous: I was racked with shame.

The shame of a man insulted by a woman; although her words had been my salvation.

The cab was stopped at a red light on Pennsylvania Avenue. The glass was not broken or cracked, merely open about three quarters of the way. I carefully turned the handle that moved the window up and down. It would not budge. I'll have to fix it, I thought with annoyance.

Meanwhile, Pennsylvania Avenue brought me to the Belt Parkway. Now for home! Enough adventures for one day. But the road led away from Brooklyn; along it flashed the chain of lights that guided pilots to the runway, and I could already make out the contours of the warehouses, fuel tanks, and hangars of Kennedy.

————

The parking lots and airline terminals were empty, naturally, but four or five cabs were standing outside the National Airlines building. What were they waiting for? I knocked on the window of the last car— "Hey!"—and only then did I realize that the cabbie was asleep, scrunched up in an uncomfortable position on the front seat. I should have slipped away quietly, but the head under the cap had already jerked up.

"What are you yelling for?" the cabbie said irritably. "What do you want?"

"When's the plane?" I asked. I had to say something now I had woken him up.

"What plane? The plane's coming in the morning. We're sleeping here."

I plodded back to the Checker, embarrassed. I had seen that cabbie somewhere before, heard that voice, that accent. But you could not wake the man up again to ask where you knew him from.

"Wait!" The burly figure was heaving itself out of the fleet Dodge. "Hey, what are you hanging around here for, you son-of-a-bitch!"

It was the Albanian! We were so happy to see each other.

"But you quit hacking!" the Albanian exclaimed, clapping me on the back.

"Didn't you quit too? And what are you doing in a fleet cab, anyway? Where's the Tirana Corporation?"

"Don't ask!" The Albanian brushed off the question. "What about you—did you buy?" He rapped on the Checker's fender.

"I'm leasing," I said.

As taxi drivers do, we got into the cab. The Albanian sat in my seat, behind the wheel, and instantly discovered that the window mechanism was damaged.

"What's this?" He scolded me as if he were the cab's owner.

"It's broken. I'll fix it tomorrow."

"Why tomorrow?"

He opened the glove compartment, got a screwdriver, pulled out the handle on the inside of the door—I was petrified!—ripped away the imitation-leather padding, stuck his hand in the resulting slit. With a groan, the glass dropped down inside the door, but a minute later it was rising and descending smoothly and noiselessly, as if nothing had happened. We lit up. Before our cigarettes were out, I had forgotten the time and that I had not called my wife and that I should have been home long ago. After all, I had to work tomorrow, which was now today.

The Albanian had been gambling all year. He had only just hit it big when we met on Park Avenue. One day a friend dragged him off to some joint where they shot craps.

The Albanian had gone in with two or three hundred on him and in an hour came out with two thousand in his pocket. After that happy evening, he neither drove the cab nor touched the dice himself again.

A Filipino and a Greek were vying for a hundred dollars. The Albanian put a thousand on the Greek. The Greek won three throws in a row, doubling the stakes each time, and received eight hundred dollars. But after the three throws, the Albanian, having risked only his original thousand, came away with eight grand!

Taking his wife and children with him, he went to Europe. Dubrovnik, Athens, Paris . . . One flying visit to Monte Carlo and the whole vacation was paid for! Then trips to Vegas, Reno, the Bahamas. He never lost anywhere, but he had real luck only in New York, at craps, in the same joint in Chelsea. He was wildly lucky!

A month after buying the Tirana Corporation, he had enough money for a two-family house. No banks, no loans; he put down cash on the nail. The Albanian's family occupied the downstairs apartment and he gave the upstairs one to his parents.

Persian carpets, Scandinavian furniture, cases of expensive brandy— he spent money like water, but still it kept on growing.

Two Chinese restaurateurs played for five hundred dollars a throw. Starting with five thousand, he bet twice and brought home twenty! Legends grew up around him at the gambling den.

Then, suddenly, the money vanished. He had to pawn the jewels he had given his wife. Now his family was living on what the Tirana Corporation drivers brought in. The money was plenty to live on but not to gamble with.

The Albanian became a careful gambler. Out of the thousand dollars the four cabbies paid him every week, he left half with his wife and took the other half to the club. The five hundred dollars easily became a thousand. But that damn thousand just frittered itself away. Something had gone wrong: he was expending his increasingly rare flashes of intuition for nothing. A man who has tasted the big time cannot play small.

His first medallion was gambled away and the second mortgaged for twenty thousand. The twenty thousand evaporated in three days. As a last resort he took out a mortgage on the house. But he lost that money, too. The mortgage cost only two hundred dollars a month, and the Albanian could easily make ends meet by working. But by now he could not stop playing.

Everything he made in the fleet cab he took to the gambling club. A hundred dollars easily became two hundred, then four, but after the next throw he would take the subway to the garage and beg the dispatcher for a cab on the night shift.

He saw neither his wife, his children, nor his parents—he did not dare show his face to them. How they were coping, what they were living on, he did not know.

"I have to be patient and wait," the Albanian said.

"For what?"

"For another run of luck."

Somewhere out of the dark, the yellow wasps were droning along the main airport road, and one of the drivers going past shouted: "What are you mooching around here for? It's stripped out on United!"

I was instantly seized by the zeal of the cabman. Now there could be no question of going home.

———

The plane arrived chock full; there were a lot of fares going to Brooklyn, which was what I was hoping for, but I ended up with a sullen black guy going to the Bronx. To avoid getting out of the car in the middle of the night in some deserted Bronx alleyway, I did not open the trunk, but simply shoved the suitcase in the backseat.

"You know the motel near Yankee Stadium, sir?"

Sir. Not bad. At least I did not foresee any arguments. And I did know the motel near the stadium: it was right next to the highway, but, more important, it was literally a step from there to a police station. There was nothing to fear. The pelting rain only cheered me, reminding me how comfortably warm and dry it was inside the cab. The bulging wad of money caressed my thigh; when I dropped this guy off I would have over a hundred and fifty dollars!

The Checker was not moving at more than about thirty miles per hour: again and again the windshield was drenched with the sheets of water kicked up by passing cars. We were driving along the Thruway, when suddenly the soaking, murky windshield was lit up by an ominous, ruby glare.

Brake!

The Checker skidded, the wipers wiped, and the ruby curtain resolved itself into two bright-red lights above the bumper of a sedan. It was screeching, swerving to a stop in the middle of the multilane highway. The right front door flew open and out jumped a woman. She sprinted toward the shoulder and ran ahead into the pitch dark, in the pouring rain.

It was extremely frightening, but I veered to the right and ended up between the car stopped on the highway and the running woman.

"What are you doing? Are you crazy?" shouted my passenger, but his terror only strengthened my resolve. Slowing down, I drew level with the woman, lunged across the seat, reached the handle, and opened the door.

"Get in!"

The other car's headlights flooded the interior of the Checker. They're going to shoot! The thought flitted through my mind. The moment the woman was inside, I tore off. Water trickled down her face. The car, from which she had managed to escape, stuck right on my tail.

"What happened?" I asked in a hoarse voice; the black man in the back had gone quiet.

"Thank you," said the woman, shaking.

"Tell me what happened, for heaven's sake!"

The woman gave a sob.

The sign for the stadium flashed past. Now I had to exit from the highway onto some godforsaken service road, and again the notion, that they would shoot, seized me. But there was no shooting.

The police precinct finally came into view. Several figures in uniform raincapes and caps were standing on the porch under an awning. By the time we reached the motel, I was quite calm. The auto mechanic paid seventeen dollars and lugged his suitcase out, while the woman rewarded me with a twenty-dollar bill.

"I really admire what you did!" she said; but something in her voice did not ring true.

The other car drove slowly up to the motel, unfazed by the proximity of the police precinct. A man about my age, wearing a suit and tie, got out into the rain. He smiled sheepishly to show that his intentions were entirely peaceful.

"Good evening," he said, and it looked as if he were greeting the Checker.

The woman I had saved unexpectedly assumed the role of aggressor. She leaped out, grabbed the man by the tie, yanked his head violently from side to side and, just as unexpectedly, got back in the cab.

"Will you take me to Bronxville?"

And how! An out-of-town trip was double the meter! My heart fluttered: I would be adding a big windfall to my $174. Indeed, today I would break the bookings records of all the liars who "only" go to Philadelphia or Atlantic City!

———

It was half past three by my watch when we turned off the Major Deegan Expressway into the pitch-black darkness of the suburbs. The woman explained which way to go and started to babble her thanks again.

"Why don't you tell me what really happened," I grumbled, bursting with pride.

"How can I tell you the story of sixteen years of misery?" the woman replied melodramatically, and my heroic exploit withered.

I did not ask her any more questions. When we reached her destination, she opened her purse again and pointedly gave me everything she had: three singles. The meter, which I had turned on again at the police station, showed $11.65.

"We're out of town," I reminded her. "I'm supposed to get $23.30."

"That's all I've got!" she replied crossly, and showed me the contents of her purse: some crumpled paper napkins, a powder compact, and a tube of lipstick. "Didn't I give you twenty bucks? That's enough!"

And there it ended. The car that had been following us moved back to allow my Checker out of the narrow lane, and I was alone once more.

The wind howled in the invisible treetops, the rain kept pouring. I drove down one hill and up another. There wasn't a light to be seen. Up one hill. Down another. Rain and darkness. Up again. Down again. What to do?

Only when a car sped past, blinding me, did the twinges of anxiety subside. I made a U-turn and followed the other car. Around a bend, a sign appeared, bearing a helpful arrow and the words NEW YORK.

But it was a long way from Westchester to Brooklyn; the rain had become a cloudburst. My headlights could not penetrate the wall of gray. I switched on the flashers and crawled along the highway, slapping my face.

I sang. I shouted. I smoked. My twenty-two hours behind the wheel had caved in on me, and my eyes kept closing. The number of cars around me multiplied, above my head flitted the shadow of the Ver-razano Bridge. If it had not been raining, the twenty-story building with the round water towers on the roof, my home, would have been visible.

An icy shower escorted me to the lobby. Wet shoes off. The frowning face of my wife peeking out of the bedroom. The couch in my little study was made up with sheets. This was my punishment. And I did so long to apologize and explain why I had not called, and brag about my unprecedented $177 shift; and I ached to deliver to my wife a lovingly cherished sentence, prepared in advance, to the effect that when a taxi driver brings home that sort of money, more adventures have happened to him in one day than happen to other people in a year.

Exhausted, I put on a dry undershirt and got into bed. Outside the window all was dark silence. The rain had stopped; I could not fall asleep.

Chapter Twelve

- - - - - - - - - -

A LETTER FROM
THE NEXT WORLD

O n the wall were bookshelves that my pillow, hanging over the arm of the couch, was propped against. By the window stood a desk.

Why did I feel ill at ease among such familiar things? A kind of heaviness was stealing over my body.

Until recently it had gone without saying that, apart from my ephemeral radio scripts, something "real" would be written at that desk: a series of short stories, or a novel, about Russian émigrés in America. I felt embarrassment recalling these ambitious fantasies, and nothing more than irritation at the sight of my massive desk, which occupied an unjustifiably large area of the room.

With the books it was different. To tell the truth, I had not bought one in the last year. But neglected and dusty as they were, they still meant something to me. Wretchedly bound and put out in tiny editions by shoestring émigré publishers, these books prompted in me a singular, aching feeling, incomprehensible to foreigners. In no other language but Russian have so many books been written for which the authors paid with their lives.

Here was a slim collection by a poet, shot to death, who bore the same name as the last Russian tsar, also shot to death. Here was another poet, who was shot somewhat later. And another book of verse:

Life dropped down like lightning flashes,
As in a teacup drop eyelashes,
Sham and rotting at the root—

Why did they throw the author of these lines behind the barbed wire where he went mad ("I was not made for prison!") and perished in the space of a few weeks? Why did they put a bullet in the back of the head of the most virtuoso stylist of Russian prose? Why did they put a noose around the neck of a woman whose poetry still lives on, fifty years later?

Before my eyes was the history of a literature created by martyrs, a literature that supplanted religion for millions like myself: prison and bullets, bullets and prison. Long live communism, the radiant future of all mankind! Amen.

———

It was getting light; one could already see to read without switching on a lamp, and it occurred to me that, although I had not added any books since I started driving a taxi, there was less and less room on the shelves, because one of them, the lowest, which I could reach without getting up from the couch, was jammed with the stacks of unsorted papers that the conscientious radio-station librarian kept on putting in my pigeonhole. She made a copy of every article appearing in the press that might be useful for *Our Daily Bread* and stuck it in there. Every issue of the *Research Bulletin*, which the Munich sovietologists prepared for radio journalists, went in, too. Into my pigeonhole also came *samizdat* manuscripts that reached us by mysterious routes from "over there." I had no time to read them, but the idea of throwing them out made me uncomfortable. Behind each of those manuscripts lay a trampled human destiny.

In deciding to commit their thoughts to paper, *samizdat* writers inevitably took a step into the abyss. They would be sought out and found. And then the searches, the interrogations, the mental hospitals, or just plain jails, followed.

It was just such a writer who had tapped out his own destruction on a Moskva typewriter: more than sixty dense, single-spaced pages which I took off the shelf. Not at all sure I was going to get through the whole thing, I picked up the first page.

On September 22, at nine-twenty a.m., I came out of our building at 8 Tarasovskaya Street—the Kiev address sent a pang of recognition through me—*and walked toward the Botanic Garden. The sun was shining; I had on a lightweight gray coat and sandals. An ordinary-looking blue van was parked next to the fire station, blocking my way. As I was about to go around it, a gray-haired man with a large head appeared from behind the van and said:*

"How do you do, Ghely Ivanovich. Please get into the car."

On the other side of the thin wall, I could hear footsteps moving through the apartment toward the kitchen. My wife was getting up; she was taking a word-processing course in Manhattan. I lay in my little study, in my Brooklyn apartment, reading a manuscript by one of my old Kiev acquaintances who I knew quite definitely was no longer alive.

A few months earlier the news had reached us in New York that Ghely Snegirev had been pardoned by the Soviet government, but had suddenly fallen ill with something and died. He had been interred in the Baikovo cemetery, the very same place my mother was buried.

This was like a letter from the next world.

The blue van drove along streets I had known since childhood. *It turned off onto Vladimirskaya.* That meant Ghely could see the red pillars of the university out the window; and then the Lenin Museum, where I had once been sworn into the Young Pioneers. Indeed, here Ghely noted that from the window of the van he saw the museum, followed by the Leipzig restaurant, and, finally, the gray KGB building, which for some reason was always covered with scaffolding.

We turned the corner, drove through the gates, and there we were!

The everyday tone of the story seemed to be inviting me on a tourist excursion inside the sinister building to which the arrested dissident had been conveyed.

The search began. There were some papers and signatures—no, that's wrong, no signatures, for I declared at the start that I was not going to sign anything. Witnesses. Some kind of big shot, who announced: "Well, Ghely Ivanovich, you dumped a regular bucket of mud on us, here at home and abroad." Then I was taken across a courtyard into a two-story building where I was frisked stark naked in a tiny cubicle. A corridor, a stairway, another corridor, two mattresses in my arms, the clanking of locks, and here I am, in the cell. My cellmate—dark hair, friendly. I do not remember those first minutes very well, but he, Ivan Ivanovich, told me about it later on: I walked around, having a good look, surveyed the polished parquet and the height of the ceiling, which was about fifteen feet (before the revolution the place had either been a cheap hotel or a whorehouse), sized my roommate up, and said: "My, it's nice here. A real palace, eh?" And, thrusting my face close to his, I muttered conspiratorially: "How about it, stoolpigeon? Do your stuff, then!"

I do not actually know whether he was a stoolpigeon or not, just as I'm still not sure if my second cellmate was snitching on me either. You never know.

So, there you are. Life went on; oh, yes, it was nice there, a real palace. And in the first few days I began writing verse.

Once a lovely lady gave me this advice:
"When you get to jail (you'll have to pay the price).
You may not be a poet, but try to write some verse;
It helps, or so I've heard it said, whenever life gets worse."

"Oh, Ghely!" I thought, recalling how, at the age of forty, still a drunk and a womanizer (like most movie people and journalists), he courted his lanky co-ed, nearly half his age, and eventually married her. As the years went by, however, the co-ed became a Soviet matron and left her husband, who had been expelled from the Writers' Union for his anti-Soviet views. Restless Gavrila. By now deprived of his livelihood, an outcast cut dead by his former acquaintances when they passed him on the street, and on the brink of arrest, he fell in love again. And married again! And now, if you please, even in a KGB jail he had lovely ladies on the brain.

I flipped through a dozen pages of verses which the prisoner had composed to ease his anguish in jail: they were inarticulate and uninteresting. And so, soon after plunging into the manuscript almost with trepidation, I was glancing through it fairly quickly.

I developed an odd relationship with the investigator from the very beginning. I did not say hello to him; I was openly rude, and in both my oral and written answers (I wrote down all the answers for the interrogation record myself) I would make as many wisecracks and gibes as I could.

It certainly was an odd relationship. At the first interrogation Ghely walked into the office of the KGB captain singing a popular song.

I offended him deeply. "Look, Captain," I said, "You are not gonna make it to Major."

Ghely's point was that Captain Slobozhenyuk (the gray-haired man with the large head) was not going to earn his major's star on this case. But the interrogator's reaction was even more unexpected. What did he do? Bang his fist on the table? Deny the prisoner food parcels, deprive him of exercise? It was not just his "pride" as an officer that should have spurred him to teach the insolent fellow a lesson, it was his duty. More than a star was at stake if he did not obtain the necessary testimony: how long would it take a tough boss to force a graying captain to retire? Nevertheless, the captain did not fly into a rage; he merely reminded the frivolous joker that, like it or not, he, Ghely Ivanovich, was in a no-nonsense institution where singing ditties at interrogations was not done. He even seemed to be complaining to the prisoner about his hardships:

"They'll really tear me off a strip for this, you know!"

There was nothing implausible in Ghely's being entrusted to such a sorry KGB man, trapped low in the ranks. After all, why use a stellar counterespionage agent to investigate a case where the basis for the accusation was that the criminal did not want to hide his criminal thoughts? If the dissident found anything unusual in the investigator's simple and forgiving nature, it was his utter dullness. He grumbled about the same things every day. "Yes, Ghely Ivanovich, that's exactly how we're supposed to do things here," or "No, Ghely Ivanovich, that's not how we're supposed to do things here." But there was no reason for amazement or wonder. The investigator was a typical product of the Soviet system: a nonentity such as the Writers' Union and any movie studio (and evidently the KGB) were full of.

True, at times it seemed to Ghely that the investigator was only pretending to be a dumb bureaucrat, a blockhead; but then, come to think of it, why would a KGB officer play such a role—almost a clown's?

Ghely treated this wretched captain as he deserved, never denying himself the pleasure of teasing the investigator when the occasion offered itself:

"*Tell me, captain, do they search you on your way in and out of work?*"

"*What makes you say that? Of course not.*"

"*Nope. They frisk you all right.*"

"*What is this nonsense?*"

"*It's not nonsense. They frisk me on the way to your interrogations and on the way back, every time.*"

"*But it's you they're searching, not me.*"

"*Well, think about it: they take me to you and I don't see anyone except you. A screw's always watching me. That means they're frisking you: either I'm bringing something to you or you're handing something to me. Don't you see? It's you they're searching, you!*"

The investigator tittered feebly.

"*What a joker you are, Ghely Ivanovich.*"

During one session the captious prisoner grabbed a page of the written record off the desk, tore it in pieces, and chucked them into the waste basket.

The investigator's face froze. There is a limit to everything; the man had gone too far. The captain stood up without a word, walked over to the steelclad safe, opened it. Ghely shivered, not understanding at first. The investigator turned, holding a bottle of glue.

Still without a word, the gray head dived into the waste basket. The officer carefully gathered up the scraps, spread them out on the table, and began to glue them together. Only when this laborious job was done did he say:

"*How could you do such a thing, Ghely Ivanovich? The record's still a document, even if you haven't signed it. I'll certainly have to answer to my superiors for your pranks.*"

Ghely felt bad about this escapade. He had not meant to humiliate the older man, and, half-apologizing, the prisoner mumbled that the captain should have warned him, then he would not have done it.

What seemed inexplicable from Ghely's notes was how he apparently developed an "odd relationship" not only with the investigator but with every other member of the KGB's internal prison staff as well.

Two warders, ensigns, would be feeling around in the prisoner's dirty socks and underpants elastic while the writer and movie director, the patrician, taunted them, *"Look how low you've sunk, lads!"*

The tough ensigns swallowed it and did not utter a word. But there was more to come. Discovering the aforementioned verses during the regular search (and not just any verses, but encoded ones), the warders put them aside, but afterward they ignored the exercise book and evidently did not even report the find to their superiors, since the episode had no further consequence.

Even the head of the investigation department, Colonel Turkin, did not disguise his liking for the dissident. "A charming, intelligent man," was how Ghely chose to describe him. The colonel seldom showed up at the interrogations, and when he did look in, it was mostly in order to check, not on the progress of the investigation, but on the health of the prisoner. And not just pro forma, out of courtesy, but in detail.

Was his heart acting up? Was he troubled by insomnia? And even, was he bothered by hemorrhoids? *"They're an awful nuisance, you know, Ghely Ivanovich, a lot of people in prison are plagued by them."*

But perhaps the head of the prison, Lieutenant-Colonel Sapozhnikov, was the friendliest of all, despite the fact that the prisoner was a thorn in his side. On the holiday commemorating the October Revolution, when the leadership all over the country comes down especially hard on any "extraordinary incident," Ghely shouted out in the exercise yard that he was calling on all political prisoners to observe the anniversary with a hunger strike.

This took place on the ninth day of Ghely's own hunger strike. Everything went dark before his eyes; he lost consciousness and was carried to his cell by the warders.

The minimum punishment for this kind of offense in any Soviet prison is solitary confinement; but the lieutenant-colonel saw fit to take gentler measures.

Two days later, when I was lying in the sick bay with a bare behind, getting a forced-feeding enema, the head of the prison came in, and, addressing my skinny ass, read out an order reprimanding me for my violation of discipline.

It makes one want to laugh and cry at the same time: a man goes to jail for seven years of his own free will, while the head of one of the most horrible Soviet prisons (the head of a KGB isolation unit *must* have been a vicious brute) slaps him with a written reprimand.

I heard footsteps again on the other side of the wall. My son was moving from bedroom to bathroom, from bathroom to kitchen. There was a crash and the scraping sound of a broken plate or cup being swept from the linoleum. Soon the apartment became as quiet as the tomb. I went on reading, no longer skipping.

A few flakes of snow were floating past the window, New Year's was approaching, and the gray-haired captain, for whom Ghely's case promised nothing but troubles, shelved all petty, personal grudges and embarked on a heart-to-heart talk with the subject under investigation about some trends in certain circles.

These humane trends were encouraging the application of a law under which a political prisoner's sincere repentance could sometimes be rewarded with a complete pardon. Particularly during the investigative stage, before the accused was sentenced. In this case, the pardon meant that the charges against Ghely's wife, who had helped—hadn't she?—to disseminate the libelous materials, and so could find herself behind bars any day—would also be dropped.

"What's this? A lot of fuss 'out there'? It's got to be quelled, eh?" Ghely asked the KGB man.

"Yes. It wouldn't hurt," the investigator admitted. *"Think it over, Ghely Ivanovich."*

And the arrogant, mocking dissident actually promised to think it over! The captain could not believe his ears. In fact, he believed it only when he realized that in exchange for his vague promise, the prisoner was asking for a favor. Ghely and his bunkmate had had the idea of putting up some kind of Christmas tree in their cell.

Needless to say, the prisoner was playing cat-and-mouse with the captain, but the simpleton fell for it, and not only permitted this unheard-of indulgence in a Soviet jail but himself even brought the prisoners two or three pine branches, smelling of resin and frost.

Having received his pennyworth of pleasure, at the first interrogation after the holiday Ghely declared haughtily that he would make no deals.

"I won't do it. Forget it!"

"That's too bad, Ghely Ivanovich," the captain said with restraint. "The conversation would have been very different."

But it did not even enter the investigator's head to take revenge on the artful dodger, although one phone call from the scaffolding-covered building would have been enough to have had Ghely's sons expelled from university, drafted into the army, and sent to serve in Siberia.

By February the interrogation sessions had become infrequent; everything had been asked, and I had answered everything, insolently and readily; but the investigator was obliged to summon me twice a week, and around February 20 I refused to go to the investigation block anymore. And once again, as he had during my hunger strike, the captain began coming to the isolation unit for the sessions.

So what did Ghely and the investigator talk about, if everything had already been asked and answered?

Well, nothing much. The odd relationship between investigator and prisoner continued to evolve; and so they chatted about all sorts of things. For instance, Ghely recounted the dreams he had in prison—some sad, some funny.

And the investigator listened to this rubbish?

Oh, yes; very attentively! Later on, almost blinded, unable to reread the words he had written, gasping for breath in his death agony, Ghely, remembering one of these dreams suddenly, observed with wonderment: *"Was it prophetic, then?"*

That night the prisoner again saw the jail in his dreams. He saw the investigator's office, and the usual view out of the window—a stone airshaft.

No, not exactly. In Ghely's dream the prison's inner courtyard appears oddly dislocated, and this dislocation permits a glimpse of the gate and the tunnel that led to freedom. The prison gates open to let out a blue van, the same one that had brought Ghely there five months before, while behind them one can see a city sidewalk flooded with sunlight and passersby! Suddenly Ghely hears a voice behind him; he looks round, and sees Colonel Turkin standing next to him. Laughing, the colonel announces to Ghely that he is free.

Ghely sees himself outside the prison gates, but he does not dare take a step toward the busy street. He is *afraid* of meeting his wife and friends. Even in the dream Ghely knows they will certainly ask him why the KGB let him go. And what will he tell them? How will he prove that he betrayed no one, never groveled? Terror grabs him by the throat; Ghely runs back and begs the guard to let him back into the prison.

> *Let me back! Let me in! Let me be*
> *In the prison of the KGB!*
> *I want to be back in my cell;*
> *My bunk still remembers me well.*
> *I should never be free, this I know,*
> *Let me in! Let me through! Let me go!*

And with that shriek of "Let me go!" I woke up, in a cold sweat, as they say. It was the perfect idyll: a prisoner reciting poetry during an inter-rogation while the investigator listened.

On March 2, toward dawn of a sleepless night, I had just dropped into a doze when there was a knocking and a groaning and a clanging, and into the cell walked Lieutenant-Colonel Sapozhnikov. I had long ago told him that I would not stand up in his presence, and merely turned and looked at him. He walked up to the bunk bed, laid a brotherly hand on my shoulder, and said:

"Ghely Ivanovich, this time you really have to stand up. Get ready to go to the hospital."

I was reading Ghely's notes and this whole story—of the idyll behind bars, of the moments of spiritual intimacy with the investigator, the kind colonel's concern, and the brotherly hand of the prison chief on the shoulder. They carried the scent of something that made my blood run cold.

I put down the manuscript without finishing it.

A Don Quixote. A veritable Don Quixote! Of course, he had been tilting not at windmills but at a real and powerful evil; still, once knocked out of the saddle, he had renounced the best of what he had achieved in life, and then his life, deprived of meaning, had come to an abrupt end. It was a pity, of course, but then it could not have been any other way.

The mass of details I had just read had not altered the stereotype I had already formed of Ghely Snegirev's image and fate.

A new day in my own life was beginning, one I would have to live through myself. The hands of the clock pointed to a quarter to eight. In the kitchen the telephone began to ring. Who could want me at this hour of the morning, for God's sake?

Part Four

HOW
I BECAME
A REAL
CABBIE

Chapter Thirteen

FRIENDSHIP FOR

A DOLLAR

The telephone rang and rang. The body would not obey. The heaviness overtaking the muscles of my back and shoulders was leaden exhaustion.

The phone stopped ringing. I was a free man, at no one's beck and call. Forget about work. This would be a day of rest, well earned and much needed. The only thing I had to do was move the Checker to the other side of Neptune Avenue; otherwise at eight o'clock its windshield would be adorned with a parking ticket. I definitely had to get up.

First thing, I looked out the window. The Checker had not been stolen; its yellow hood protruded from behind the hefty dumpster next to which I had parked the cab at dawn, close to my building's entrance.

On the kitchen table, underneath the sugar bowl, was a compact wad of damp green bills. I had purposely put the money in an obvious place so my wife and son would count it and discover my $177 record before leaving the house. The bundle looked a bit thinner, though. With a sigh, I extracted the money from under the sugar bowl, counted it, and sighed again: $154. My wife had taken twenty bucks and my son three.

I knew my wife was careful with my taxi income; she was still wearing the overcoat she had brought from Russia. My son's extravagances were as yet limited to an extra slice of pizza or a movie. I had nothing with which to reproach my dependents; but I could not help begrudge the money anyway.

The next thing I remembered was the criminal court summons. No, I had not torn it up or thrown it away. I got down the English-Russian dictionary and hunted for the illegibly scribbled term that defined my "crime." S—I deciphered the policeman's scrawl with difficulty; *o*. The next letter looked to me like an *l*. There was no English word, in my dictionary at least, beginning with *sol* and ending with *ing*, but I did come up with a verb whose stem matched. The various senses of this verb, however, had nothing to do with yesterday's incident: "beg for alms," "accost men for immoral purposes," "incite the population to revolt."

Wonderful! What a good thing I had not thrown the summons out. I would definitely go to court and even felt slightly vexed that the hearing was still a couple of months away. I would walk into the courtroom in pressed suit and polished shoes and, keeping my righteous indignation in check, I would recount in dispassionate tones everything as it had really happened. I would ask the cop point blank what exactly he was accusing me of. Begging for alms? Or inciting the population to revolt? That dolt in policeman's uniform—the judge would teach him a lesson all right!

––––––––––

The red-eyed visage of a perfect stranger faced me in the mirror, as puffy as if I had been out drinking. I should have some kind of wash, but I could not cup my hands to bring the water to my face; my left hand was shaking.

The phone clanged again.

"Sorry I woke you," said my wife.

"You didn't wake me, I'm up."

"You haven't forgotten the car has to be moved right now? I called once already."

"I was in the bathroom," I said.

"Do you realize what time you got home?" My wife was trying to keep the note of exasperation out of her voice. "I was worried sick!"

"It just worked out that way," I said, pulling on my still damp jeans.

"Please don't drive today," my wife said.

The last thing I wanted to do right then was get back on the job. But there was something contradictory in the fact that after taking twenty bucks out of the money I had brought back, my wife was now trying to persuade me to stay home and rest. I put the keys in my pocket and slammed the front door.

Out of the $154 remaining, about twenty would go to refuel the car, I thought as the elevator hummed its way down. Sixty-two fifty belonged to the owner. If I took the whole day off, the debt would double. If I let the Checker sit beneath the window, I would have to pay for it with yesterday's take. For twenty-two hours' work I would net seven dollars.

I was a free man, my own boss. What boss could get me behind the wheel again without a moment's sleep? I had no intention of pulling a number like that. I would move the car, come back, wash up, take a nap, and then, somewhere around noon . . .

My smoke-clogged lungs dragged pleasurably on the bracing, rain-refreshed air. I walked around the dumpster—and saw a sight that cut me to the quick. The small triangular window on the driver's side was broken, the door was open. The lid of the trunk was bouncing up and down in the wind; its lock had been wrenched off and hung from the bent rivet, tinkling slightly. The businesslike auto thief had not wasted time fiddling with picklocks in the rain. He had opened the car the quick way, with a hammer and chisel, and had stolen the brand-new spare wheel and jumper cables, the jack, and the flashlight. The trunk was empty. Water had collected in the bottom.

Had the meter been stolen? The electronic meter cost over six hundred dollars. I did not leave it in the trunk, unlike most cab drivers. Either I took it home, or, as I had yesterday, wrapped it in a rag and hid it under the seat.

"Never again! I'm never leaving the meter in the cab again!" I vowed, and began frantically to search for it under the seat, realizing instantly that the thief had looked there too. The changer and its coins, the carton of cigarettes, and even a paper bag containing two bottles of Coca-Cola, had all disappeared; however, despite my worst fears, the meter, wrapped in its rag, turned up just where I had left it. Providence had taken pity on me that morning after all. But there was no getting around it: yesterday's money would not even cover the cost of replacing the window and equipping the trunk with a new lock, spare, and jack.

There was no counting on the owner's sympathy. I would save a little by buying a used spare wheel and jack. The lady owner never looked inside the trunk.

I tied down the lid of the trunk with a piece of rope, and told myself not to depart from my original plan: move the cab, eat, take a nap.

I circled my own block and the next, but there was no place to park. One more block, then another. Even if I found a space for the Checker now, I would not have the energy to drag myself home almost a mile on foot. I lit a cigarette, let fly a healthy obscenity along with the smoke— and set off for the highway to Manhattan.

Numb with chronic fatigue, steeped in the smell of gasoline, I was driving some woman with a boy, about five years old, along Park Avenue. The child's fidgety heinie refused to settle, whether next to Mommy, in her lap, or on the jumpseat. He decided the best thing to do in a cab was to *stand*, clutching the lower track along which slid the thick glass partition, open at the time.

My tongue, stuck to my nicotine-corroded gums, could not twist itself around the words needed to lecture the woman about making her boy sit down; if, God forbid, I should have to brake unexpectedly, the kid could get hurt. So, instead of delivering a homily to my customer, I drove very carefully, keeping an eye on the boy in the rearview mirror. What was the point in my telling his mother anything if I was meeting her for the first and last time on the long road of my life, which we happened to be traveling together from the Pan Am building to Seventy-second Street?

But my passenger adhered to a different set of rules. If she did not like something, she did not deem it necessary to hide the fact, at any rate not from a taxi driver.

"Why did you stop at the yellow light?" she asked irritably.

I could have explained to her that Park Avenue is one of the most dangerous thoroughfares in the city; that one should never try to beat the lights there; that right here I had seen with my own eyes—But I kept my mouth shut; we had only ten more blocks to go.

The traffic lights on Park Avenue change at intervals that allow a driver to cross about five streets at city speed limits. If you hustle you can make a sixth. With the boy in mind, I went a little slower; I traveled only four blocks and again stopped at a yellow light. This time the mother was positively convulsed with fury at my petty ripoff.

"You think I don't know why you're doing this?" she said.

"Well, why?" I asked nastily.

"Because while you're stopped the meter keeps going!"

She was implying that I was purposely dragging out the trip so as to squeeze an extra dime out of her.

I growled: a surge of anger made my throat contract so tightly that the foulest abuse I knew in English and Russian stuck in it. And it would have been a great deal wiser to have spewed my entire working vocabulary in this lady's face, because what I actually did was worse. Blinded by the insult, oblivious to where the child's hands were at that moment, I slammed that heavy, transparent guillotine of a partition shut with all my might—and heard a heart-rending shriek.

Shrinking with horror, burying my face in my hands, I could visualize the blood and the little butchered fingers.

The shriek was not abating behind me, and, clamped to the steering wheel, I did not dare tear my hands away from my eyes. Only when I grasped that it was not the child who was screaming, but the mother, and that something articulate was escaping from her— "I tell you, this is the last time you drive a cab!"—did I look round.

A passerby was holding the hysterical boy. The child was stretching out both hands to his mother, and they were whole.

"Don't try to sneak off!" a cop in plainclothes hissed at me, showing his badge.

I got out of the car. Somewhere nearby a siren was wailing; the plainclothesman had called a patrol car on his radio. The boy was sobbing in his mother's arms, and I leaned against the Checker and kept saying to myself: "No more. I can't take it anymore. I can't!"

"What the hell did you do?" A policeman came rushing up.

"I don't know why she called the cops," I said.

"He nearly crippled my child!" the woman shouted.

But the New York City police do not take complaints about what might have happened. The horror subsided. Yet I realized I could not go on working the way I had been. I was in no condition to carry on driving. I had to get some rest. And at the same time I had to make money. The cab rental must be paid.

———

If a cabbie wants to take a break and yet not waste a valuable hour, he need only spend a buck to buy the friendship of a doorman, under whose wing he can dine peacefully on a soggy cellophane-wrapped roll and afterward doze sweetly, scrunched up on the front seat.

For the doorman won't be dozing. If the guest is only going a short distance, the doorman you have bribed would never disturb you. He will stop a cab driving past. But if the passenger is going to an airport, Long Island, or New Jersey, your splendid patron in the gold-braided uniform will clap his hands and shout: "First cab!" And then the line of drivers who pay the doorman tribute will move up, and you will be one car nearer.

If the hotel is busy, and the line keeps moving, in thirty or forty minutes, after a short rest, you will be first in line. Time to finish the roll, clamber out of the cab, walk over to the doorman, look at him admiringly, pat him on the shoulder—not too familiarly: *pat*, not slap— smile humbly, and say: "Would you give me a Kennedy, please?"

If the doorman signals his imperial assent by the droop of his eyelids, or at any rate by nodding, even if it is with a frown (as long as he does not snap that he's fed up with the constant pestering, the absurd demands the cabbies make on him; as long as he does not bark, "Stay with your cab!"), consider the deal done. If the next guest with a suitcase is going to the nearer of the airports, the doorman may clap his hands, but he will shout "LaGuardia!" and it is nothing to do with you how the drivers waiting *behind* you in the paying line agree on which of them will take this LaGuardia. Someone will take it and pay the doorman his dollar. Now you just have to be patient.

Another forty minutes go by, an hour, perhaps; I try not to worry. I am taking a break, gathering strength, and who cares if "LaGuardia!" resounds time and again, and the cabbies waiting for airports whisper spitefully behind your back: "What's the matter with that guy?"

"First cab!"

Hurry, open the trunk. Stuff *two* bucks in the proffered hand. Yup, this is *two*-dollar service. A bit dear, of course, but worth it. Oh, is it worth it!

An hour and a half wait and forty minutes to JFK, and it may be three or four hours before I get back with a city-bound passenger. But there will be money in my pocket. Then back to the hotel, another Kennedy. Wait. Would I really make any more working the streets?

Just a little, maybe fifteen dollars. However, after eight hours cruising daytime Manhattan, a cabbie is like a squeezed lemon. His tongue hangs out. If a dead hour comes along, he won't win the race.

The cabbie who enjoys a doorman's patronage is full of energy. After those easy airport bucks, putting in the three or four hours needed to reach the quota is child's play. At ten p.m. he is already in bed, glancing slyly at his wife, already sinking into slumber. He whispers, "Tomorrow morning my darling isn't going to work on the subway. She'll travel by taxi, like a big executive!"

A doorman can bestow anything in the world on a taxi driver, even domestic bliss.

But what about the brown-nosing? The humiliation? Hunched against the rain, an old acquaintance of mine from Riga, an assistant professor of Marxism-Leninism, is trotting across the avenue, cupping his hand around a hotdog with sauerkraut as if it were a candle in the wind and bringing it as a present to the honcho in the hotel uniform. The honcho takes the hotdog and pretends to fish in his pocket. But the former assistant professor, who would choke the last nickel out of a fare, nervously fends off the doorman with both hands, as if the great man were about to take a gun out of his pocket instead of a dollar. No, no, the cabbie wouldn't dream of taking money for the hotdog! It's not a buck he's expecting from the doorman.

There are cabbies who value a doorman's favorable disposition so highly that they take their patrons home from work every day for free. And so that the doormen's capital will not lie idle under the mattress, these enterprising cabbies seek out suitable investments for him: in laundromats, gas stations, and honest, reliable lads—mostly hacks like themselves, who have fallen on hard times and need ten grand desperately for a new cab . . . at thirty-three percent per annum.

Parking the cab outside a hotel, I go up to the doorman.

"My friend!" I say tenderly, and stuff a dollar in his pocket. "Give me an airport, please."

I am paying in advance. And I am not fussy. I'll take a LaGuardia. But the doorman recoils like a well-brought-up young lady from a pickup artist. He puts one hand over the pocket and with the other thrusts away mine.

"Get lost!" he mutters through clenched teeth. "Leave me alone!"

And I *know* the louse takes money from other cabbies. Some months before, my buddy Uzbek, who seemed to have vanished into thin air, had promised to introduce me to this very doorman who sold airports right and left. So why wouldn't he take *my* payoff? How was my dollar any worse than the others'? And wasn't I ready to hand over a second buck if a Kennedy showed up? But he turns me down. Because he doesn't know me. Maybe, he thinks, having paid a buck, I'll get cheeky, loitering around the entrance and questioning the hotel guests myself. Totally out of line.

I smile but the doorman does not even *want* to know me.

"Listen, are you a cab driver?"

"Sure!"

"So where's your cab?"

"That's my Checker, over there."

"Can you do me a favor?"

"Glad to, my friend! What?"

"Stay with your cab."

———

My first friendship with a doorman, like a sixteen-year-old boy's first woman, came as an unlooked-for gift from fate. That first woman always finds her pimply Cupid herself, after all.

Late one evening, on that ill-starred corner of Park Avenue and Forty-second Street where I had gotten the criminal court summons, and where buses not only take passengers to the airports but also bring them back, a grizzled man carrying a battered suitcase with a British Airways label got in my Checker and gave an address somewhere near Carnegie Hall. He had just flown in from London and prattled about the weather. I was simply dying to hear about the weather in London, of course. All day I had thought about nothing but how to find out whether they were having rain or fog. Suddenly the old man sighed and said, hurt, "You don't recognize me, do you."

An eyebrowless, inexpressive face.

"No, I don't. Who are you?"

And here he threw me for a loop.

"I'm the doorman at the Washington Hotel."

This was no joke! A chance meeting could turn my grueling toil into a delightful pastime. It seemed that heaven itself had taken pity on my lot, and all I had to do was not thwart a Higher Design.

"Please don't be offended that I didn't recognize you, *sir.* The fact is I'm new to cab driving."

The explanation was accepted graciously.

"By the way, sir, you didn't say how long you stayed in London."

"Two days."

"And what were you doing there?" I coaxed.

"Oh, nothing much. I'm a widower, you know, I don't have anything to do on my vacations. [What an amazing doorman, so approachable!] While I was in London I dropped in at the Washington Hotel."

"That's great! Hmm, well . . . And what did you go there for?"

"To meet the doorman."

"How interesting! And what did you talk about?"

"Tips."

"You've got to be kidding! How can he put himself on *your* level? New York and London? There's no comparison!"

"That's not true, I'm afraid. He does a lot better, actually. You see, my problem is that the bellboys, the young guys who bring down the luggage, won't ever tell me where the guests are going. And if I don't know that, how can I take airport money from the cab drivers?"

What kind of a doorman was this? A dud. Hence the battered suitcase.

"But why do you need to ask the bellboys, sir?" said I, astounded. "Ask the guests. Who but the doorman should ask?"

"Well, that's the way it ought to be. And which hotel do you usually work out of?"

"The Statler," I fibbed.

"You make good money there?"

"So-so." I made a face, but the ground did not open up under my feet. "The lines at the Statler are too long. Is it like that at the Washington?"

"I wouldn't say so. And how much do you pay for airports?"

"The same as everyone. A dollar for LaGuardia, two for Kennedy."

"I'll be back at work the day after tomorrow," the old man said. "Come over then."

I did not come — I flew! The doorman greeted me as if I were his own son. He ran over to the registration desk to find out how many people were leaving that morning. About thirty guests were checking out. And piles of suitcases soon mounted up, both in the lobby and at the entrance outside. And a gang of greedy cabs, engines running, gathered behind my Checker. And my febrile anticipation was agony!

But the Washington guests' suitcases were picked up by some minibus drivers, who were taking the economical travelers in groups, five bucks apiece to Kennedy, four to LaGuardia. For a guest of a third-rate hotel like the New York Washington, where people stay to *save* money, the expense of a taxi to the airport is too painful. It isn't the Plaza, nor even the Roosevelt.

Having wasted two hours, I left empty. The old man spread his hands helplessly. He was upset too: we had come to such a capital business arrangement!

————————

Yes, there are hotels and hotels. And the doormen are all different, too. Blacks, Puerto Ricans, WASPs. The man at the Plaza is Ukrainian. At Halloran House there is a toothsome blonde, a door*woman.*

The most prestigious, most splendid hotel in New York, of course, is the Waldorf-Astoria. This is where the heads of state stay, the majority shareholders, the stars. This is the hotel for the elite that rules the world, and here limousines are favored, with their telephones and televisions, refrigerators and bars. If you order a limo like this for a week — the length of your stay in New York — it will set you back three or four grand.

The doorman who arranges such a match for an independent, lone-wolf limo driver gets a *twenty percent* commission.

"'Kennedy'!" the chauffeurs of the limousines sneer at the cabbie. "He wants a Kennedy! Ha!"

Some heads of state may enjoy the pomposity of the Waldorf, but frankly we cab drivers are not too crazy about it. Waiting for a job at the Waldorf or the Pierre, a cabbie feels like a second-stringer: they'll put him in if something goes wrong with the limos. No, to all the palatial hotels I, like every New York cabbie, prefer the Hilton, propping up the sky above the top of Sixth Avenue.

In the whole of the uncrowned capital of America I doubt you could find a taxi driver who does not stop at least once a week at the Hilton to have a go at our "lottery," where a win means a trip to the airport and the bet is a ten-minute wait in the ceaselessly crawling line. The odds of winning the lottery are the best.

The thousand rooms of this skyscraper are occupied not by those who rule the world, not its "generals," but by a class one rung lower on the social ladder, the "colonels." These are the busiest people in America; nobody values his time as highly as a resident of the Hilton. They are always in a hurry. They are in a hurry to become habitués of the Waldorf. It is only six blocks from the Hilton to the Waldorf, but for the majority a lifetime is not enough to overcome the distance.

And "colonels" are more lavish than "generals." Three hundred dollars a day is normal for a doorman at the Hilton. On Fridays they get five; on the eve of a holiday they can take home a thousand!

Every now and then I would get a lucky ticket: just as my cab had moved up to the head of the line, out would come a passenger accompanied by his luggage on a cart. But the doorman will not give me the win that is rightfully mine. With a bow, he asks the guest something, while putting someone else in my cab—a Circle Line or a Chrysler Building—$1.75! I say, what's the matter? And at best I merit the reply that the gentleman with the luggage has to wait for his wife, or a friend.

Fine! Nothing to fret about, it would seem. He will wait, and I will wait for him. I will load up his suitcases, move a few yards away from the main entrance, and wait, as we always wait for customers whom we pick up by appointment. But the doorman has put the Circle Line in my cab on purpose, so I will clear out quick and not hinder his wheeling and dealing.

Two or three cabs behind me, a driver who *pays* the doorman is blowing him a kiss—and the doorman has already whispered to the guest that he'll put him in a *good* cab, with a *good* driver (and reap an extra good tip to boot).

Lying in wait for my win, and hearing "Checker!" I was about to pull out of the line, only to be stopped by the doorman.

"Stay where you are!"

"But you called for a Checker yourself."

"The guest wants a *fleet* Checker. He needs a trunk with no spare wheel so there's enough room. Capisce?"

Crap. When I drove a fleet Checker, nobody ever needed *my* trunk with no spare.

"What you need is a spare dollar, not a roomy trunk, you top-hatted pig!" I yell.

The cabbies guffaw. They detest the honchos in gold-beribboned uniforms. But who is willing to make an enemy at the hotel he works out of? No one is going to stand up for me. Shouts, a ruckus, and the upshot is, I leave empty. You can all fry in hell!

———

I could not get on with doormen. I loathed them!

I did not want to waste my time at the hotels. Usually I roamed the streets. But at about four in the afternoon, when the bumper-to-bumper traffic had my nerves shot, the grotto of the Hilton's covered driveway and a line of customers in a hurry to get a cab was forming. The yellow snake crawled forward without stopping. As if fleeing danger, I would join the line and try my luck. Perhaps this time I would manage to yank myself out of the city's inferno!

However, during the rush hours a second line of cabmen, the chosen few, would always appear alongside the regular one. These were the wily cabbies whom the Hilton doormen had chosen to assist.

Standing half in and half out of the cab, like a horseman in the stirrups, the driver signals for attention with a wave or a whistle. The doorman nods, and, without interrupting his main task of putting passengers on short trips in the ordinary cabs, he watches for the approach of the next suitcase. Here it is!

"Where are you going? You're not sure? Let me take a look at your ticket, please. Ah, the airport. For you, sir, I'll get a reliable driver who knows the way. Oh, thank you very, very much, sir."

The favored hackman bursts into the Hilton's grotto, skirting the head of the yellow line.

"Hey, where d'you think you're going!"

"Can't you see there's a line?"

"Don't give him a job!"

But it's the doorman who gives the jobs here. The drivers' revolt is subdued with a wrathful glance and a single word.

"Appointment!"

The trunk is already slammed shut. He has already whirled away on a forty-buck trip to New Jersey. The doormen's vassal and favorite; it's too late to kick up a fuss.

The outraged cabbie choked on his own abuse and swore. The belly of his cab scraped against the sloping curb at the exit from the grotto onto Sixth Avenue, and there was the next vulture, flapping his wings to get the doorman's attention.

"How did you manage to get on the gravy train?" I ask one of the craftiest of the predators, Felix, quite recently a black-marketeer in Moscow and, frankly, a pretty fair scoundrel. He had no qualms about stealing jobs, even from the Russians at the Madison, and when Crewcut or the Sculptor held him up to shame, he would explain it quite artlessly.

"You've been sitting around here for years and you don't steal jobs from each other because you're all friends. But I don't need any friends. All I need is money!"

However, Felix was still a cab driver. And a Russian. And he began hacking about the same time as I did, carrying around his neck the same millstone of the $62.50 rental. Or maybe he just wanted to astound me with his gamesmanship—I don't know. At any rate, he shared his ingenuity with me the way a starving man shares a crust of bread with another.

It is unthinkable for a cabbie to approach a three-hundred-dollar-a-day doorman, especially an immigrant who cannot even express himself clearly in English. On a dead Saturday morning, having shaved and put on decent clothes, Felix parked his Checker not far from the Hilton and went into a liquor store.

"One bottle of Martell, one of Chivas Regal, and one of Absolut vodka. Together, gift-wrapped."

This was done.

"And another package exactly the same." Since the Hilton doormen work in pairs.

A heavy shopping bag in each hand, Felix set off.

The hotel was still dozing; the sentinels as well. And the yellow line, stretching three blocks, slept too. There was almost no one about at the entrance.

Felix showed both the doormen his hack license. Yesterday a guest from the Hilton left these two packages in my cab.

"Who was it? What's his last name? His room number?"

"How should I know?"

The two doormen exchanged glances; it smelled fishy. But the beribboned packages were very alluring. And this Russian cab driver looked at them with such honest eyes. Maybe he was just another fool.

"The boss says never take anything that doesn't belong to you. No good."

"Okay, pal! In America you gotta do what the boss tells you. And of course you can't take something that doesn't belong to you. Give us the packages. You're a good cabbie."

Felix, growing bolder, winked. "I didn't look inside, but I think you'll find Martell, Chivas, and Absolut. See you next Saturday, my friends."

Half an hour later, Felix's Checker, in line with the rest of them, crawled into the entry grotto. The doormen saw him and exchanged glances again. Some luggage was coming out at that very moment. But Felix was third in line.

Now Felix's heart was fluttering. Did these scumbags have no shame? Would they insult him after all? They did not.

"Checker!" barked the doorman.

What a vulture. I had seen Felix hit bottom. Dirty, unshaven, deserted by his wife. Worse yet, she went off with his cab owner, an Israeli.

One day Felix ran over to the coffee stand in the LaGuardia parking lot. When he came back, the Checker was lying on its belly, all four tires slashed. The message: don't steal jobs from your own at the Madison!

Nobody had seen anything, of course. So whose head should he split open with the jack crank?

But now Felix is reborn! He is bright and cheerful, works about ten hours a day, makes about fifteen drops; his weekends are sacred. Every Friday he brings his benefactors their cut in an envelope.

I listened to Felix; I watched him count the bookings—six twenties, four tens (a hack doesn't have to *tell* me how he made his money. Like any cabbie, all I have to do is glance at the dough: the handful of change, the bundle of crumpled, soggy singles.) I thanked the guy for the lesson, for his openness, and promised not to blab. And I thought, "Really, why shouldn't I take this tempting—and, above all, well-trodden—route? It's always easier to follow in someone else's footsteps. Why shouldn't I risk a hundred for a deal like that?" And then Felix had invited me to join him.

Early Saturday morning I put on a clean shirt, shaved, parked my Checker outside the liquor store, and went in. The salesman swooped down on me, but I waved him away. "Hang on. Let me think about it first."

Did I want to plunge into this swamp? I couldn't look these bastards in the eye. No, I'd better do it some other way. The Hilton wasn't the be-all and end-all.

"A bottle of Smirnoff, please," I said to the salesman, who had just about given me up. And I bought a bottle of cherry brandy for my wife, too.

Chapter Fourteen

AN HONEST DOORMAN

The number of drops, the harsh indicator of the quantity of passengers taking my cab, rose daily: twenty-eight, thirty-six, forty-
four. I was making money, of course, but I sweated blood for it. More
and more often I lacked the energy to get up in the morning, unable to
cup my hands to bring water to my face.

A sultry summer, meanwhile, was turning Manhattan into an oven; I
had to close the windows and turn on the air-conditioner.

"It's wonderful in here!" the passengers would say as they got in the
cab. But a driver pays for the privilege of using the air-conditioner with
more than extra gas. When he basks thirty minutes or so in the gentle,
breezy current of air—suddenly, zap! a red signal lights up on the
dashboard and the hapless Checker stops short in the middle of the
avenue. The overheated engine has cut out. Now push the cab to the
curb and wait until it cools down.

I had to go back to the Madison Hotel and the pack of Russians.
There they were, the Boss, Long Marik, the Sculptor, the same old
dreary faces. I never wanted to lay eyes on them again! You sit there for a
couple of hours and get a ten-dollar customer to LaGuardia. Like
porters unable to hoist a heavy burden onto their shoulders and thus
obliged to lessen its weight (although now they have to make two trips

instead of one), we paid for the hours lost at the hotel by working late, and in the morning, unrefreshed, barely able to turn the wheel, we camped outside the hotel again. I had started on a slippery downward path.

On a slow holiday afternoon we were parked at the Madison when a Ford with the number 8W12 joined the line. It was Uzbek's medallion; but the man behind the wheel was an American. He came over to us.

"Been waiting long?"

"Five minutes. Three cabs went to Connecticut already."

He laughed, appreciating the joke.

"You renting?" Tomato inquired cautiously.

"No, it's mine."

"Did you buy it from a Russian?" Tomato probed.

"How should I know if he was a Russian or an Eskimo? I bought it from a broker."

Uzbek lived at a remove from the Russian colony, somewhere in the Bronx; none of us knew his name. We remembered only his medallion number. Where he had gotten to we did not know either.

"They took his medallion away, sold it to pay the debts!"

"They've got no right, he's sick."

"He's in a wheelchair."

"He's pushing up the daisies!" the Doctor pronounced. But we could not tell whether he had heard something or was simply flaunting his perspicacity. "Remember what I told him?"

We remembered. If anyone did not hustle around the hotels, it was Uzbek. What had happened to him? What would happen to each of us?

Our only comfort was derived from chatting about our hero. Provoked intolerably, a valiant taxi driver, Richie, had clouted the insolent doorman, Sean, and had become our standard-bearer. His glory rose on the crest of a new wave when Sean came back from the hospital Richie had put him in.

Richie did not get cold feet and slink off. He sat there, waiting for an airport, as if nothing had ever happened. Sean did not try to reimpose order at the hotel anymore, and we chortled maliciously.

But Richie's star waned as unexpectedly as it had risen: he stole the portable TV from Frank, the young replacement doorman. Like many hotels, the Madison has two entrances, main and side. When Sean came back, Frank, the novice, was moved to the lower-ranking post, and there, in the doorman's cubicle by the side entrance, our hero perpetrated his shameful theft, giving every taxi driver a bad name and after that was seen at the Madison no more.

Chapter Fifteen

- - - - - - - - - -

THE CRIMINAL CASE

I went to the hearing for my no-standing ticket; the criminal charges would be dealt with later in an actual court.

"How do you plead?" asked the hearing arbitrator.

If I succeeded in getting out of this minor ordeal, it would be a big step toward winning the later criminal case as well. Acquitted here, I could produce documentary proof of my innocence there. "This strange policeman," I would say, laying today's acquittal on the judge's desk, "at first charged me with standing in an allegedly forbidden area. But when I pointed out to him the absurdity of his action, out of pure spite he could think of nothing better than to accuse me, a taxi driver, of 'incitement to riot'."

"Not guilty!" rang out my response to the arbitrator, a good-natured man whose sympathies were clearly with the real live people who occasionally happened to deviate from the dreary bureaucracy of the traffic regulations. I was not imagining this: the hearing immediately before my own, had ended with a promising "Case dismissed! Next!"

"Your honor!" I began solemnly.

"I am not 'your honor,'" said the arbitrator.

"Sir!" I corrected myself. "You know better than anyone the disgraceful tricks some policemen get up to on the streets of New York."

"Get to the point, please," the arbitrator interrupted.

If they are interrupted, especially in a formal situation, most people get flustered and start to waffle. Most people, but not I. Well in advance I had elaborated a highly persuasive if not, perhaps, entirely truthful version of the events. However, there was nobody here who could deny it. The cop whom I would be meeting face to face in criminal court had not been summoned to today's hearing, and I could say anything that came into my head. Nonetheless, my testimony was distinguished by its brevity.

"The taxi I was driving was stopped by a woman with a child in a stroller. I got out of the cab in order to put the stroller inside."

Who would raise a hand against such a cabbie? Besides, no one could doubt my truthful tone, and I could see that the arbitrator believed me.

"Is that all?" the arbitrator asked.

"I stopped for less than a minute." I said, and straightened my impeccably knotted necktie.

"I find you guilty," the arbitrator said.

"What!" I yelped.

"My decision is based on your testimony," the arbitrator explained readily. "Not only did you stop near a no-standing sign, but you got out of the cab as well. The fine is twenty-five dollars. Next!"

———

About ten cabs were gathered at the main entrance to the Madison; there was no point in my staying there, but among the drivers languishing in line I noticed Shmuel.

This legendary cabbie did not chase Madison guests away from his shiny Impala. He was never less than polite, but somehow, after talking with Shmuel, the customers took themselves off to the corner of their own accord.

"Excuse me, sir. You can't do things like that at this hotel," Shmuel would rebuke an impatient type who already had one foot in his cab. "Ask the doorman. Give him a dollar, he'll put you in a taxi."

And the antsy guy would flounce off to the corner. He would rather hail a cab himself. But quite often the guests, muttering "Daylight robbery," would indeed shove a green bill at the doorman. The doormen adored Shmuel.

I had to have a talk with this worldly cabbie: my day in criminal court was approaching, and after the hash I had made of the no-standing ticket, my confidence in my legal talents had diminished.

"Can you advise me what to do?" I asked Shmuel, beckoning him aside so the other Russians would not get involved in our conversation. But there was no getting away from those windbags; everyone wanted to put in his two cents.

"It's too late to ask for advice now," said the Sculptor.

"If you tell lies in court, they better be smart." The Boss wagged a didactic finger. "How come you told such a dumb one, Bagel?"

"Who asked you?" I said angrily, showing Shmuel the summons. "Can you figure out what they're hauling me into court for?"

Long Marik peeked over my shoulder. "Bagel, you still aren't through with the suitcase trouble? By the way, Shmuel, he doesn't have citizenship yet. That suitcase could cost him."

"What's citizenship got to do with it?" I said heatedly. "What suitcase? What are you babbling about?"

Shmuel gave me back the summons and said, "I have no idea what really went on there. You want my advice? You're welcome to it. Before you go to court, see a lawyer."

———

There was nothing to hang around for at the side entrance either: Frank, the junior doorman, was on the rampage. It would be futile to get in line behind Kim Il Sung and the Greek rookie, who was trying to "join the club" at the Madison. Nevertheless, I slowed down as I drove past, noticing an unusual disposition of the figures in front of the revolving door. The doorman was standing by the first cab, instead of where he was supposed to be, by the hotel entrance. The Greek and the Korean were sitting next to each other on the hood of the yellow Dodge; Frank seemed to be interrogating them.

"Who is this beggar?"

Something probably got stolen again, I thought and, not wanting to get drawn in, drove away.

The asphalt undulated under the feet of the passersby. My attempt to switch on the air conditioner, even at low power, was scotched when the engine died. I barely managed to make it to the Madison. Now I had to wait until the motor had cooled a little.

Just as they had been an hour before, the figures at the side entrance were not deployed according to the rules. The cabbies were not with their cabs. Frank had herded them into a straggly rank and was pacing back and forth in front of them, dripping sweat inside his heavy coat and repeating, in time to his footsteps:

"There is a beggar . . . the beggar has a brother . . . but . . ."

Here Frank had to pause; Ali Baba, standing in the ranks, spoon and thermos in hand, had gone AWOL in order to shoo away an old woman lingering by the revolving door. The unruly Syrian finally came back, whereupon, enunciating each word, the doorman uttered something incomprehensible.

"But the brother has no brothers!" He cocked his hat jauntily to one side and squinted slyly. *"Who is this beggar?"*

Had the ninety-degree heat had sent him slightly off the tracks.

"Who is this beggar?"

"My friend, how do you expect us to know?" Ali Baba protested obsequiously, spreading spoon and thermos in the air. "We're not educated people. We can't answer such complicated questions."

"May I get a taxi, for heaven's sake?" The old lady popped up from behind the Syrian and went for the doorman.

Frank clutched his head in his hands. He could not be in two places at once, to put peevish old women in taxis while simultaneously trying to enlighten a herd of dumb cabbies. He showered the rank with scorn, and, as if to say, "I'll do this to every fool who can't hack it," flung open the door of the first cab. The old dame who had caused all the trouble jumped in.

"Alexander's!"

Ali Baba ground his teeth but got in and started the engine.

———

I was hustling around the city, looking for suitcases. By now I could scent them as a hound does a hare; but time after time nimbler cabbies would snatch up the baggage from under my nose. I was tired, and kept losing the race.

I stopped at the Hilton.

"Checker!" the doorman called.

Carts piled high with luggage were standing at the door, but the command I was expecting, "Open the trunk!" did not follow. The jumpseats crashed: my cab was boarded by five chortling guys with nametags pinned to the lapels of their slick jackets, while a sixth, a nerdy type, was tugging at the handle of the front passenger door so as to get in next to me.

I would have been quite within my rights not to let him in, and to throw the whole bunch of them out: a Checker is not supposed to carry more than five passengers. But the guys were going to Wall Street, which was not a bad trip. I unlocked the door and, as the nerd got in, told his pals that in principle a driver had no right to take six people, and they ought to have hired two cabs; and, of course, they were saving themselves some money, while my head was on the block. My transparent hint was picked up immediately.

"We get it!" the crew roared cheerfully. "We'll be terribly grateful!" That was enough for me—a couple of bucks over the meter.

The more a cabbie knows about what is going on in the city, the more money he makes. The nametags on their lapels showed there was some kind of convention gathered at the Hilton. I did not give a hoot about what sort of convention it was, but I certainly did want to know when it was going to end. On that day a thousand checkouts from the hotel would mean a thousand airport trips, and then I should not waste a minute on the streets or at the Madison. With so many suitcases in the Hilton driveway, there would be enough for everybody, hustlers *and* regular drivers. This was why, while we were still outside the hotel, I asked:

"So when are you going home, gentlemen?"

"Tomorrow! Tomorrow!" the gentlemen shouted, and only after this did I inquire who they were.

"Attorneys! Attorneys!" Look what luck had dropped in my lap: a legal consultation, gratis, would be very timely.

"The Hilton's stuffed to the rafters with stupid lawyers!" the lads went on noisily.

"What about smart ones?" I said, playing along. "Aren't there any?"

"Sure! Sure there are!" they howled. "Larry Fishman's smart!"

"The smartest!"

"Brilliant!" And they started chanting: "Lar-ry-Fish-man! Lar-ry-Fish-man!"

The nerd sitting next to me blushed.

"Joking aside, Mr. Fishman," I said, leaning on his lap to open the glove compartment and extract the summons from it, "I would like to consult you about this."

What a nice bunch they were, not yet grown out of their student ways. They were dying to lark around and crow about it—Wall Street! The Hilton! The world had become their oyster only yesterday, but some pesky cabbie (what did they care about me?) was asking their advice, and they quieted down. They even stopped teasing their Larry, who looked as if he were sniffing my summons as he studied it with nearsighted eyes. He seemed embarrassed about something, even a little guilty.

"You see, *Vladimir*"—he read my name without stammering; his tongue was trained to twist itself around unpronounceable foreign words—"your problem isn't really our province. We work for corporations, you know."

My anxiety was aroused: a professional was having trouble with my case.

"Cut the crap, Larry! Give it here!" Several hands were held out through the partition at once. Larry looked questioningly at me and, when I nodded, gave his friends the summons.

"What did you make of it, anyway?" I asked impatiently.

"It's a criminal court summons," said Larry.

"I know that. But what am I accused of?"

A boyish face peeked through the partition. "Don't take it personally."

"Take what personally?"

"This is the law they generally use on"—and here the young lawyer let drop yet another strange word I did not know.

"What does that mean?" I said.

"Prostitutes."

Very funny! I went right off those cutups. They had picked a terrific target for their razzing.

"I did warn you not to take it personally," the boyish voice said in self-justification. "We're not specialists in this area." Larry said.

But I had no desire to listen to them. I took back my summons and, inscrutable, drove on to Wall Street: a hump-backed, twisting alleyway, which, as everyone knows, governs the entire financial world and yet is so narrow that even two tiny Volkswagens, let alone a pair of potbellied Checkers, could not pass each other in it.

———

I had done the right thing in snubbing the bumptious youths and cutting short a conversation on a topic that mattered greatly to me; I had no regrets. Manhattan was teeming with legal conventioneers that day, and I did not have to seek out a lawyer in the crowd. He found me himself.

"Will you go to the Hilton?"

A tired, important-looking businessman, a fat brown folder bursting with papers under his arm. He awaited the cabbie's decision submissively: would I take him or not?

"Are you a lawyer?" I peered at the nametag on the lapel. Was he or wasn't he?

The important-looking man suddenly blew up.

"What is this, you won't take a lawyer but you will take a stockbroker? Or is it the other way around?" He got into the cab with an autocratic air and slammed the door. "The Hilton!"

"No need to get so worked up, mister," I said amicably. "I just wanted to ask you, if you were a lawyer, to sit next to me up front: I have a problem I'd like to ask you about."

And there it was again: no sooner had this man—not a recent graduate, but an American getting on in years, to whom, moreover, I had been impolite enough to put a stupid question before asking him to get in the cab—no sooner had he understood that the cabbie's tactlessness was unintentional than he expressed his willingness to hear my story.

"Well, what seems to be the trouble?"

"Take a look, please, sir. What is this?"

"Hmm. I'm not really a specialist in criminal cases."

But I had already heard this excuse and I asked him straight out:

"Could a prostitute receive a summons like this?"

"Hmm. If you put it that way, well, yes."

"But there's no rhyme or reason to it!" I burst into a passion; some legal quirk that confounded common sense had turned against me in earnest. "How can a taxi driver, a hardworking man, and a prostitute be charged with the same offense?"

"The law does not take into account the occupation of the lawbreaker."

Now it was my turn to say, "Hmm." Trying to conceal the timidity that possessed me, I articulated with effort: "Could the judge's decision in such a case affect my chance of getting citizenship?"

The man was already tired of answering my questions, however.

"Look, I don't want to scare you. As a lawyer I can say one thing: you should never go to criminal court without an attorney."

"But how can I get an attorney? Where would I get the money to pay for one?"

My passenger took out a business card, jotted something on the back of it, and said:

"This is the phone number of a very good lawyer, a friend of mine. Call him; he won't ask you for a lot of money."

The word "sir" as a form of address was gradually disappearing from my vocabulary; I made more and more use of the sassy "mister." When, for example, an improperly closed rear door began to rattle alarmingly on the bumpy pavement, I would say, "Mister, if you go flying out of the cab when we make the next turn, who's going to pay the fare?"

When my Checker was overtaken by a police car, signal lights blazing and siren deafening, I would say, "Mister, can you guess where they're going in such a rush?"

"Where?"

"To get a cup of coffee."

I treated tourists to the sights of New York, and, since I did not know the city well enough to be a real guide, I invented things shamelessly.

"Rockefeller and Nixon lived in this building," I would inform my customers quite truthfully as we drove past 810 Fifth Avenue, but once begun it was hard to stop.

"Elizabeth Taylor and Richard Burton were married in this church."

The ladies would gasp. I never got caught, and my biggest success involved my compatriot Mikhail Baryshnikov.

"Did you have a good day?" a typist, worn out with working overtime, asked me. She could not afford to ride around in taxis, of course. She took my cab because she was afraid of the subway at night. But after yielding to the modest luxury of my Checker for a few minutes, feeling her tired face become more youthful in the half-dark of the cab, the woman began to unwind and, hearing that I had had a good day, interpreted my answer quite superficially. "You probably picked up some celebrities."

How could I disappoint her now?

"You won't believe it, but just before you got in I drove Baryshnikov and Liza Minnelli to the Russian Tea Room."

A barely audible, stifled moan: "Oooh!"

An American woman cannot give less than a dollar tip to a cab driver who picked up Baryshnikov. Even a typist. I was already sorry I had lied to her. But my passenger was in such joyous anticipation of the stories she would tell tomorrow to her co-workers and her boss and her neighbors—about *the* cab she had ridden in yesterday—that she just could not help wanting to be more generous than all the stars who had graced my Checker.

I regularly had my cab cleaned at the car wash, thanks partly to Baryshnikov's reflected glory—and partly because I used to show my gullible passengers the "women's prison."

When you drive onto the Triborough Bridge (which I did every day), level with the roadway, rising high off the ground, stands a trio of gray buildings with barred windows. I don't remember who happened to mention that this was apparently a women's prison. I had no idea whether it was true or not, but I pointed out the buildings to everyone.

"By the way, that place over there is the women's prison."

And the loudest, most cheerful of my passengers would stop talking and become quiet and thoughtful. A women's prison!

———

In the line at the ship terminal I ended up with a mother hen, all freckles and fussiness, extraordinarily attentive to her brood of four daughters. The equally freckled sisters, diminutive replicas of their mom, were so like one another as to differ only in size, like Russian matryoshki dolls. I put the mother in the front seat so she would be more comfortable, but her whole being was there, behind us, with her offspring, whom even now, on the road to LaGuardia, she tried to stuff with everything good and beautiful (but above all educational!) that one could possibly extract out of a cab ride.

"Shall we go through Central Park?" I dropped the hint with a view to an extra trip across the Triborough.

"Fancy that!" the mother exclaimed. "Now you're going to see Central Park!"

"Christopher Columbus is buried here." As if to an old acquaintance, I nodded toward the statue of the great navigator, standing in the middle of the circle named after him.

"Fancy that!" the careworn mother nudged her matryoshki.

We sped over the Triborough Bridge, past the gray buildings.

"By the way, that place over there is the New York women's prison."

"Fancy that!" The kids peered out, silent.

The mother was warm-hearted as well as funny. With an effort, she managed to tear herself away from her freckled daughters for long enough to give a particle of her attention to the cab driver. And her questions were not reduced to the vulgar "How's business?" She wondered when I had left the house that day. Did I still have a long time to work?

I replied that, like many New York cabbies, I worked roughly eighty hours a week. "But there isn't a cabbie in America," I said, quite reckless by now, "who works as hard as a mom with four kids!"

The poor woman was all choked up. It was as if her husband had wished her a happy birthday on the radio. Her blue eyes grew moist and she gazed at me, pressing a hand to her breast.

For a month afterward I would tell other drivers about the tip I was rewarded with for my improvisation, but, since I was speaking the truth, nobody wanted to believe me.

When was this? Spring? Summer? Fall? Running around and around the city, like a hamster on a wheel, a cab driver loses his sense of time.

————

I called the number the helpful attorney had written down, and his colleague, the "inexpensive lawyer," explained over the phone that it was not necessary to decipher the policeman's scrawl immediately; we would meet in court and would have plenty of time to discuss everything there.

My case would undoubtedly be settled; however, if I wanted him actually to appear in court on the appointed day, *three hundred* dollars must be paid in advance. Not because he did not trust me; that was the general rule among criminal lawyers.

I did not know what to do. I was afraid of the court, but I begrudged him the money too.

In the late afternoon rush hour, when taxis are in great demand, I was dropping a customer off at the entrance to Central Park when I heard a doorman whistling from the other side of the street. Outside the Hotel St. Moritz I could dimly make out a fiberboard suitcase. There seemed no guarantee that this unimpressive object was going to the airport and we were separated by a double yellow line. If a policeman were to spot me crossing it . . .

Understanding my hesitation, the doorman gave another blast on his whistle and flapped his arms up and down like a bird to show he had an honest-to-goodness airport job. A doorman would never deceive a cabbie with this pantomime; you don't joke about these things. I turned against the traffic pouring into the park from the Avenue of the Americas, and not in vain. The fiberboard suitcase was headed for LaGuardia.

"Go through the park," ordered my passenger. This was playing right into my hands: through the park meant taking the Triborough Bridge. However, once I had made the illegal turn, I could not deny myself the taxi driver's innocent pleasure of lecturing the customer.

"What a nerve, asking a driver to do things like that! The doorman let me know you're late for a plane, and I already made one three-point moving violation for your sake. So why ask me to make another?"

We were well into the park by then, but I kept on picking at it like a scab.

"I don't suppose you would have paid my fine, would you?"

In answer to my attack he simply yawned.

"A cop can't give you a ticket when I'm in the cab."

I went off the deep end. "Aren't you ashamed, bragging like that?"

The passenger raised his voice too. "Watch your mouth, driver! You know who I am?"

"That's the last thing I want to know, mister. And why should I care anyway?"

"I'm the Chicago police commissioner," the customer snapped at me. But this did not pacify me at all.

"Aha!" I shrieked, more enraged than ever. "I've got my hands on one of you at last!"

"What do you mean, 'got your hands on me'? You'd better think about what you're saying, driver."

This fiftyish wiseguy, who had taken it into his head to tease me, obviously had not guessed that I was not really angry; for what could give a beat-up cabbie more joy than a means to bare his soul and unload his burdens on somebody else?

"The only thing you know how to do is take it out on cab drivers," I rumbled, as if I really believed he was a police commissioner. "You don't have any time left to catch real criminals!"

"Don't talk crap about stuff you know nothing about!" snapped this impostor. "I always tell my guys to leave a cabbie alone if he wangles a couple of extra bucks, like you figured you'd do just now, dragging me all the way to the Triborough. I saw through you right away."

"But you told me to go through the park yourself," I said, really upset now.

"Imagine the fuss you would have kicked up if I'd asked you to take the Queensboro Bridge," my passenger muttered. He knew his way around. "Never mind. But if you ever try moving drugs, you sonofabitch, the New York commissioner and I will put you away like that! You follow me?"

"Then I will!" I exclaimed. "Sure I'll move drugs, because you don't give a guy a chance to make an honest buck. You won't leave us in peace. You hand out criminal court summonses for nothing!"

"Bullshit! Cops don't write criminal summonses for nothing. You can tell that to anybody but me."

"Oh, they don't, huh?" I exclaimed, performing the acrobatic feat of reaching into the glove compartment without slowing up. "What do you call this, then?" I shoved the grubby summons toward the backseat. "You tell me what this is!"

"Ah! SOLICITING!" My knowledgeable customer, deciphering the indecipherable gerund and the essence of my crime, shook with malicious laughter. "Forty-second and Park! Now I get it."

"What do you mean, you get it?" I retorted automatically.

"It's the airport bus stop outside the ticket office. You were stealing fares from the bus company. How many people did you manage to pull in before you got pinched?"

"Three," I admitted, and this strange man actually slapped his knee in a surge of incomprehensible emotion.

"I knew he must be a good guy!"

"Who?"

"The cop."

"Oh yeah, really wonderful," I said sarcastically.

"You better believe it! A heart of gold," the passenger said, nodding his head in affirmation. "Let me tell you, he was totally within his rights to stick you with a busing ticket, fare-doubling, misconduct—but he felt sorry for you."

"He gave me a no-standing."

"While he could have booked you for overcharging. Then you really would have had something to bellyache about!"

"What do you mean, 'overcharging'?" I said indignantly. "I was asking six bucks apiece to take them to Kennedy. I had no idea that taxi drivers can't pick up passengers at a bus stop. And this is the first time I've ever heard this word 'soliciting.'"

My customer believed me at once and his tone softened.

"That's how you got into this pickle," he said. "You slipped up out of ignorance, and the cop thought you were just an out-and-out hustler. Put yourself in his position: he's standing at his post, and some cabbie starts playing dirty pool right under his nose. You follow me? What do you think he should have done?"

"But what should *I* do now?" I said bitterly. "I have to go to court next Monday, the lawyer wants three hundred bucks—"

"Why do you need a lawyer at the first hearing anyway?"

None of the professionals had told me anything about this.

"You mean there'll be a second one?"

"Sure! This is only the preliminary hearing. All the judge will ask is how you plead, guilty or not guilty. He won't give you more than thirty seconds. There'll be hundreds of poor assholes like you there. You follow me?"

The barrier lifted to let us onto the Triborough Bridge.

"The women's prison." I nodded in the direction of the trio of gray buildings, treating the guest from Chicago to one of the sights of New York.

"Bullshit!" The guest brushed it aside. "It's a mental hospital for the criminally insane. You would have done better telling the passengers that Son of Sam's in there."

Scratching the back of his head, the passenger went on. "Listen to me. Your only chance of getting out of this mess is at the first hearing. If you plead not guilty, for the second hearing the judge will call on the policeman who wrote the summons. The cop will testify, and that'll be that."

"And if I say I'm guilty, what will happen then?" I asked. But at this my benevolent consultant suddenly became annoyed.

"You poor schmuck, if all you took was six bucks apiece and now you're going to plead guilty, why the hell am I bothering with you? When they accuse you, you have to defend yourself!" My well-wisher was so carried away that my faintheartedness made him sick. "It's not a big deal to beat this summons, but the problem is, the judge won't let you open your mouth. You follow me?"

Irritated by the fact that I could not follow a damn thing or discuss my case seriously with him either, the passenger began to think aloud, biting his lip.

"The judge will only let you give one of two standard replies. 'Guilty' or 'Not guilty.' You can use a third, 'Guilty with explanations,' but you don't have any explanations. What can you say? That you didn't know? Judges can't stand that. He'll get mad and slap you with something that'll make sure you'll know next time. By the way, don't even think of talking to the judge the way you were talking to me. There's nothing worse than making a judge mad. You follow me?"

We were getting near LaGuardia, and as if to spite me, he fell silent. He turned away and looked out the window. He was probably just fed up with my problems. We had reached the ramp leading to the main terminal when the Checker trembled at his thunderous "Ha!" and a sort of satanic inspiration lit up my customer's face.

"*NOT* GUILTY—WITH EXPLANATIONS!" he pronounced, in a voice that was hoarse with excitement.

"What sort of nonsense is that?" I thought sadly.

But my customer repeated the nonsense again, savoring each word.

"NOT GUILTY—WITH EXPLANATIONS!" He was in raptures over this ruse, which I could not make head or tail of.

"Supposing I say this—"

"Don't you understand, no judge has ever heard anyone say it before!"

"So what?"

"The judge will be surprised!"

"But what good will that do me?"

We were facing each other under the American Airlines sign.

"Oh, please," he said, "What have I done to deserve this?" He had put such inventiveness, such emotion into my case, and I repelled him with my obtuseness. "If the judge is surprised, he'll say, '*What happened?*' and that'll give you a chance to speak. Good luck, Lobas!"

He picked up the suitcase, which was standing between us.

"Sir, where are you going?" I cried in despair. "After all this, how can you leave me to my fate?"

"Give me a break! What else do you want?"

"What else! The judge will probably say 'What happened?' But what do I tell him?"

My good fairy looked at his watch. At this rate he might miss his plane.

"Listen carefully. When the judge says 'What happened?' you just repeat this: 'Your honor, let me draw your attention to one circumstance—'"

But I was not listening. With a cry of "Hold it! Hold it!" I flung myself into the cab, grabbed my pen and my trip sheet, and scribbled all over that day's list the words of the great speech I would give to the criminal court taught me by a stranger passing himself off as the Chicago police commissioner.

Chapter Sixteen

IN COURT

D riving up to the Madison, I remembered I had not eaten since breakfast. At the side entrance I gave the keys to Alberto, an Argentinian, to shift my Checker if the line moved up, and ran two blocks over to a cart under a striped umbrella. Instead of a measly hot dog I bought a whopping sausage with all the trimmings. And ran back to the cab.

I sat on the hood, and, alternately blowing on the sausage and testing it with my lips, settled down to observe the loony doorman.

Frank had mustered the cabbies again (unless he had never dismissed them). He was pacing back and forth in front of the "rank," repeating in time to his footsteps:

"A father and a son . . ."

Left, right!

". . . were driving in a car."

Left, right!

"They got into an accident . . ."

Left, right!

". . . and the father died."

"Poor man!" said Kim Il Sung in sham sympathy for another's misfortune. Frank frowned and continued.

"When they got to the emergency room, the doctor said, 'I cannot operate on this boy. He is my son.'"

"I've never had an accident," Ali Baba boasted, fishing a piece of meat out of his thermos. "I'm a good driver!"

Shutting up the chatterbox with a commanding gesture, Frank stopped dead and flummoxed the drivers with an unexpected question: *"Who is the doctor?"*

Kim Il Sung, Ali Baba, and Alberto remained glumly silent.

"Who is the doctor?" the doorman repeated, but the unfortunate cabbies, cowering beneath his irascible stare, were mute.

A guest emerged from the revolving door, and Frank snickered mockingly.

"Taxi, sir?"

"Yes, please!" the guest responded to the nice doorman opening the cab door for him.

"Mister Frank!" Alberto whined. "Better I pay you a dollar."

"Two, if they bring out a Kennedy," the Korean wheedled. In vain. Frank put the customer in the first cab and sent Alberto off to the Time-Life building. Kim and Ali glanced at each other like condemned men.

"So, *who is the doctor?*" The implacable Frank went on torturing the cabbies.

I swallowed the last of the sausage, and at that moment an unseen angel flew down to me out of the sky, alighted beside me on the hood, and whispered, *"Mo-ther."*

"The boy's mother!" I said aloud.

A heaping spoonful of rice froze on the way to the Syrian's mouth. Frank squinted in my direction. I sensed that another important moment in my life had arrived.

The squeaky voice of the Korean broke the silence. "Of course the doctor is the boy's mother," he said casually. "That's why she didn't want to operate on him."

Did you ever see such a chiseler? I never would have thought my friend Kim capable of such meanness. But Frank ignored his blather and strode up to me.

"How did you guess?"

I looked down modestly.

"Terrific!" said Frank. "I was the only one of all the guys I bunked with who could guess the riddle."

The doorman looked me over from the bald spot at the top of my head, past the grizzled curly hairs on my puny chest and the shirt coming untucked from my jeans, down to my long-unshined shoes. There was probably not a single sailor this sloppy on his entire battle cruiser.

"Well then, listen to this one," Frank said, giving me a penetrating stare.

"A train one mile long is traveling through a tunnel, which is also one mile long."

The scheming Kim Il Sung pricked up his ears; gluttonous Ali Baba thrust the spoon into his thermos like a sword into a scabbard.

"Traveling at sixty miles an hour, how long will the train take to get out of the tunnel?"

"One minute!" the Korean blurted out. Frank did not even glance at him, while I racked my brains in agony. Somewhere, trapped in the folds of my gray matter, were there not the remains of the wisdom battered into it long, long ago, when my head was still shaggy, by our physics teacher, a veteran of Stalingrad with a wooden stump where his right leg had been? Seemingly he had not been wrong when he bawled me out: "Lobas, you're dead from the neck up! You'll end up scrubbing floors." He had turned out to be a prophet, since I had indeed ended up, if not a janitor, then at best a cabbie.

"So how long does the train take?" Frank, growing impatient, asked again, but once more I sensed someone breathing gently in my ear: *Two minutes!*

"Two minutes," I said, and Frank slapped me on the back. "Beautiful!"

"One minute," the Korean argued.

"One!" Ali Baba was getting sore.

"Stay with your cabs!" Frank squelched them and put his arm around me. He contemplated my visage as joyfully as if it had been the Hispanic girl's.

"You're Russian?" he asked.

"Yes," I replied. There, however, our conversation petered out.

Frank sincerely wanted to make friends with a man possessed of a similar level of intelligence, but he did not know what to talk to me about. I wanted to strengthen our budding friendship even more than Frank; yet I did not know how to do it, either. What could I talk about with a young doorman? Girls? Baseball?

Well aware that if I were ever to retell this story nobody would believe it—this one you must have made up, they would say—I asked Frank to write down for me the riddles about the doctor and the train. Frank agreed eagerly, found a place to write, and even added another, very complicated riddle about ten apples, which afterward neither I nor any of my acquaintances, including my old neighborhood friend Professor Stanley, could solve. On the other hand, Stanley did say that Frank had not made a single grammatical error in transcribing the riddles, and that all the commas were in the right place.

While Frank was writing, Kim and Ali Baba chased customers away from the hotel entrance, but then the doorman returned to his post and the airport guys looked dejected. A bulky woman carrying a smart briefcase emerged from the revolving door.

"Taxi?" asked Frank.

"Yes, please."

"Where are you going?" Frank inquired, and all three of us were instantly on the alert. This was something new. Up to now the honest doorman had never asked such a question of anyone.

The woman replied that she was going to Kings County Hospital in Brooklyn, and added something else which none of us could hear. But even without hearing it we realized it must be important.

"Do you *want* to go to Kings County Hospital?" Frank asked the Korean.

"I've been dreaming of it all my life!" Kim snapped, indicating that he had noticed the change in the doorman's approach.

"What about you?" Frank asked Ali. "You *know* this hospital?"

"I don't go to Brooklyn," the Syrian answered cockily.

However, the doorman did not bother to curse out the impudent drivers, merely opened the door of *my* Checker and invited the woman to get in.

By now convinced that the doorman had been bluffing and was twisting them around his little finger, both cabbies gnashed their teeth.

"The first cab gets the first job!"

"There's a line here!"

"You, and you!" Frank barked at them. "Move those crates of yours out, right now. You got it? This is the first cab!" He pointed to the black driver's Dodge parked behind me.

A few minutes later, as I drove out onto the highway, I found out what the word we had not heard was. "And *back* . . ."

"Kings County Hospital and *back!*" That was what the woman with the smart briefcase had said to Frank.

Did I know where it was? Of course not, for heaven's sake. All I knew was that Frank was *wangling* this job for me. How could I stutter that I did not know the way? The only time a taxi driver does not know the way is when the trip is unprofitable. If the address you want lies outside the city limits and therefore pays double the meter, we know everything! The harder it is to find the address, the more the cabbie will get lost and the more you will pay.

And what if the passenger becomes indignant when you ask for directions? You undertook to get me to the hospital, she may say, but you haven't a notion where it is.

Just let her try! If she dares let out a squeak I would make her blush to the roots. For what? For ingratitude. Haven't all the other cabbies refused to take her outright?

But the woman was not the least indignant. Driving south along the FDR Drive, with only the vaguest impression of where in the enormous borough of Brooklyn my passenger had to get to, I knew something much more important than the location of some stupid hospital. I knew that my passenger was a psychiatrist from Houston; she had flown into New York for one day only. With a clear conscience, I skimmed along the most roundabout route there was—the Belt Parkway.

———

By the time I found the hospital, there was already more on the meter than I would have made if I had gotten a passenger to Kennedy. That day, naturally, the money came quickly and easily, and I was home by eight in the evening. Seeing me walk in so unusually early, my wife turned white as a sheet, but immediately realized from my expression that nothing bad had happened. I took a quick shower and the whole family sat down to dinner in splendid friendliness. The next morning I drove my wife to school in Manhattan, and by nine that evening was home again. This time my wife was no longer frightened to see me walk in, and asked, "So you saw your Frank?"

"How on earth could I have seen Frank," I replied, barely containing myself, "when the wine wholesalers' convention at the Americana finished today? You think Frank works at the Americana?"

Only then did my wife realize how ridiculous her question had been.

"I didn't think," she said.

"One ought to think at least now and then," I joked, tempering my wife's little slip, but neither she nor my son seemed to appreciate the witticism.

They sat staring dumbly at their plates, and listened unenthusiastically to my highly diverting account of that day's two LaGuardias and two Kennedys picked up at the Americana, and what big spenders the wine wholesalers were, even better than lawyers: one had left me a four-dollar tip, another $3.65! But neither my wife nor my son managed to evince delight even for decency's sake; they did not say "Wow!" or "How about that?" as any cabman would have done in their place.

Hurt by my loved ones' indifference, I did not even bother to mention the merry band of rich people slumming it whom I had picked up that day. One of them, whose name was Charlie, put his friends in my cab for "a lark" (instead of a limousine); they chuckled over this the whole way, and prodded that wag Charlie to tell them what caper he would think up next. If they had started the day in a yellow cab, what could they expect later? Eh, Charlie?

"Dad, I need new sneakers." My son interrupted my thoughts.

"Didn't we just get you sneakers?" I said, quite without meaning to reproach my son; my wife, however, felt she had to stick up for him.

"But you know he's playing soccer!"

I did know. And I was pleased by the progress he was making. Unfortunately, the sort of sneakers he was buying now cost about the same as two Kennedys. It was hard to explain how much I begrudged the money made in my Checker.

"I've got an idea!" I said brightly. "Let's try to have the old ones repaired, and if that doesn't work—"

"They don't repair sneakers in America," my son muttered, gazing fixedly at the floor.

"But we're not Americans," I riposted playfully. "There's a Russian shoe-repair shop in Brighton Beach. Why don't you stop by and ask?"

What was so hurtful about that? But the boy flared up. He left the table without thanking his mother or pushing his chair in. It was abominable. I raised a finger, but my wife grabbed me by the arm. I wanted to tell the young man to come back and push the chair in, but my wife covered my mouth with her hand.

The door slammed. I tried to free my arm.

"I'd like to know why, whenever I call, you both always tell me to come home as soon as I can."

My wife let go of my arm. "Because we never see you."

"Well, here you are—you've seen me."

"I've always been proud," said my wife, "that we don't fight about money in our family!"

I was also proud of this, which was probably why I said, "The fuss wasn't because of money."

"Then what?"

"It's because of the uncalled-for way you take sides!"

My wife got angry: she was being sincere, and I was not. Her green eyes blazed, and she looked so unfamiliar, and so beautiful, that I instantly wanted to repent and explain why I was turning into this petty domestic tyrant and at least tell her about today's good-time rich guys: how Charlie the joker gave me a five when he settled up (with $3.95 on the meter) and told me to keep the change, and how all his cheerful pals suddenly got mad. They saw nothing funny in *this* stunt at all; they were too embarrassed to take the dollar I held out to them, and began to tell Charlie off even more, saying that this time he had really lost all sense of proportion. Charlie defended himself. He had left me a dollar-five because I was "a nice guy." But one of his friends, voicing the opinion of the rest, replied, "Sure, he's a nice guy, nobody's arguing. But why spoil such a nice guy?"

I could not tell my wife about this, however. If I had explained to her what the work I did now was really like, her face would have shriveled like a party balloon the morning after, and she would have said something I had already heard a few times from her during this taxi-driving year:

"Tell me: what did we come here for? Tell me that!"

———

The vestibule of the Manhattan criminal court is semidarkness beneath an immensely high vaulted ceiling, a flagstone floor, the unceasing hum of the crowd, and an unaccountable, oppressive commotion.

"Not guilty—with explanations!" I kept repeating to myself, like a mantra, but all the while a cold, repulsive toad of an idea was creeping into my mind: had the passenger from the St. Moritz Hotel just been pulling my leg? For all I knew, the whole thing could be a practical joke, which would really screw me up now. What if the judge got angry about this *not guilty with explanations* and clapped me behind bars for thirty days?

The clerk at the information window searched for a long time but finally found my case number (they hadn't lost it, dammit!) and sent me to Room 6, which was as long as a subway station and chock full with two or three hundred swarthy criminals, half of whom were black teenagers. Finding an empty chair with difficulty, I took up my place in the next-to-last row.

Everyone stood up; a stately-looking Jew in a black gown mounted the rostrum. A court officer, revolver on hip, began to call the criminals up to the foot of the bench. He shouted out the charges in unintelligible accents, and the criminals, one after the other—to a man—pleaded guilty.

They probably realized that the judge deciding their fate was a particularly terrifying one, I reasoned, noticing that none of the accused dared even suggest to the judge anything about "explanations," let alone declare their innocence.

"Guilty!"

"Guilty!"

"Guilty!"

However, after a short time had passed—half an hour, perhaps—my hearing, growing sharper as it became accustomed to the acoustics of the booming hall, suddenly caught the words of the sentence that the judge passed on the hoodlum pleading guilty at that moment.

"The fine is five dollars!"

I started. It couldn't be! I must have misheard. But the next dialogue between judge and criminal repeated the preceding one word for word.

"Guilty."

"The fine is five dollars."

My overhasty opinion of the judge's harshness instantly switched to the opposite one. "What a revolting travesty of justice," I thought, observing how all these—murderers! muggers! rapists!—were leaving the courtroom smirking impudently, no doubt in order to go straight out and do it again.

I find this scene extremely instructive, in the sense that too often and too incautiously do we take any nonsense for the truth, so long as the story-teller begins his yarn with the magic words "I saw it with my own eyes." After all, I was also an eyewitness to the farce taking place in Manhattan's criminal court. I heard it all with my own ears! And if the officer with the revolver had called my name early on that morning, that is, had I not ended up hanging around the courtroom for several hours, I would un-doubtedly later have told every one of my passengers that in my presence the judge sentenced a good hundred cutthroat recidivists to five-dollar fines. And my listeners would have boiled with righteous indignation.

The officer appeared to have forgotten about me, and as seats closer to the bench became vacant, I began to tiptoe toward the front in short rushes: at least there I would not get stabbed by one of these bandits. Reaching the third or fourth row, I could now hear not only the sentences but also the charges that the officer shouted out, and I soon realized that all the felons in my courtroom fell into two distinct categories. The teenagers' crimes consisted in either running across subway tracks or across a highway. It was they whom the judge fined five dollars apiece, while the older offenders were Harlem gypsies, those who say about themselves, "We are not yellow, we go anywhere." These unlucky cabbies, who earn their crust in the ghetto, carry passengers whom the yellow kings will not usually pick up—in cabs with no medallions or insurance, in beat-up old wagons. One man's cab, it was revealed, did not even have license plates.

The judge determined the severity of these sins by weight.

"Illegally operating! Unregistered cab! Uninsured! Uninspected! No livery plates! No driver's license!" boomed the officer with the revolver, tossing the tickets one by one onto the table standing between himself and the guilty cabbie. Then the officer gathered the tickets up into a bundle and held it up so the judge could see it better. His eyes narrowed, the judge would assess the bundle. "Fifty dollars!" or, if the bundle was fatter: "Seventy dollars!"

After a few hours, I was so at home in the courtroom I began to get bored.

"*The People of New York versus Vladimir Lobas!*" cried the court officer, as if suddenly recollecting me, and I tottered toward the bench on unwilling legs.

The black audience went quiet, and in the silence I could read their thoughts as though they were my own turned inside out: this honky must have really done something if he's ended up in criminal court along with us.

"Soliciting!" the officer informed the judge, with a morose expression.

"NOT GUILTY—WITH EXPLANATIONS!" I blurted out, and fell silent, choked with terror.

The court officer sniffed skeptically and adjusted the revolver on his hip, just in case.

And here the first prediction of the passenger from the St. Moritz came true. The black-gowned figure stirred; the judge leaned over the edge of the bench and looked down at me, his blinking eyes round with astonishment.

"What happened, cabbie?" asked the judge.

It was too late to back out now. The speech which the "police commissioner" had taught me, and which I had learned by heart, burst out of me like champagne out of an unchilled bottle.

"Your Honor! I ask you to consider one circumstance only—the location of the crime I am accused of. It's that godforsaken Forty-second Street. My cab was surrounded by scores of prostitutes soliciting men. Scores of pimps were approaching passersby inviting them into whorehouses! Scores of drug dealers were offering people marijuana, pills, cocaine, whatever. But out of all of this wonderful bunch the policeman singled *me* out. The most dangerous criminal was a cab driver, who labors seventy-two hours a week by the sweat of his brow. I ask you, your Honor, is that fair?"

The courtroom rocked with laughter. The judge waved both hands and shouted, enveloping me in a Jewish accent thick as honey.

"Sha! Sha! Enough already! Cabbie, will you shut your mouth? You'll maybe let *me* get a word in?"

I lapsed into obedient silence.

The courtroom went quiet in anticipation of the sentence.

"Criminal case number . . ."

The judge read an endlessly long number aloud, smacking his lips, and, having reduced me to jelly, concluded thus:

". . . dismissed due to lack of evidence!"

Chapter Seventeen

--- --- --- --- --- --- --- --- --- --- ---

ENCOUNTER IN A JEWISH CEMETERY

Only two days had passed since I had last seen Frank. A month before we had barely been on speaking terms, and now we met like bosom buddies. To begin with, Frank told me the news: last night, in Room 2214, a prostitute had killed a guest.

The German travel agent, who was accompanying a group of tourists from Munich, kept a substantial wad of cash in his wallet for unforeseen expenses en route. The prostitute, whom he had picked up on his first evening in New York, somehow got wind of the money. She managed to slip her customer a Mickey Finn, and, when he fell asleep, not only took the money, but, instead of a goodbye kiss, slit him from ear to ear with a razor.

We got into an argument. I was sure they would not catch the prostitute, while Frank was equally certain they would. Chuckling and slapping each other on the back, we switched to the episode of the psychiatrist from Houston and the neat trick my new pal had played on those morons Ali Baba and Kim Il Sung.

"And *back!*" I chortled.

"And *back*, Vladimir!" Frank winked.

I pulled the two dollars I had ready, out of my pocket.

"Oh, no, Vladimir, no!" Frank said. He was an *honest* doorman, wasn't he? And so I stood there like a fool, holding my two bucks and not knowing what to do.

But why did you feel bound to do anything at all? Was it really necessary to drag Frank down into the muck along with you by foisting your lousy bribe on him? All I wanted was to get home tomorrow, and the day after tomorrow, at ten in the evening rather than three in the morning. But what doorman will keep asking every hotel guest where he's going, and swindle the line of cabbies by giving me the choicest morsels, out of mere chumminess? And wasn't Frank always complaining that he made less than the other doormen? Apart from this, it also seemed to me that his "No!" was uttered in a somehow uncharacteristic tone for him. This "Oh, no!" sounded quite categorical, yet not absolutely final, as if Frank were saying, I may be refusing, but I can't prevent you from asking me again.

While the doorman and I were dickering, Kim the Korean and Alberto the Argentinian questioned the guests at the doors. They did not chase them rudely off to the corner, however; they stopped taxis driving by, opened the doors, and collected the tips. After amassing a fistful of quarters this way, Kim Il Sung came over to Frank and dropped them in his coat pocket. Since this was not a bribe—the money, collected on his "territory," did belong to Frank—the honest doorman made no objection, but, so as not to feel himself indebted to this obsequious cabbie, appeared to notice nothing at all.

Catching the chink of coins which Frank chose not to hear, I suddenly realized that yet another vastly important moment in my career as a cabman had arrived.

"You've got a ton of quarters, Frank," I said, "and I don't have anything but bills. Would you change five bucks for me?"

There was no whiff of a bribe in this, and Frank trustingly took my five dollars. He made a stack of four quarters and gave it to me, saying "One." Another stack, "two." He appeared to be piling up the next four quarters a bit more slowly; perhaps he was thinking about something else.

"That's enough, Frank," I said, taking the third stack, and our eyes met.

"Come on!" Frank protested uncertainly. "I've only given you three." But at that moment a bellboy brought out some suitcases, and I ran to open the trunk. Frank shook a finger at me in parting, as if to say, I'm wise to you now, Vladimir, you won't trick me next time!

"Skip it!" I shouted. "I'll be back!"

———

I was back two hours later. Frank had finished for the day; he had not left yet, however, and was chatting with the doorman relieving him. Beanpole Betty was standing at the corner, swinging her pocketbook impatiently. Frank was due a dollar for LaGuardia, from where I had just returned.

"Frankie, change another five for me," I said. "Seriously. No fooling."

"Not again!" Frank wagged a finger at me when I pushed his hand away after taking the fourth stack.

"That's a pretty good exchange rate," the second doorman remarked, nudging Frank.

"When my Checker's at the end of the line," I said, "and gets called up for a Kennedy, I give an even better rate."

The doormen laughed.

"Get acquainted," Frank said, and introduced me. "This is my friend!"

"Mario."

We sealed the acquaintance with a handshake, and just then a third top hat, belonging to the seventy-year-old doorman, Monty, emerged from the entrance.

The old fellow was out of breath and could not speak: he had been running. Out by the main entrance, where Monty was on duty, the manager of the hotel had been beside himself for ten minutes already. He was late for a train, but none of the airport cabbies wanted to take Monty's boss to Penn Station. There wasn't an empty taxi to be had on the street, and Monty was seriously afraid he might be fired. Who needs a doorman who cannot keep the cab drivers in check?

Frank gave me a meaningful look.

"Hop in, Monty!" I said. We dashingly ran one red light, then another, circled the block, and came bombing up to the main entrance.

"Thanks, Monty!" said Mr. Kraft, holding out a dollar to the doorman; the manager was a decent man.

"Thank *you* very much, Mr. Kraft," Monty replied, grateful more for the forgiveness than the dollar.

With me Mr. Kraft settled up even better. On the way he jotted down my name and hack number on a notepad and said, "Go back to the hotel, find my assistant, Tim Barnett, and tell him I asked you to get the Finnish athletes' luggage to Newark."

I went back to the hotel, gave the assistant the boss's message and added, without specifying whether the source was Mr. Kraft or not, that he, Mr. Barnett, should write down my name and number, as the manager himself had done, in case the need arose for someone to do a similar job.

"You can reach me through any of the doormen," I said. "Frank, Monty, Mario—they all know me!"

———

Frank matured with every passing day. He had mellowed, and his head stopped turning at the sound of clicking high heels. All his thoughts were now focused on a woman whom I thought of as popeyed Beanpole Betty. I was honored with an introduction.

"Elizabeth."

"Pleased to meet you."

An uncomfortable pause.

"Frank, didn't Monty tell you? Your uncle's upset with you again. He was on the warpath here just now, wanted you to go and see him."

I expected Frank to wink at me and say something like "That crazy old fogey again!" But the "nephew" did not pick this up and run with it. Betty was a forty-year-old married woman with three children and it was her own husband who had brought her and the doorman together.

Every time the husband strolled past the Madison he would take a long look at the neat, well-groomed—if uncouth—lad. Having sized him up, he went over, started a trivial conversation, and invited the young man home.

Frank, in his soldierly way, did not beat about the bush, and replied that he was not homosexual. But the husband was well aware of this. He himself was an experienced, confirmed homosexual. Being attached to his children, however, he had no desire to change his life in any way, and repeated the invitation.

Frank went, and was warmly received. A large scotch, some light banter, and he was already in the bedroom with Betty, hearing the timid voice on the other side of the door.

"You okay, honey? Is everything all right?"

"Yes, yes! Get lost!"

Unbuttoning his coat, Frank displayed the monogram YSL on his shirt. Her present. Then he pulled out a silver watch with a cover. The husband's present.

Frank had no illusions about the reason for his success.

"I'm not in their social set. I couldn't break up that family even if I wanted to. And what would I want with that woman and her kids at my age anyway? But believe it or not, they both care about me. They want me to take accounting classes. Betty says she'll set up me up for life."

———

A new order now reigned at the side entrance. The first cab waited with open trunk. Kim Il Sung, Ali Baba, Alberto, and any migrant drivers who happened along paid the doorman a dollar for the right to open the trunk and wait for an airport job. If the bellboys brought out a LaGuardia you were quits; for Kennedy there was a surcharge.

Mr. Barnett set up Frank as an example to all the other doormen: people at the side entrance who needed a cab for a short trip were not shooed away. While receiving tribute from the airport cabbies, Frank had not halted the flow of licit tips from the guests. Passengers going a short distance were taken by the cab at the tail of the line. But on his return the cabbie kept his original place in the airport queue. We liked this rational way of doing things.

The Madison doormen's gratuities were relatively modest. Monty made about fifty dollars a day in tips, Mario seventy. Frank, the youngest, who had been there no time at all, never went home with less than a hundred. The source of his surplus profits was the yellow line painted along the curb in front of the Madison's entrance.

"Hey, you!" Frank would yell, turning purple. "Don't try leaving your buggy here. This is the hotel loading zone, not a parking lot!"

A green bill rustled.

"Sir, leave the keys! I might have to move your car."

But if there was no rustle of bills, if the careless motorist, hurrying about his business, shouted at the doorman over his shoulder, "Don't worry! I'll see you later!" Frank would dive into his cubicle, call the tow truck, and, as he watched them hauling off the "unattended" car, would remark sardonically: "See me later? See me now!"

"Vladimir, do you play the numbers?" he asked one day. And, confidingly, as if understanding another man's weakness: "Sometimes, right?"

However, even for Frank's sake I had no desire to waste several dollars on a bet. But he would not give up.

"If you know a cabbie who wants an honest bet, send him to me."

Frank had become the most wanted man at the hotel. I never heard guests wonder when Mario, Monty, Mr. Barnett, or Mr. Kraft's other assistant would be on duty. But somebody would ask for Frank every day.

———————

Since I did not play the numbers and did not procure any other cabbies either, Frank's attitude toward me soon cooled. But even so, I never came home later than ten in the evening. By now this had nothing to do with Frank, Mario, Mr. Barnett, or the Madison Hotel at all. Once inspired to exchange a five-dollar bill for four dollars' worth of quarters, I realized I possessed a key to the hearts of even the haughtiest, most well-heeled doormen.

The fat cats of the Waldorf-Astoria could not resist when I asked, "Will you give me change for a five?" Every doorman wants to get rid of the handfuls of coins that constantly weigh his pockets down.

"Two . . . three . . . four . . ."

"That's enough."

"Thanks! That's a pretty good rate of exchange."

"If they bring out a Kennedy and you call for a Checker, I'll do even better."

"Okay, my friend!" That's the way the doorman was addressing me now!

"Hi, Irving!" I greet the big cheese as I drive up to the Sheraton. "Give me some change."

"Happy to!"

"Take the keys, please. I'm going for a pizza."

And off I run across the street. If the line moves up, Irving won't shift the Checker himself, but he will tell one of the other drivers to. Should a Kennedy show up—

My pizza is in the oven. I sip my coffee. Suddenly I hear a piercing whistle. I look round and see Irving waving to me: move it! And the bellhop is already slamming *my* Checker's trunk. Hey, sister, put my pizza in a bag! Gimme a lid for the cup. The coffee will do cold just as well. We'll wolf down the pizza later. No time to hang around—it's a Kennedy!

As I drive along the streets, with or without a passenger, I say hello to every doorman. Manuel at the Edison, Basilio at the Astoria, Fernando at the Empire, Robert at the Holiday Inn. How come Bruno didn't smile at me, only spread his arms in an odd fashion? "Excuse me, miss, I have to stop for a minute," I say to my customer. "I work for this hotel. The doorman has an important message for me."

"Bruno, you wanted to tell me something?"

"But you're busy."

"I'll be back in a flash. You won't know I've gone."

"Come back right away!"

"Two minutes flat, my *friend!*"

And what of it? Now he really is my friend.

On returning I change my traditional five.

"One, two . . ."

Wow, it's a very good sign when a doorman gives you only two bucks in coins for a five-dollar bill. And so it proves.

"Tell the receptionist I sent you to take the attaché case to Lufthansa. It got left behind. Quick!"

That's fine with me; I don't mind the three dollars. Delivering an attaché case is a special service. The Taxi and Limousine Commission strictly forbids us to carry anything without a passenger. I won't forget to mention that to the absent-minded German. I won't lose anything on this deal.

"Hi, Vlady!"

"How are you today, Jimmy? Change this for me, would you?"

The bill has vanished, but this time I don't get any change at all. Fantastic! I don't grudge five dollars.

"Be here at three p.m. on the dot! Wash the cab. You're going to the cemetery."

———

Never before had I pondered the fact that every city on earth was built for the living by the dead; and that we, the living, wherever we live, keep on building around the cities of the dead.

Such were the thoughts triggered by the scrap of paper I was handed in exchange for my five dollars by this doorman acquaintance, as he put a silent man in a black suit in my freshly washed-to-order Checker. Moreover, as he saw the guest into the cab, the doorman impressed on me, with assumed severity, that I should give this customer good service, since he was a *real gentleman* and from Melbourne besides.

This geographic precision sounded quite irrelevant to me; however, its meaning became clear as soon as I glanced at the piece of paper, on which was written

S. COHEN

Jewish cemetery.

An electric charge coursed through my back somewhere between my shoulder blades. I looked round and asked, "Jewish cemetery?"

"Mr. Melbourne" nodded indifferently, and I floated away on a gentle wave of joy.

Do you understand how I felt? If you don't, try to imagine that you've undertaken to find a person in New York called S. Cohen, and think about it: how long will it take you? Do you have any idea how many Cohens with the initial *S* there are in the phone book? Sams and Samuels, Seymours and Solomons, Sylvias and Sarahs, Susans and Sophies. And what if your S. Cohen is beyond the reach of the telephone? And if you consider that there are many more dead S. Cohens than living ones? And bearing in mind that you've arrived in New York from distant Melbourne and don't seem to have any idea how many Jewish cemeteries there are here? Try to picture what the gangster whose cab you ended up in (after you were bought and sold by a hypocritical doorman), what that gangster will do to you! However, I was not that sort of guy. At first, with commendable restraint, I drove toward the Queensboro Bridge.

"But why exactly did you go to Queens?"

"What do you mean, 'why'? Because I'm not a barefaced thief, and the closest Jewish cemeteries are in Queens. I had no intention of fleecing the defenseless man from Melbourne. There was only one thing I wanted: to make it my last job of the day."

"But would a decent man have acted this way in your position? Shouldn't you have told the visitor from Down Under that there are a great many Jewish cemeteries in New York, and he needed something more specific to find the right grave?"

"'A decent man'? My, my, what expressions we're tossing around! Well, for your information, if I had really lost all sense of shame, I would have dragged a Melbourne like this one—had I paid five dollars for him or hadn't I?—straight across the George Washington bridge and begun the search in New Jersey."

"Whew. You certainly like to have the last word, cabbie. But one more question, if you please: who is it you're talking to all the time? Here and there, as we recall, you've addressed the reader directly: no harm in that, of course. One can pardon a taxi driver's use of such a "fresh" literary device. But who is it you're always elbowing so playfully? Whom are you crossing swords with? Who is it you've selected to serve as such a convenient opponent, whose every argument is known to you in advance and whom you vanquish so easily and without fail? Eh?"

"None of your business. 'Opponent'!"

Have you never seen a cabbie busy arguing and arguing about something as he drives? He scowls. He gets angry. He gets sarcastic.

You take another look, but there's no one in the backseat. The cabbie's alone in his yellow cage. He must enjoy talking to an "intelligent person." I developed a taste for this myself back when I was learning the ropes in the fleet Checker. Oh, yes. I would drive along, and "we" would chat. Those were fascinating conversations: the witticisms flew thick and fast on both sides, while from behind I would hear "Blah blah blah blah!" Some cretinous passenger butting in. Ah, go jump in the lake! Mister, what do you want from me? But the passenger gets angry: "Leave me alone! Why should I want to talk to you? I'm talking to myself!"

New York, New York.

What places had I not managed to visit as I went gadding about New York in a yellow cab? I had driven my customers to the thoroughbred classics at Belmont and the night harness races at Yonkers; to baseball games, zoos, jails, country clubs, and golf courses; but I had never yet been to a graveyard.

While Mr. Melbourne was talking to somebody in the cemetery office, I wandered among the graves, marveling at the number of compatriots from my emigration, the Third Wave, who were already buried here. Like me, they had striven to reach the New World in pursuit of a better future. Beneath these stone slabs reposed a refusenik, who had paved the way to freedom for all of us; and puny Yulik Shmuelson with his child-size violin, to whom the road to music school had been closed over there, in the Soviet Union, because he was Jewish; and plain Sofochka Butz, one shoulder playfully lifting a strap of her open Russian summer dress, just a notch too revealing for a cemetery.

Such familiar, homey faces smiled up at me from the white ceramic ovals affixed to the tombstones.

A Jewish grandmother in a Russian kerchief; a Jewish grandfather, a Young Communist of the twenties, in an embroidered Ukrainian shirt; Jews with sad Georgian eyes and Georgian surnames.

In Brooklyn, in a graveyard one side of which abuts the northern section of Ocean Parkway, the taciturn man from Melbourne at last found his needle in a haystack: a fresh mound, not yet beaten down by rain, marked by a tablet driven into the ground.

SHIRLEY COHEN
1961–1979

I glanced around, then gasped with surprise and stepped back. Looking out at me from a vertical slab as tall as myself was the vanished Uzbek. I could not be mistaken, it was he, 8W12.

Uzbek's widow had chosen for the headstone not the photograph of that pitiable man of my own age who had nursed his sick hand and asked me for an aspirin with a forced, steel-toothed smile, but of the hard-working, sinewy fellow, confident in his own strength, who was the father of her children and whom she had so doggedly nudged out of his native Samarkand to America.

Why had he died so young, this sturdy bulldozer driver, this true

Jewish husband, who did not drink his pay away but brought it all home to his wife, down to the last penny? He drank hard, but only on holidays. He used to say he could "knock back a bottle of vodka, no sweat." Look what the yellow cab had done to this stalwart fellow in a mere two years.

But, come to think of it, the sad fate of Uzbek held little that was instructive for me; here was a man who had not listened to anyone—neither the Doctor, nor wise Shmuel, nor Long Marik, though they had all wished him well. Uzbek thought he was smarter than all of them: he did not hustle at the hotels, did not want to get to know the doormen, but toiled from dawn to dusk, and this was the outcome. My driving career was turning out differently. I had been on the job only a little over a year, and already I was returning home more and more often before dark. And this had nothing to do with the magic words ("Gimme change for five bucks!") or the chance trips to Long Island or Westchester, which I averaged no more than once a week, after all.

What did matter, as I now realized, was that, after traveling fifty thousand miles, dealing with twenty thousand passengers, losing out on my first, no-standing ticket, and beating the second, "soliciting"; and after also learning to deceive my comrades without blinking an eye—for at whose expense did I get the good jobs without standing in line?—I had become a real cabbie.

Chapter Eighteen

- - - - - - - - - - -

"WE, THE FRIENDS OF GHELY SNEGIREV . . ."

T he better things went for me in the taxi business, the worse they became at the radio station. I taped only nine and a half minutes a week in the recording studio, but the microphone there possessed the unpleasant property of penetrating like an X-ray everyone behind whom the soundproof door closed. Far better than any lie detector, it read your most secret thoughts like an open book. And should the mind of an employee of a radio station broadcasting to the socialist camp be occupied with bonds or stocks, with ocean cruises, mink coats, ski condos, or other Western "temptations," the microphone would turn him into a sponger, a nonentity, afraid of losing his easy émigré pittance and a toady to his American boss.

The only immigrant whom the microphone would allow to feel himself a journalist of value was one who, in the free world, went on year after year living the spiritual life, sharing the sorrows and the pain of the country he had left. Though I had no dreams of sumptuous possessions or stock-market windfalls, the price of the gasoline with which I fueled the cab still worried me more than the international prices of grain, the topic of my talks to Soviet listeners. And in an effort to excuse myself for this and for the fact that I could not absolve myself of my friendship with doormen, I would pore over the confession of Ghely Snegirev again and again. *"I betrayed no one."*

Why does he say that? I thought. If he really had betrayed someone—the people who smuggled his manuscripts to the West, for instance—everyone would have known about it long before he died, since new arrests, new trials, new repressions would have followed.

And yet I could not rid myself of the feeling that these pages guarded some suspicious, impure secret.

Here is cheerful, forty-nine-year-old Ghely, striding along the quiet, sunny street in the direction of the Botanical Garden. He has been preparing himself for arrest for a long time, and then, in prison at last, he is glad of every walk in the cramped exercise yard. He is glad of the musty herring at breakfast, glad of the pipe and tobacco sent by his wife from outside, and he notes with childish surprise: "Yes, one's glad of everything in this place!"

And here is another mention of the hunger strike that Ghely gave up after failing to achieve anything at all. Why do I focus on the details, which seem to illuminate nothing of import?

After the month-long strike Ghely recovers his strength hourly rather than daily. He notes that his heart is as strong as a sprinter's, and that a feeling of happiness permeates him through and through.

How was one to make sense of the fact that this essentially healthy prisoner was suddenly surrounded by whitecoats dancing attendance?

What were they doing in his cell? The prisoner was not and had not been sick. Occasionally depressed, maybe, occasionally complaining of chronic backache, but . . . well, the doctors knew better. They raised the alarm when it was discovered that Ghely Ivanovich was not sleeping too well. The pills did not help? A stronger concoction of three medicines, administered intravenously, was prescribed. No sooner were the words "minor heart trouble" mentioned than the prison cell—as if it were a private suite in the Kremlin hospital for government members—was visited by a solicitous cardiologist, who ran an EKG every day, stuffed Ghely with a special heart medication in short supply (derived from young stag antlers), and called in three other doctors for a consultation.

A month passed, then another, but the physicians' watchfulness showed no sign of slackening.

Knowing full well that this degree of attention—not merely to a prisoner but even to a sick KGB captain—was unheard of in Soviet practice, the irrepressible Ghely did not waste yet another chance to tease the investigator. Wasn't the KGB afraid of getting stuck with the fresh corpse of a fifty-year-old man while the investigation was still in progress?

However, the usually pliant investigator put a stop to this line of talk at once.

"No, Ghely Ivanovich, we're not afraid of that. What do we have to fear? One can get sick anywhere; anything can happen."

And Ghely had no witty comeback. This time logic was not on his side.

———

The first émigré family to leave our housing project, the "poor man's paradise," was moving out. All the Russians spilled into the courtyard. The women watched the bustle of the move from a distance, while the men went over to offer their help. Émigrés are thrifty people who abhor wasting money on a job one can do oneself.

The departing family thanked their well-meaning compatriots, but declined their disinterested services: the furniture was toted out by the capable moving men. We were seeing our neighbors off to a better life; the fish store had freed Rosa from her job as a waitress in a nursing home.

Misha peeked out from the bowels of the moving van.

"Ah, Volodya! The very person I wanted to see."

But to begin with we talked about the new house in Great Neck. Four bedrooms, three baths, large yard, pool, garage.

"Volodya, my address is easy to remember. Nine ninety-nine Elmira Avenue."

Elmira was in the "jungles," and Misha was not inviting me to the housewarming; he wanted me to go see him at the store.

"Drop in when you have time."

No offense was intended; we had not visited each other's apartment when we lived in the same building.

"Isn't it time you quit breaking your back in that Checker?" Rosa said with significance.

"You won't make any less with me," Misha added.

"And what would I have to do?" I inquired.

"Nothing," answered Misha artlessly. "Not a lick. Then you'll come by?"

"He will," Rosa promised.

I pined for the past I had once erased so easily. I was only twenty-one years old, a provincial journalist, when I tackled my first film script, about the workings of a hospital from the inside, and got myself a part-time job as an orderly in the Neurosurgery Research Center in Kiev.

I lugged oxygen cylinders from the storeroom to the operating block, past the small, out-of-the-way one-story building that housed the morgue, and would find a moment in an inconspicuous corner to jot down my observations in a notepad: "Before entering the morgue for an autopsy, the doctors take off their white coats."

Armed with mop and pail, I was washing the cellar floor in the main building one day when I found myself in a tiny, windowless room, where roughly hewn shelves held thousands of gray clerical folders. I opened one: it was a patient's case history. "Final diagnosis, sarcoma." I opened another, "medulloblastoma"; then a third, "astrocytoma."

Spellbound by these sonorous and terrifying words, with no idea of how it would look onscreen, I scribbled: "This is a *parade of tumors*. A parade of shapeless, slimy malignancies, and behind each one is a person who wanted to live. Hats off. Here the dead teach the living."

The reward for the orderly's diligence was that within a week or two I was bossed around by anyone who was inclined to, right down to the alcoholic technician who cleaned out the experimental animals' cages. One such errand sent me to the hospital's vivisection department.

As soon as I crossed the threshold of this suffocating place, pervaded with even fouler smells than the morgue, the first time I heard the groans of the beasts tortured by researchers and condemned to agony and death, I realized that the plot of my screenplay would be the fate of a *dog*.

A homeless, emaciated mongrel is wandering around the wintry city.

The shop windows shine, people and cars hurry by; a street vendor, selling pies, lands the dog a kick.

None of the sybaritic Afghan hounds, German shepherds in fancy collars, or well-groomed Pekineses out for walks on leashes pay any attention to the frozen stray.

Some boys tease the mangy dog; a passerby, whom it tries to follow, stops and brandishes his cane threateningly. Only one human being has noticed the wretched animal, pitied it, tossed it a morsel of sausage, called to it, petted it—and tied a noose tightly around its neck.

The dog is shoved into a pickup and taken to "jail."

The cages of the vivisection department, the canine jail. But there's plenty of food here. Moreover, the dog now has a new master. It quickly gets used to the man in the white coat and his queer games: X-raying, weighing, taking blood pressure, listening to lungs and heart.

But one day, when the researcher was sure that the dog was healthy, it was given anesthesia and went to sleep.

And it dreamed a naïve, drunken dog's dream.

The new master, meanwhile, filled a syringe with fluid drawn from a sarcoma and injected it into the test animal.

The scientists keep constant track of the fast-developing tumor inside the dog's skull. A contrasting substance is injected into an artery, and in the X-ray pictures there appears and grows, from frame to frame, the "shadow of a sarcoma," a network of neoplasmic vessels which supplies the tumor with blood.

The researchers await the first symptoms, so important for early diagnosis. And in due course they manifest themselves: the dog becomes uneasy, loses its appetite, and sleeps badly.

The tumor grows, inducing an epileptic fit. The animal's body is convulsed and racked with seizures.

A second attack follows the first, after which paralysis sets in, the field of vision narrows, and peristaltic failure occurs.

The dog's life hangs by a thread, but it is taken to the operating room, and the tumor is removed.

As the surgical wound heals, the dog's strength returns. It eats, crawls, stands, walks, runs, and greets its tormentors with a joyful bark. But once the new master is certain the animal is cured, he kills it, so the autopsy will show whether the cancer has metastasized to other organs.

Why was I trying so hard to restore to memory only those drafts of the screenplay where my imagination contradicted the real state of affairs?

Malignant tumors were indeed induced in animals as part of research into new anticancer drugs, but, for this, less valuable "biological material" than dogs was used. Guinea pigs and rats were employed; dogs were kept for more complicated experiments.

In the vivisection department, special plastic models of tumors were implanted in dogs' brains to enable the researcher to control both the size of the "tumor" and the speed of its "growth," and to determine which of the brain's vital centers the model would exert pressure on. Sometimes it was the center of movement coordination, sometimes respiration, sometimes unconditioned reflexes. When the researchers slowly reduced the size of the "tumor," the compressed brain center recovered, and the animal's epileptic attacks ceased.

Around the period when I became "one of them" in the vivisection department—when I had several times tied down an animal on the operating table, held the dilator for the cut during the operation, and so forth—it became clear that the aim of many of the experiments was incomprehensible not only to me but also to the lab technicians; every day people came to pick up the records of these efforts from the new building for "experimental neurosurgery," which stood in the depths of the hospital compound, behind the morgue and the vivisection department.

I knew that one of the best surgeons in the hospital operated in the new building, Professor Mikhailovsky, an unsociable man who never smiled. The patients whom he operated on there never received visits from relatives.

Any door was open to an orderly carrying mop and pail. No janitor or secretary ever asked who had told me to clean in the doctors' staff room, the department head's office, the recovery ward, or even the hospital pharmacy. But they would not let me in the new building. As soon as I climbed the front steps some grizzled watchdog, a retired veteran, rose up in front of me and inquired in an unfriendly tone what I wanted.

I put on an innocent expression and goggled at him.

"Alexander Ivanovich was yelling that nobody's cleaned here in three days!"

But even the mention of the most important person in the whole research center did not help.

"Scram, kid. Out."

Why did I remember all this each time I reached the place in Ghely's manuscript where there was such an unexpected and inexplicable change in the style of the physically and mentally sturdy, mordantly cheerful prisoner's notes?

———

I must record everything about my six months under investigation. But I do not know how much time I have left, and, albeit in haste, lying hunched up and almost unable to see my scribble, I am putting on paper the most important thing, March. All the horror, all the loathing, and how I broke down.

The half year that Ghely spent under investigation divided into two distinct and unequal periods: five months in the KGB internal prison, and March, "that accursed month of March," as Ghely writes, when he found himself in the prison hospital.

The KGB doctors' recommendation that the dissident be moved, from the investigation unit to the prison infirmary, came just in time. Ghely was hospitalized on March 2; only three days later his right leg was paralyzed.

Within a week the left leg was paralyzed, too. The mysterious illness that had interrupted the flaccidly moving investigation was progressing at a gallop: the lower part of Ghely's body, immobile and insensate, was convulsed with spasms. The paralysis had affected peristaltic function, and now the prisoner could not relieve himself without the doctors' help.

Through the expanding pain, high fever, and delirium, he drifted somewhere, poisoned by his own body's waste products, which his organism had ceased to eliminate.

They gave me an enema, and the orderly, Shurik (another prisoner, and an interesting character), and a soft-hearted guard heaved me onto the wobbly seat above the bucket; some liquid came out, but I couldn't bear down. And then, bending over and swaying, I stuck my own finger up my backside and for half an hour dug out pieces of petrified excrement. Shurik watched, horrified; the screw fled the dirt and the stench. Then Shurik poured water on my hands and thighs. No way to wash it all off—everything stank of crap. When they were heaving me off the seat and onto the bunkbed, Shurik suddenly shouted, "Hey, you're pissing!" The urine that had been sitting there for twenty-four hours gushed out. The guard jumped back, cursing. I collapsed onto the bed, soaking it; somehow I fell asleep, lying in the wet.

When he woke up, the investigator was sitting by the bed. He stroked the paralyzed man's fingers and said that treatment under prison conditions was no treatment. He had to be moved to a specialized clinic. Gentle, loving care was needed even more. He must take pity on himself, finally.

"*It's all in your hands, Ghely Ivanovich. There's only one way out.*"

"*The same old thing?*"

"*Yes.*"

"*A sincere recantation under medical torture?*"

"*Now, now, how can you say things like that?*"

"*I call a spade a spade, captain.*"

They were silent for a moment. And again the investigator said, over and over, that perhaps it was still not too late and that the authorities would agree to it, that a pardon before trial was a very different matter from a pardon afterward, and who knew when that trial would be—since Ghely Ivanovich obviously could not go to court in this condition—and the charges against his wife, who was an accomplice (had she not helped distribute the libelous materials?), would be dropped; and nobody would touch his children.

"Think it over, Ghely Ivanovich, think it over hard. There's still time, but it's running out."

The light dawned on Ghely in a flash, and he said:

"You knew it all from the very beginning. My illness is your ally."

My new teeth had the glorious bluish sheen of an expensive toilet bowl, and I did not owe a penny to anybody in the world. This was very nice, of course; but now that I had finished paying the dentist, my work as a taxi driver had lost its point.

Meanwhile the length of my radio program, *Our Daily Bread*, had been increased from nine and a half to thirteen and a half minutes. Now each script was divided into two parts, the first of which was called "Food for Mankind," while the second, as before, was devoted to Soviet agriculture.

My seasoned editor, tired of lecturing me, had made a very wise move: henceforth the scripts of my shows, channeled into a quietly flowing stream by his skillful hand, no longer elicited adverse comments from the political department. Against a background of starvation in India or Africa, the discussions of food shortages in the Soviet Union were seen not as evidence of a congenital defect of the socialist system, unable to feed itself, but as criticism of some of its deficiencies.

It was pointless to argue with the editor, and I did not have the courage to give up the weekly check. In my pigeonhole I found a magazine I had never heard of, *Farmer's Digest*. The editor explained that from now on my show would consist of *three* parts. Besides "Food for Mankind," I had to introduce another new rubric: "America as Agricultural Superpower."

How and what could I write about agriculture in the U.S. if I had never seen a single American farm or spoken to a single American farmer? But my editor was adamant.

"You must learn to work the way most of our writers do, basing your scripts on press material."

He was not a Soviet agent charged with sabotaging Radio Liberty from within. He was an ordinary bureaucrat with only two years left till retirement. A journalist whose scripts are based on "press material"—i.e., a hack, with no angle or personality of his own—is the most convenient employee an editor can have: he will cobble a piece out of anything you toss at him.

In for a penny, in for a pound. Why sweat hours over translating stuff from English into Russian when the *Soviet* press was full of the very material my editor would like to find in my program? I came on a gold mine in *Young Communist* magazine: "The Shadow of Starvation Over the World Today"; in a year-old issue of *Atheist* I dug up a preposterous "futurological" essay on the oceans that described how trained dolphins would eventually pasture schools of fish for man. In *Engineering for Young People* an intelligent paragraph on a new American berry-picking machine caught my eye.

"You see! You can do it when you want to," the editor said enthusiastically.

The red light I once yearned for, had played a dreadful joke on me: my show on Radio Liberty had become my shame. The microphone had turned me into a sponger, scrounging that easy émigré pittance; and now when I greeted the "influential American" in the hallway, I would peek devotedly at his eyes behind the glasses, trying to guess whether he knew the sources from which I was extracting the material for my broadcasts.

"When they catch me, I'll be out on my ear!" I thought. I had to prepare a bridgehead for the retreat.

———

For thirty minutes the crowded bus bounced along a wide thoroughfare that became progressively narrower. We had long ago left behind the shady little streets lined with private houses, and there were almost no white passengers remaining. Those commuting to the poor slum neighborhoods were black.

Number 999 Elmira Avenue jutted up in the middle of a burned-out, weed-grown block. The entrance to the shop gave off a smell like a garbage dump, and I found myself in a wide-open space that buzzed like a disturbed beehive. They sold everything here!

On my left rose pyramids of oranges and apples, on my right were carcasses hanging on metal hooks; a deli counter shimmered against the back wall, while in the middle of the store the fish counters were set up in a circle. On a wooden dais in the center of this circle Misha stood behind the cash register.

Four salesmen dropped frozen gray lumps, from which fishheads stuck out, onto the clanging scales, while Misha took the customers' money. This retail conveyor belt worked without a halt, and it was

251

several minutes before a teenage black assistant with darting eyes noticed me (the only white face in the crowd) and whispered to the owner.

Misha flashed me a smile and called loudly, "Haim!"

A decrepit man with hands that shook from Parkinson's got up on the rostrum, and Misha surrendered his place behind the cash register.

"He's the old owner's brother. I feel sorry for him, but he'll steal twenty or thirty bucks while we're talking," Misha said. "That's what he's used to."

"Maybe we should talk some other time?" I suggested.

"Come on!" Misha brushed this off, and added, "I'm not so hungry for money anymore."

The young sales assistant entertained the customers in a whisper loud enough to carry all over the store.

"Yo, lady, come over here quick. I'll sell you anything you want for half-price while that Jew isn't watching us! Hey, bro, let me take care of you right now, while our Jew's blabbering with the other Jew!"

His face wrinkling with pleasure, Misha commented, "He gave that drunk twenty-six cents' short weight and then overcharged him another eighteen cents. That fat woman he gave fourteen cents' short weight and overcharged another twelve cents—he doesn't miss a trick. He's served four customers in a row without giving a single shopping bag!"

A real salesman, Misha enlightened me, brings down the cost price of a product even as he sells it to the customer. With the money this black teenager had just stolen from his fellows, Misha could buy several more pounds of frozen gray lumps wholesale, sell those, and again give people short weight and overcharge them.

We went outside, and, as we walked around the burned-out block, I learned that although Misha's shop was stocked with a large variety of seafood, including live fish, salmon, and expensive shrimp, he made his money on the cheapest frozen stuff, which he bought at $500 a ton and sold for a dollar-fifty a pound. Eight tons a week. I tried to calculate what the weekly profit from the frozen gray lumps would be, but the numbers were astronomical and, feeling slightly dizzy, which can happen when you come out of a stuffy room into the fresh air, I lost count.

Evidently guessing what had made me so thoughtful, Misha changed the subject.

It appeared that these thousands had not showered down on Misha all of a sudden. Across the street from the burned-out block there stood another shack, to which we now repaired.

A cement floor and the same stench, but the store was empty. Rosa was languishing behind the counter. On some boxes at the entrance a ragged-looking black man was arranging a pile of potatoes, a pile of onions, a pile of bananas. It was a sorry parody of the empire of thriving trade we had just left.

"Make us a snack!" Misha ordered, and Rosa came to life and bustled around. On the ledge under the impenetrably dirty window appeared a bottle of Stolichnaya, pickles, smoked eel, and four shot glasses; Cliff had joined us.

Misha let him sell his stuff here rent-free, so Rosa would not be alone in the store. She was afraid of being all by herself. Cliff cleaned the shop and paid only the electric bill.

A shot of vodka had the fishmonger reminiscing.

A year or so earlier Misha had given the owner of the fish department in the "supermarket" next door the eighteen thousand dollars in cash he had made from the hot dogs, donned a canvas apron, and started behind the counter.

What had he known about fish? He knew how to eat it, but nothing about selling it.

The two of them, Misha and the former owner's old brother, worked together. There was no point in hiring help: the housewives would ask the price of the fish, but took their food stamps to the chicken counter. At the end of the week Misha toted it up: he had made a loss of four hundred dollars.

The next week he was in the red again. Rosa moaned into the pillow night after night.

"What did I tell you? We've given away everything we had."

No one interrupted our conversation, burbling gently along with the vodka. The door through which Misha and I had entered half an hour before had not opened since. The customers from the black ghetto had no desire to know what vegetables Cliff had today or the price of Rosa's fish.

This had also been pretty much the state of affairs a year earlier in the fish section in the middle of the crowded store. Misha's trade was being stifled by a competitor. The fish Misha bought at the wholesaler, and not by the ton, nor even by the hundredweight—the freshest and tastiest—was expensive.

The housewives asked the price of Misha's fish, but bought from the competition.

Misha got together with three or four other unsuccessful fishmongers and started buying in larger quantities and paying less. Every cent saved at the wholesaler's he passed on to every customer he managed to get. He was lowering his prices.

He would sell huge fresh carp at cost, cheaper than the neighboring store's frozen porgies. Every week at a loss left a bleeding hole in Misha's budget, but he knew that each thousand dollars' profit that slipped through his fingers was a nail in his competitor's coffin.

Sniffing trouble, the competitor began keeping the store open seven days a week and closing later than Misha, but he had caught on too late. The housewives were already converted: the Russian's fish was cheaper and better.

Rosa made a sortie: "Is it true you want to sell the store?"

The competitor did not risk losing his chance to dump his moribund business. But in buying the store that had gone bust, Misha had no intention of deriving any profit from it.

When the vodka bottle was already empty, two women came into the shop. They bought potatoes from Cliff and inspected Rosa's counter skeptically.

"How come this fish costs $2.10? We always get it for a dollar-fifty."

"Get it where you like, then," said Rosa.

The women went out.

"Great salesmanship!" Misha snickered. "How much did you take in today?"

"Twenty-eight dollars," said Rosa coyly.

"Boy!" Misha said with glee. "At least today she won't ask me for cab fare!"

The happy couple turned toward me.

"Volodya, she's got a house and two kids to look after—she shouldn't have to work. But we can't close this store: if we close, someone else will open up another. We need you in the shop."

"I don't *do* anything here at all," Rosa said.

"If things are good for me, they'll be good for you too," Misha said.

I realized these were not empty words, and I was tired of being a pauper. The flat fee for my radio show, now longer and divided into three sections, had not gone up; I was still getting the same $190 a week. But had I really come to America to sell fish?

———

Our memory is so designed that any distressing bumps are smoothed away incomparably faster than are the bright milestones. Having fallen out with my latest cab owner and finding myself, for the umpteenth time, without a cab, I felt like a sailor onshore whose ship has left without him.

When my wife and I went into Manhattan, I could not walk past the Hilton or the Madison unmoved. "Look, a Kennedy!" I would nudge her, pointing to the bellhop rolling a cartful of suitcases onto the sidewalk; and I thought with pride, "Was it really I who cut in front of that sinister car, at night, in the rain, and fearlessly picked up that hysterical bitch running along the highway?" The arguments with passengers; the child's hand in the partition; the cigarette butts that I had to scoop out of the change cup every day; the busted trunk and the windows smashed by vandals—all of this blew clean out of my head as soon as the weariness left my muscles.

I introduced my wife to Long Marik, the Sculptor, and Shmuel. The only category of persons connected with the taxi business that aroused my antipathy was cab owners. I switched them now as easily as Frank used to switch girls.

They did not reduce my rent for the hours I lost while the cab stood idle in the repair shop, and I repaid them in kind. If the cab I was leasing had to be fixed, the best mechanic, as far as I was concerned, was the one whose lift happened to be free at the moment.

"What's the problem?"

"It's overheating."

"Leave the keys and come back in a couple of hours. Don't worry, we'll fix it."

How many times did the cab owners answer my reproach—"Why won't you put a partition in the cab? It's dangerous!"—by *shaming* me?

"Why are you such a coward? Don't pick up blacks and everything'll be okay."

I would leave the mechanic the keys. I could not care less whether he flushed out the radiator for thirty bucks or put in a new one for a hundred and fifty: the owner would pay the bill.

One Sunday, about an hour before daybreak, two white youths stopped my cab in deserted SoHo. "Twenty-first and Eighth," they said.

When we reached their destination, we saw a group of sequined and tuxedoed partygoers, from some all-night bash in a Chelsea loft, wandering along in search of a cab, or perhaps breakfast. Suddenly, the building my passengers wanted was apparently not there. "Let's try Twenty-second," they said.

There was nobody about on the avenue I had come out onto; there was no partition in this cab either, just when it would have been the right moment to slam it shut; and I had already heard many times that when passengers start changing the destination a cabbie has to be on the alert.

It was pretty scary driving into quiet Twenty-second Street, but right there on the corner I saw a motorcycle policeman writing a ticket for a car parked next to a hydrant. When it appeared that the building my guys were looking for was not to be found on that block either, I thought that even if I had stopped where the cop was, what could I have said? That my customers had changed the address and therefore I was afraid of them?

"Sir, it's on Nineteenth Street. Between Sixth and Seventh."

"Please. We'll pay well."

Why had I suddenly become "sir"? What were they "paying well" for? At five o'clock in the morning nobody pays cab drivers *well*. And they kept on whispering to each other. And how could I tell if they were looking for a building or just an empty alleyway? Turning onto Nineteenth Street, I glanced in the rearview mirror again, and my heart did not tingle or sink. It said, quite distinctly: "Killers!"

The cab leaped forward like a mad thing.

"Hey, what're you doing?"

But I knew what I was doing. Somewhere nearby there was a fire station! The accelerating cab lurched as the brakes bit the wheels, and skidded across the pavement, wet with dew.

"Are you out of your mind?"

But I was already out of the cab and running toward the red-painted doorway, where two firemen were standing, invisible from the middle of the street. They were drinking coffee out of paper cups.

"What happened?" Both firemen jumped; coffee trickled onto their fingers and down the sides of the cups.

"You hurt?"

I was panting so hard I could not speak.

"Did you get mugged?"

"N-no."

"So what's it all about?"

"N-nothing. I just got scared."

The firemen were angry at the fuss and the spilled coffee, which was probably why they started to laugh. Meanwhile, my two passengers climbed out of the cab and one of them, hearing the firemen's laughter, shouted, "I bet he's a Jew!"

The young men set off unhurriedly in the direction we had just come from, away from the fire station and toward Sixth Avenue. They walked down the street, easy, slim, in summer shirts tucked into tight designer jeans.

"They don't have anything on them," one of the firemen said to me. "You must have seen when they got in, they didn't have anything."

I was upset about the nearly three bucks clocked up on the meter; and I felt ashamed.

"They had a package," I said.

The firemen glanced at each other and headed over to the cab, holding their cups in front of them. The youths, who were halfway down the block by now, quickened their pace and disappeared around the corner.

One of the firemen put his cup on the roof of the cab and looked inside.

"Well, looks like he's got to be a kike!" he said. "Who else would try to save a hundred by not putting in a partition?"

On the floor next to the backseat lay a heavy cobblestone, which had fallen out of a crumpled paper bag.

The warning was crystal clear. Enough adventures. Don't go near a yellow cab ever again! But I interpreted the incident to mean that the prediction the gypsy had made long ago had at last come true. She had prophesied that I would someday find a bagful of money in my cab; it turned out that I had found something far more valuable.

———

My beloved story of the experiment dog never actually became a film; it was buried in the approval stages. But the death of one idea gave life to another, and I signed a contract with the Kiev movie studio for a screenplay about a famous physician, the head of the same neurosurgery research center for which I had worked as an orderly.

Even before the final draft of the screenplay was finished, our klieg lights were set up in the main operating room where the hero of our documentary removed aneurysms and tumors, and in the morgue ("Here the dead teach the living!"), where he analyzed his mistakes at autopsy. The lighting men bustled around and the cameraman made his tests; the doctors gradually became so used to the movie crew that they ceased to notice us.

In the vivisection department we were filming the episodes that showed how the researchers mined their "nuggets" of new medical knowledge; how the model of a tumor, implanted in an animal's skull, compressed the cerebrum. There was only one place in the whole research center where Professor Mikhailovsky operated to which the film crew was not admitted—the "experimental surgery building." There neither wives, mothers, nor husbands visited, before or after operations. We did try to gain entrance there, but we were told, "This entire area is kept especially sterile." Our curiosity was satisfied.

Only now, many years later, was I led into that "experimental building" by the last five pages of Ghely Snegirev's manuscript, the pages that were written *after* his death.

The government's announcement of Ghely's pardon was signed on the last day of March, and on April 12, in the closed, top-secret department of the Ukrainian Neurosurgery Research Center, Professor Mikhailovsky operated on the dissident and removed from the region of the second vertebra some kind of embracing, compressing tumor.

"It's benign," Professor Mikhailovsky declared to Ghely's wife. But the patient was not discharged after the successful operation.

The prisoner, who had been officially released from custody, had 272 days left to live; yet not one of them did he spend at liberty.

We, the friends of Ghely Snegirev, succeeded in obtaining permission to visit him when his sudden transfer to the top-secret building of the neurosurgery research center, his operation [on a vertebra in his neck, as Professor Mikhailovsky said], and his equally sudden appearance in the October Hospital, had already occurred.

When they first let us in to see Ghely, his emaciated, shriveled hands were still capable of holding a pencil. Paralyzed, able to move only one hand, scrawling and tearing the paper, he wrote down for us everything he wanted to say but could not; this hospital cell was distinguished from the one in the prison only by the greater number of microphones. Thus the people who wished to hear something important from Ghely, or tell him something, deciphered his zigzags and wrote down in capital letters the words they wanted to say and could not. And that was how — at the end of the summer, when his fingers were gripping the pencil with his last ounce of strength — he transmitted to us, his friends, his final request to compile a chronicle of this, his last hospital hell, and add it to his confession in the form of an epilogue. We are carrying out that wish here.

From Ghely's note to a friend: "They're talking about a repeat operation. I suppose they haven't covered all their tracks yet."

Speaking to Ghely's relatives, the doctor often said: "His condition is not improving only because some scar tissue formed around the spinal cord after the tumor was removed. That's what is causing the paralysis." In answer to a proposal that Western anticancer drugs be used, he said: "Whatever for? The tumor was benign."

From the tape of Ghely's conversation with a friend: "I think they'll finish me off soon."

———

Ghely informed his friends of his final decision to summon the KGB representative and demand permission to seek treatment abroad.

"I am taking this step in the understanding that it will be the end.

They cannot possibly expose themselves. But I cannot go on this way any longer."

During the next few days Ghely gave his final instructions, orally; he could not write anymore. Among them he asked that a pathologist friend of his be invited to the autopsy.

On December 28, 1978, Ghely Snegirev passed away. The KGB informed Ghely's wife of his death after the autopsy was completed.

The official diagnosis was cancer of the prostate with metastases in all parts of the body.

Following the orders of the KGB, the burial took place the next day; the body was cremated and interred within a few hours. During the service the crematorium was guarded by KGB men.

The facts available to us are doubtless insufficient. But we still cherish the hope that, sooner or later, this secret will become known to the world; proof will emerge from KGB files bearing witness to yet another despicable crime of an evil power, while the name of Ghely Snegirev will take its place alongside those of other martyrs to truth, crushed by a totalitarian machine.

The friends of Ghely Snegirev

Anyone who reads Ghely's last manuscript, with the purpose of understanding it as a history of his illness, inevitably arrives at the suspicion that the doctors in the special medical team attached to the group of KGB officers—top-class, enterprising agents, whose task was to break the dissident (and it was essential to break him, primarily for *humane* reasons: in order to keep other hotheads away from the path to disaster)—that these doctors had injected some cancerous extract into one of Ghely's intravertebral spaces and then, during the stalled investigation, had observed their "ally" reveal itself, germinating in the connective tissue of the spinal column and at the same time actively metastasizing.

But after much ruminating over the manuscript, its chief meaning (at least for me) was revealed not in the clues to and proofs of the "medical techniques" of the KGB, but in the fact that even the horrible fate of Ghely Snegirev had not stopped the people who had resolved to carry out his last wish, to write down the epilogue to his aborted confession.

After all, they are indeed the friends of Ghely, of whose names we are still ignorant, and of whom we know only that they were able to overcome their fear, while understanding better than anyone that they were taking a step into the abyss; that they would be sought out and found, and none of them could predict what might be awaiting him tomorrow: getting hit by a car at night, perhaps; getting shot by a "mugger," or being put away for raping a child; and they would make sure guilt was proven beyond doubt: with vile photographs, and the testimony of witnesses and medical experts; and the newspapers would scream in horror and wrath—and what defenders of human rights and political prisoners would stand up for such a monster?

I was in the studio, taping the next installment of my program, copied from Soviet magazines. "A certain influential American" popped up behind the glass partition. He waited for a pause, and said into the microphone:

"When you're done, come and see me, please."

I wonder how they set these scenes up? I thought. The American way—they'll say they've had another budget cut, there's no more money for my program—or the Russian way: "How could you stoop to copying stuff out of Soviet publications?"

In the spacious office, where I had never been before, sat the "news professor" Kukin and my editor. When I entered the conversation abruptly stopped.

"The panelists in Munich have been listening to your recent broadcasts," said the boss.

"That's the highest review stage we have at Radio Liberty," Kukin hastened to explain.

"Here, read it yourself," said the editor, holding out a sheet of telex paper.

The letters danced in front of my eyes, and I made out with difficulty:

". . . deep understanding of the topic . . . tone respectful to Soviet listener . . . Recommended for repeat broadcast . . . Consider possibility of increasing program length to 18½ minutes."

The three respectable gentlemen in well-tailored suits were graciously nodding their heads, as if inviting me to join their pleasant company, while I felt my face breaking out in spots, as if they were slapping my cheeks. The panelists were lauding the innocuous hack work? In a hoarse, disagreeable tone I said, "I've been in the West a relatively short time, and I don't know how some things are done here. Would you advise me, please? If I take exception to what you are making me do, to whom can I complain about you?"

I did not see their reaction, because I was looking at the floor.

"If a writer does not agree with the radio station's policies," pronounced the imperturbable editor—but in a forced, unnatural voice—"then he hands in his resignation."

Somehow this expression, "hands in his resignation," did not gibe with my shabby mien, or my miserable paycheck, or my puzzling social status. I myself could not figure out what I was: a radio journalist, the author of a weekly broadcast, who was obliged to moonlight in a yellow cab—or a taxi driver, moonlighting for an émigré radio station?

"Thank you," I said to my superiors. "I'll have to think about it."

I had no idea what would become of me now; but I did know for certain that with my fifth year in America drawing to a close, the time had come when I would have to make yet another abrupt change in my life and begin it all over again.

Chapter Nineteen

A BUSINESS FOR FOOLS

"Raise your right hand," said Judge Wang.
There followed a pause charged with sacramental solemnity.
"Swear that you will tell the truth, the whole truth . . ."
But the story of our naturalization in America will come later; now it
is time to keep a promise. A writer's first book is not a campaign speech,
in fact what makes it special is that on every page—literally every one—
you, the reader, are deciding whether I am a writer or not. If I deceive
you, you will slam the book shut.

At the very beginning, as far as I remember, I promised that anyone
who opened my book would discover how to find, amid the maze of life's
criss-crossing tracks, that hidden path leading to the land of milk and
honey, to carefree prosperity for all, even those who are fed up with
going to work and nonetheless want a taste of the sweet life.

Well, once spoken, a word takes flight. Now the secret of that path
must be imparted.

But that is not all, unfortunately. I seem to have also let it slip in the
heat of the moment that my route somehow circumvents years of
sleepless labor, years of soul-destroying scrimping on an ascetic's diet of
bread and water, years of living in a fifth-floor walkup.

Okay, what's done is done; now there is nothing for it but to trace that winding path with a careful dotted line; it's no big deal, really. And since some people will probably wonder if those with not much basic capital—well, none at all, actually—can get a foothold on the road to wonderland, here's my answer. Anyone can. No problem!

Hey, are you sure you're all right, cabbie? You don't have a headache? Maybe that's enough with all the writing and writing? Maybe we'd better go for a ride, get a breath of fresh air, and stop off on the way at that establishment by the Triborough Bridge which you used to pass off as the "women's prison." They will listen carefully to anything you say; they know how to listen. And nobody will contradict you or doubt a word of it. You just tell them all about this "route" that seems to be your very own discovery.

In order to pour oil on these waves of sarcasm, let me set things straight. I am not an unknown genius. I am a very ordinary person. But are ordinary people so rare among the well-to-do? Who says they are scintillating intellectuals one and all? They are no better than you or I. And now, if we can agree on this at least, give me your honest hand, my unknown friend, and, through the fading darkness of your disbelief, we shall stride toward the station from which your train for the future is about to leave.

———

Getting on this train is as simple as getting on any of the trains that leave Grand Central or Penn Station every minute. Anyone who wants can board it. There is nothing you have to know or be able to do in order to ride a train, of course; but, on the other hand, neither natural intelligence, dimples in your cheeks, nor degrees from prestigious universities will help or speed things up one iota. For the first year the train will run strictly to schedule, at a speed of one dollar per hour.

No, it's not an express. And so if you have your own ideas—if you plan to open a dry cleaners or a newsstand, if you are expecting an inheritance or some other switch in your fortunes—good luck to you. But if you have nothing to hope for, if you are no good at anything, then come with me!

Just one more thing—you're not a wishful thinker, are you? Maybe you have fantasies of untold millions, yachts, private jets. If so, I can't help you. I do not know the road to incalculable riches. Remember this:

all I can promise you is a nice condo in Kew Gardens and a modest Buick. Still, you will be able to put away a couple of thousand a month for a rainy day and neither you nor your wife will have to work. Does that suit you? Then let's go!

Hark! Hear the sound of tools banging? That's the track walkers checking the lines.

Hear the buffers clanking? That's the train pounding along.

What a juggernaut, eh?

The lights have flickered past, the clack of the wheels has died away; what's the matter, pal? Why so sad? Ah, you thought we'd be off at once. Don't despair, your turn will come! And not traveling as a stowaway, not riding in a boxcar like a hobo, but in comfort, as befits a man of business.

What's today? Thursday? On Monday—Tuesday at the latest—I swear, I'll make you a real businessman.

You know nothing about business? So what? You don't have to be Lee Iacocca to do what I have in mind . . . You're no good at anything at all? Don't worry! . . . No dough? That makes it a bit harder, of course. You really don't have any money? How about a subway token?

Ah, you see! And who was just making a poor mouth? We will pop into a couple of offices, meet some other businessmen, scribble our signatures on a piece of paper, and in two shakes it will all be fixed up—the simplest, most reliable business for anyone—the business for fools.

The business meetings that transform a cabbie dreamer into an entrepreneur number only two, and the first takes place in the office of a broker who buys and sells taxi medallions. There are taxi brokers' offices all over New York, at Columbus Circle, in the Pan Am building, and on dubious Tenth Avenue, but also in the wilds of Queens and the south Bronx, where hoods hang out in packs on street corners.

But as soon as I start talking business—as soon as I open my mouth, I think—my fellow businessmen will have my number. No matter how thoroughly you've been coached, any broker will realize instantly not only that you're on your uppers, but also that you're a loafer with no intention of driving a cab, and he will know exactly what kind of cheap trick you've got up your sleeve. That's why we need a special kind of broker, a mean little guy, awash with debts, entangled in crummy rackets, whom somebody punches out at least once a week and whose entire office consists of a scratched-up desk tucked away in an abandoned warehouse, among mountains of parts from stolen and cannibalized cabs.

Pull yourself together as you go up to the desk. But don't try to make a good impression. Don't beam, don't fawn, don't say hello. Just look straight into those rotten, angry eyes and get right to the point.

"Jerry, I want to lease a medallion."

"You got a cab?" Jerry asks.

"Jerry, I would like to lease a medallion and *buy* a cab."

"A new one?" Jerry asks, just in case, and his face brightens ever so slightly when you reply that you don't actually need a new cab and a used one will do fine.

"What make d'you want, then?" asks Jerry, though what he's really after is you—who you are and what's your game. So don't play hide-and-seek with your broker. Tell him frankly:

"I don't care whether it's a Ford or a Dodge. All I want is a good deal."

And now Jerry is sure you won't be driving this cab yourself. But don't be shy, let the crook know he can't take you for a sucker and you wouldn't dream of overpaying for any old piece of junk. It all has to be on the up-and-up. But, for the medallion and the car, you're prepared to shell out the full downpayment, *fifteen hundred dollars*.

Boy, you're some piece of work. You haven't forgotten you don't have any money, but you have to talk as if you did. That's the way businessmen do things. If you don't say it, Jerry may think you're a worse thug than he is. When you mention that fifteen hundred, though, he will see you don't have two pennies to rub together—but he will appreciate your tact. Jerry is used to scrounging his living out of people like you. Customers with money don't come looking him up. So there's no point in standing on ceremony with him; don't beg, *demand*.

"Jerry, I'd like to start Monday. Can you make it?"

Jerry scowls as his gorge rises with his loathing for you but he'll say, "Sure!" and put a piece of paper on the desk. Your first business contract.

But what if he doesn't put that piece of paper on the desk? Isn't it likely that Jerry will snort scornfully, make a scene, and refuse to do business with the possessor of some imaginary fifteen hundred bucks?

However, that fifteen hundred is not at all imaginary, and Jerry knows very well where it's coming from. But he may ask for *some* money—five hundred, or at least three hundred—up front, and if you don't have any . . . what then?

Then you act offended; you say everyone knows how honest you are, and if somebody thinks otherwise, he's not to be trusted himself.

Well, and then?

We'll take our business to Abdul.

And what if Abdul—

We'll try our luck with Anastas or Sakhir.

But what if they won't either?

Look, it just doesn't happen that way. Brokers always need customers who don't have money.

They *need* them?

And how!

Why?

People who don't have money will agree to any conditions. If a lease on a medallion costs $450 a week, Jerry will stiff you for $500; that's why he was in such a hurry to stick you with a one-year contract.

But why on earth sign it?

Because you-don't-have-any-money! Who else would agree to buy that heap of junk, with two hundred thousand miles on the clock, which Jerry is foisting off on you?

I don't want a heap of junk. What am I, worse than anybody?

No, you're not, but *you-don't-have-any-money*. The main thing is to swing a deal. And, anyway, you're not going to be driving that decrepit cab yourself.

But a worn-out car needs a lot of repairs.

You won't be repairing it.

But who's going to pay for it?

You. And Jerry will skin you alive. People with empty pockets always pay double. But don't get upset about it. Just remember this: despite the fact that you'll end up buying the beat-up jalopy for real, despite the fact that you'll hand over the promised fifteen hundred in full, and fork out the monthly payments, and the interest, and the rent, and *like* it—try to console yourself with the thought that it won't be you who'll be *working* for these mind-boggling sums of money.

You leave the broker's with a heavy heart and the feeling you were screwed—but this impression is deceptive. Signing the contract, and clinching the deal on whatever kind of cab, is a step toward boarding the train.

Now dozens of people will be wanting to do business with you in any of the five boroughs. But we go back to Manhattan, to the Russian kid, Itzhak-Schpitzhak, who was too shy to pee on the street and carried around a jar with a lid. He did not spend long driving a yellow cab; he came up with a different angle. Itzhak in the last few years has settled down, married, and become the father of two girls and the owner of eight medallions.

He is in the west Twenties, at the repair shop where he fixes his crates. He is a big customer who brings the mechanics a lot of work, so the shop owner lets him use the phone.

Itzhak-Schpitzhak's shabby van, stuffed with spare parts—springs, bumpers, drums, radiators—is usually parked at the entrance, while Itzhak himself hangs out inside. When the phone rings, he lunges for the receiver, and the call often turns out to be for him.

"Day or night?" Schpitzhak snaps, and with joy in his voice declares: "You got it! I have just what you want!" Then he shifts into the earnest tone of a straight shooter. "Why even bring it up? . . . Of course . . . Like new!"

And he closes as firm as granite. "I give you my word. You'll start today!"

You don't address the owner of eight medallions as "Itzhak-Schpitzhak." You had better call him Joseph, and say:

"*Joseph*, I need drivers."

"Two?" Itzhak asks.

"No, three."

A dog-eared exercise book appears from under the seat of the van.

"The car's in good shape?" Itzhak-Joseph inquires, and you don't need to be told how to reply. A person who has already promised a downpayment of fifteen hundred dollars, real or unreal, will himself find the appropriate words and the only correct way to couch them—in a tone of injured pride.

"Joseph, what are you talking about? The cab's like new!"

"V.g. cond.," notes Itzhak, lowering the evaluation somewhat, and he himself writes out the work schedule that will keep the old crate—for which you still have to pay through the nose—going nonstop, since *three* hacks are going to be driving it.

> Dr. #1   5 a.m.–5 p.m., Mon.–Fri.—$350
> Dr. #2   5 p.m.–5 a.m., Mon.–Fri.—$375
> Dr. #3   48 hrs. Sat. & Sun.—$235

Even a person with no imagination at all can see beyond this simple arithmetic to a cozily curtained sleeping compartment in a railroad car rattling along the tracks. Hacks 1, 2, and 3 will bring in a pile of dough at the end of next week! However, the lion's share will go on the lease of the medallion and the first payment for the cab. The remainder, unfortunately, is only a couple of hundred, and is the game really worth the candle? But be fair: it won't be you who will bust a gut to make that two hundred, after all.

Meanwhile, Itzhak-Schpitzhak-Joseph closes the exercise book, thanks you heartily, and shakes your hand, wondering how to get rid of you. You sense that it's time to go, but you can't take a step. (Damn it all! I'm done for!)

Those business contacts you had such simple faith in, that beautiful formula—"Dr. #1 + Dr. #2 + Dr. #3"—and, most of all, that real live money you thought you would be getting in just a few days (oh, that hurts!)—they are all a snare and a delusion.

Will Jerry, who gets punched out by someone every week—will that wolf give you the keys to the old crate without the agreed fifteen hundred? It's more likely the Hudson River will reverse its flow and go back toward the Adirondacks.

What? What are you mumbling about . . . ? The contract? What kind of a contract do you think you've got? At the moment the only person who has signed that piece of paper is you. Jerry just produced it for the customer to sign; he would never sign it till he's counted the cash twice. So where to find those miserable few bucks without which the whole thing will unravel?

————

O my friend, my friend—on some moonlit night, waking in a high-rise hotel overlooking the ocean in Miami Beach (or the Bahamas, or some other medium-priced resort), you will caress the two-hundred-dollar goddess sprawled next to you, thinking you have every right to rouse her—but it won't do your heart any good, so you will grope for the cigarettes on the nightstand, and, blowing a stream of smoke at the ceiling, you will ponder your extraordinary fate: what you were and what you have become.

Most likely you will remember the pleasant, heartwarming moments during your ascent: for example, how you managed to buy up pen-sioned-off police cars at auction for a song and then painted them yellow; your first broker, Jerry, will come to life before your eyes, and you will go roving back in time to that harrowing instant when, on the point of slipping in a puddle of oil at the repair-shop gates, you grabbed convulsively at the sleeve of Itzhak's jacket. But never remember that flash of despair with shame!

So what if Itzhak stared at you as if you were insane? And who cares if you came off as a greenhorn who didn't know beans about business? The main thing was that once you had fallen into this *illusory* financial trap, you did not beg for advice, trying to wriggle your way out of it; no, you showed some character, turning red in the face and bawling out the blameless guy with a wild, senseless fury that was in fact the guarantee of your ultimate success.

"Listen, Joseph!" you yelled. "I consider I have a driver only when I see the moolah. Nobody gets *my* cab without putting down the full deposit!"

"You think we're playing games here?" Itzhak took a step back, astounded by this onslaught. "Every driver puts down five hundred bucks, cash on the barrel."

And you're saved. The fifteen hundred Jerry wrung out of you will come from the hacks. But, while sighing with relief, you did not let Itzhak off the hook yet. Breathing fire, you began making long-winded, superfluous provisos should someone steal the meter, force the trunk open, take off the wheels, or break a window.

Itzhak, however, soothed you with a mother's patience. Before setting foot in your cab, every driver would have to sign a paper attesting to his total responsibility for it.

But what if he breaks his neck in an accident? What if, God forbid, he gets shot by a mugger? The widow will drag you through the courts and take you for everything you have!

No way. Itzhak-Schpitzhak knows what he's doing. Not one driver will get behind the wheel before he has signed yet another paper that says you have not hired him, that he is not working for you and so you bear no responsibility for him. He is an *independent contractor.*

In the eyes of the law you are two equal partners: he because he is crippling himself in "your" yellow cage, and you because you are taking his money away.

———

The birth pangs of a business are accompanied by more than fears and flaps. They bring their own small, inimitable joys, too. Every five minutes your wife will be smitten with a new terror and you will dispel her anxieties.

"And the gas? Have you thought how much will go on gas alone?" your wife will blurt out, and you will explain that the drivers will buy the gas.

"And who's going to pay for the insurance?"

"The medallion owner, of course," you respond wearily.

"And what if the driver gets sick?"

"Then he'll probably go to the doctor."

"Who needs your silly little jokes?" Your wife has lost her temper. "Who'll pay for the days he misses?"

And how pleasant it is when your spouse gives you a chance to show off your legal erudition! A driver leases a cab under the same conditions by which a tenant rents an apartment. There are no valid reasons for missing payments. Any debt is automatically deducted from the five-hundred-dollar deposit.

"And what if the driver quits?"

"Joseph'll send another one."

"But who is this Joseph of yours? Why should he look for drivers for us—and where does he get them?"

The best way of calming both your wife and yourself on this score is to buy a *Post* or a *News*, open it to the Help Wanted section, and look for the column with that irresistible appeal, TAXI DRIVER—BE YOUR OWN BOSS! Under one of the ads promising fabulous earnings and brand-new cabs, you will undoubtedly find a phone number you know—Itzhak's.

He pays seventy dollars for every ad. But every driver who gets a job through Itzhak pays him fifty bucks, and every owner also gives him thirty—for every driver. Sounds good? Fancy it for yourself? We won't miss that tasty tidbit either.

———

Attention, please! Your train to the future has already left the station. So smoothly and naturally you did not even notice it. At the start, this metaphorical motion is almost imperceptible; but somewhere, curled up in the depths of the naïve, fledgling businessman's soul, there's already a cuddly feeling, tender as a kitten, of secret pride in yourself; no kidding, you have managed to put three "own bosses" in a heap of junk bought, in essence, with *their* money; and now, among thousands of other yellow cabs, yours is roaming the streets of New York, too. And it does not really matter if your life is just as meager and wretched as before; from now on you know it won't be like that forever. Far, far away, over yonder, above the blue horizon, a flame of hope is already burning: through rain and blizzards, from dawn to dusk, twenty-four hours a day, the three "own bosses" recruited by that son-of-a-gun Itzhak will keep cruising and cruising in your old crate, and with every hour you are richer by *one dollar.* Only one dollar, maybe, but still, when you're rattling along in the subway, and when you're watching TV, and when you're sleeping, that unstoppable meter will be ticking away in time to your heartbeat. Just beware, my novice businessman, in the name of everything you hold most sacred, don't touch the dollars it's clocking up. He who violates this commandment is courting inevitable disaster.

The more often your cab breaks down, the more often you will have to run to Itzhak for new drivers, and the day will arrive when it is clearly time to change the vehicle operating under the medallion you have leased. This ordeal will roll around as inexorably as the sun sets, and not even Jerry will have any truck with a squanderer of those early dollars.

But if you are sensible, in six months that successfully invested subway token will become four or even five grand, and so, when the need arises, you will be able to buy a new old cab, which, despite the curses of the hacks, will do the job and go on doing it, and when the money you have squirreled away has grown once more, it will be time to expand the business.

Another medallion leased with another wreck purchased, and now six "own bosses" will be pushing your train; and before you have had time to turn around those six will have become nine.

The more money that passes through your hands, however, the more painful will be the feeling of injustice at the crumbs you are getting compared with the income of the medallion owners, who do nothing at all and are lining their pockets with the money you have made.

You will begin by sniffing around those inordinate prices; you will call on a medallion broker to find out about the conditions for a bank loan. But time and again, as you peek into the brokers' offices on Lexington or Tenth Avenue, you will run up against a brick wall — the monstrous size of the downpayment.

Even assuming that by now there are three fully staffed cabs of yours driving all over New York, it is virtually impossible to raise the necessary amount.

"So, put another three units on the road and get nine more hacks — let them do the work!"

Huh. It's easy to talk. Something's always going wrong with cabs — if it isn't a breakdown, it's an accident. And those drivers wear you down. Just think about the phone calls at three o'clock in the morning.

"The steering wheel won't turn, find yourself somebody else to drive this thing!"

The idiot doesn't know that if the wheel won't turn you have to step on the gas — then it'll work.

"I'm stuck in Far Rockaway."

Stuck? He locked the keys in the car and now he gets the owner out of bed in the middle of the night. Find a rock, blockhead, bust the window, unlock the door, and put the glass in tomorrow! If you've paid for it once, you won't get stuck again. But you can't talk like that to the cabbie. Get up, get dressed, and take him the spare keys.

And even so—as long as you don't give up, as long as you keep looking for ways of restructuring the business, keep nosing around, asking the same questions over and over again—in the end, a peculiar rule of thumb will become apparent: if the downpayment is fifty thousand on Columbus Circle, on Lexington they will take forty, and in the black sections of Brooklyn, twenty-three.

You have prudently taken off your gold chain, gotten on the subway, and surfaced in a neighborhood of abandoned warehouses. There are the familiar heaps of hoods and fenders from stolen cabs. Pull up a wobbly chair and straddle it backwards.

"Jerry, if I buy a medallion, how much do I have to put down?"

"Depends what kind of car you want, new or used."

"I have a car."

"Twelve Gs."

Where Abdul wants twenty-three, Jerry will take twelve.

"And what's the interest on the mortgage?"

While Jerry is writing down the numbers—17 percent for the first loan, 22 percent for the second—hang on tight to the back of the chair you're straddling so you won't accidentally fall off when you see that the interest on the third loan Jerry is offering you, as an old and valued customer, from his own personal assets, is only 4 percent.

"Per month," Jerry explains. "Four percent per month."

This little figure sends a sepulchral chill washing over you, but at the same time common sense reminds that it is not you who will be slaving to make those percentages.

———

Having parted with everything you have managed to scrape together, you close yet another deal on crushing terms, but your business has nevertheless undergone a revolution: now, two dollars grow where before there was only one. You are getting the same dollar an hour for the cab you lease to the drivers, but beyond that, as the owner of a medallion, you are now gaining a second, mysterious ghost dollar. A dollar which you receive but which instantly vanishes—into the pockets of a loan shark or through a bank teller's window. You cannot buy a bag of peanuts with that dollar, you cannot change it into four quarters. It is as if it were not there at all—and yet it is.

The real value of this dollar becomes apparent only a few years later, when the formerly inaccessible broker on Columbus Circle meets you at his office door, offers you an armchair, and, glancing perfunctorily over your documents, announces that merely by signing this paper here, and then this one, and putting your initials on the back, you will become the owner of a corporation—that is, of *two more* medallions.

Your tongue, glued to the roof of your mouth, gets out the words with difficulty.

"Holy moly! But the downpayment on a corporation is a huge amount."

And here Noel Greenbaum, son of the great Andy Greenbaum, presses your hand reassuringly. "From you, sir, not a cent!"

Those dollars that you did not exchange for quarters, those ghost dollars that vanished into the bank teller's window, have fallen like crystals to the bottom of the paid-up part of your loans. Don't be chicken—sign! Here and here. And don't forget to put your initials on the back.

Now your problems never let up. Early in the morning you are at the repair shop, then you have to make time to stop by a tire wholesaler's, then it's off to the junkyard, where they sell stolen cabs for parts, to ask the price of a door, a front panel. Plus you have to hunt down a cheap van and call the *Post*.

DON'T PASS UP THE CHANCE TO EARN $600 PER WEEK! GET BEHIND THE WHEEL RIGHT AWAY!

From now on your telephone will be your curse: it will ring off the hook. Before you have hung up it will be ringing again.

"Yes, absolutely. Why even bring it up? The cab's like new!"

But every call is money in the bank. Every cab driver who gets a job pays you fifty bucks, and every sucker of an owner who isn't capable of finding drivers for his own rattletraps gives you another thirty.

The leased medallions will come flocking around the debt-burdened corporation, charging your budget much as an alternator charges a battery, and your gravy train keeps gathering speed — twelve, sixteen, twenty-two, thirty-six dollars per hour! While you are eating and while you are sleeping, the wheel on the magical meter goes round and round. On the other hand, the midnight phone calls, the worries, the bother, the problems your drivers give you get so numerous that you will find yourself wondering if you are choosing them right. They keep calling and calling, and though you try to pick the most honest ones for yourself, they turn out to be scoundrels to a man. Is there a story they didn't tell you just to rip you off for a few measly bucks, or at least pay later — tomorrow, next week? Either it was a dead day, or a cop wrote a ticket "for nothing," or somebody broke into the trunk and stole the spare wheel, or a kid got sick.

You gave preference to careful middle-aged family men, and they wrecked your cabs. They crashed into lampposts or buses; they reduced expensive Volvos and Cadillacs to twisted piles of metal. And always, without fail, whatever happened, they swore that some other motherfucker was to blame.

Only with time do you grasp that they are all the same. You are giving them the chance to work and support their families, but do they appreciate it? Hacks are the dregs of society, degenerates, scum! Pity them, give in to them for a second, and they will sink their teeth in and never let go. They will drive you to the poorhouse; your gravy train will derail. And so, if you're white, put blacks in your jalopies; if you're a Hymie, you can't do better than with those dirty Arabs; if you're a genuine Yank, hire Greeks and Chinese. It will be easier for you to despise them.

Bad day? Do I raise the rent on a good one?

A cop broke the law? Sue him.

The kid? I have children too.

You want to work? So, pay up and work. If you don't pay, I'll keep your deposit, and you can get the hell out of my cab!

Day or night? It's a deal! Take my word, you start today.

Chapter Twenty

--- -- -- -- -- -- -- --

DO YOU LOVE

AMERICA?

"**R**aise your right hand," said Judge Wang. "Swear that you will tell the truth, the whole truth, and nothing but the truth."

I swore, and then came the question that everyone who applies for American citizenship must answer.

"DO YOU LOVE AMERICA?" asked the judge.

"Yes," I lied. "I do."

Waiting to be called into the immigration judge's office—as my wife told the story later on—she feared most of all that she would forget whether it was the Speaker of the House who swore in the Secretary of State, or the other way around. But Judge Wang was not about to torment my wife with tricky questions. In fact, he did most of the talking during the interview.

"You're *Russian*," Judge Wang said to my wife. "So don't try to be more American than women who were born here. Fix Russian dishes, try to observe Russian customs and holidays, buy your son Russian records and Russian books. The American ones he'll get for himself."

I listened to what the judge had said to my wife, and it occurred to me that it had relevance for me too. Had I not tried to be more American than any of my American supervisors at the radio station? And, in the end, had I not reached the point where my work at Radio Liberty, which had once been my dream, had become my shame?

Five years spent living in America might not be much, but still something in my way of thinking had changed, and now I sensed dimly that, in laying claim to a particular "mission"—*telling the Soviet people the truth*—I myself had probably remained a "Soviet man;" only upside down, turned on my head.

Every day I lived in America was making me a little more like the people around me, and I was gradually beginning to acknowledge that if I wanted to tell the Soviet people the truth I should have stayed there; and that now, in New York, trying to live the spiritual life of Russia, which I had left of my own free will, was merely a pose; and that one should not attempt to subordinate or devote one's life to a single, albeit worthy goal—even the red broadcaster's light that I had once so yearned for. *One must simply live.*

———

By now I had been to at least a dozen taxi brokers on Columbus Circle and Tenth Avenue; I had already made a deal with Jerry for an old cab and resurrected my former acquaintance with Itzhak-Schpitzhak, but I decided not to finally sign the lease on a medallion until I had paid one more visit to the ex–hot dog vendor at his fish store.

The frozen gray lumps were clanging on the scales; the black kid was putting on an inspired performance, giving short weight, overcharging customers, and entertaining them all at the same time.

When Misha noticed me in the crowd, he did not look particularly pleased. "You took a long time to think about it," he said from across the counter. Another man had taken the job I had once been offered.

But I had not come to Misha with any intention of getting work. I wanted to propose a business deal to my wealthy ex-neighbor. He and I would go shares on a corporation—*two* taxis, one for him, the other for me. I would drive one cab myself, and we would lease Misha's. I would look after the second car as if it were my own, and hire the drivers. In five years the bank loans would be paid off, and without lifting a finger Misha would have tripled his original investment and become the full owner of a paid-off medallion. What was wrong with a deal like that?

"And who says there's anything wrong with it?" Misha responded, and inquired how much money was needed to invest in two medallions.

"Thirty-six thousand." I gave the lowest amount I had come up with, from a broker in the south Bronx.

"Good!" Misha nodded, and asked about another detail: what would be his share of the money, and what mine.

Needless to say, I was fully prepared for this question. My share of the investment would be exactly fifty percent, but in the form of eighteen checks of a thousand dollars each, which Misha would deposit in his account every month.

There was nothing more I could add; now it was Misha's turn to speak, and he said, "Look, if I give you the money, and you give me checks that aren't covered, that's not what they call business."

I said nothing. It was stupid to expect any other answer from a fishmonger.

"Maybe it would be better to buy one taxi instead of two." The huckster was mocking me openly now. "What do you think?"

"You know better," I said. "So buy one."

"Volodya, don't you understand what I'm talking about?" Misha could not hold back. "I'm not interested in cabs myself. How would you feel if we bought one medallion, for you?"

Only now did I grasp what he was driving at.

"How much interest would you want, then?"

The smug face darkened.

"What do I want with your interest?"

"So where's the profit in lending me the money?"

"Profit?" The huckster was offended. "A big one! If things are good for me, then I want them to be good for you too—that's my profit."

I had been expecting anything—a churlish refusal, a loan shark's traps—and the only thing I had not allowed for was the fishmonger's right to act the way I myself had never acted. And so, after stammering words of gratitude (which Misha was indeed expecting), I began to enlarge on the subject of guarantees, getting a notary to verify the loan agreement, which would put down in black and white—

"Volodya, if you take it into your head to steal my money," Misha interrupted, "that piece of paper won't help me."

And although it did not happen the next day, or next week, but about three months later, when the price of a medallion had jumped by six thousand, when the bank loan conditions were stiffer—Misha gave me eighteen packets of a thousand dollars each, and from that moment my life once more began anew.

At the brokerage office in the south Bronx I met my future partner, John—a taxi driver who had slogged away in a fleet cab for seven years to get together the eighteen thousand for his downpayment—and we put our flourishing signatures to the documents bearing witness that from this day on, medallion number 2i25 belonged to John and 2i26 to me.

An inspector from the Taxi and Limousine Commission hung these precious ornaments on the hoods of two brand-new Checkers, and John and I drove toward the city across the Queensboro Bridge, awaited at the other end by the homeless traffic lady.

Blown by the wind from the East River, her thin dress, its hem unevenly ripped, clung to her body. The wind had tousled the heavy sheaf of her wheat-colored hair, while she, swigging from the bottle in the paper bag, urged our Checkers toward Manhattan. Manhattan! Choking from the wine, her own laughter, and the wind . . . As I drove past, I was not a whit less happy than she.